JOHN W. MACKAY
JAMES G. FAIR
JAMES C. FLOOD
WILLIAM S. O'BRIEN

These were the lords of the Comstock Bonanza.
When miners worked for an unprecedented 4 dollars a day in mines where air temperatures exceeded 130°, these four men demanded the best and got it. Six trainloads of supplies a day were sent over Senator Sharon's fantastically crooked railroad, and in return a broad stream of bright minted dollars flowed back to San Francisco, endowing her with homes, hotels, theatres, banks and factories, rivaling the most luxurious in the world.

SILVER KINGS

The Lives and Times of
MACKAY, FAIR, FLOOD and O'BRIEN

Lords of the Nevada
Comstock Lode

Oscar Lewis

BALLANTINE BOOKS • NEW YORK
An Intext Publisher

BALLANTINE BOOKS, INC.
101 Fifth Avenue, New York, N.Y. 10003

CONTENTS

FOREWORD

In recent years the story of Nevada's Comstock Lode has been told in numerous works of history and fiction; it is not the purpose here to cover again a subject that has already received extended treatment elsewhere. The present volume is primarily biographical. Its aim is to present, objectively and in some detail, the life stories of the four men who, by their discovery and control of the richest strike of precious metals in American mining history, amassed very large fortunes and for many years made themselves potent factors in the affairs of the entire Pacific Coast.

The writing of these biographical sketches presented certain problems in both the assembling of material and its interpretation. The last surviving member of the bonanza firm died almost half a century ago; all four lived in obscurity until they were well past thirty, and the record of their early years is incomplete and sometimes conflicting. After they had become important figures in Western industry and finance, their activities were reported at length in newspapers all over the Coast. But these references were almost exclusively concerned with their then current enterprises, and such light as they throw on their lives and characters is usually both indirect and unintentional. Yet it is on this mass of newspaper comment —much of it biased, for few of the Coast journals took an impartial view of the group's activities—that the biographer must mainly rely.

Thus, although the Comstock era is one of the most

fully documented chapters in Far Western history, the four men who rose to power on the profits of its mines have received comparatively little attention. Few extended sketches of their lives or serious appraisals of their characters appeared during their lifetimes or later. No full-length biography of any of the group has yet been published. Such biographical material as exists is scattered through Coast newspapers and magazines, in books on the history of the Comstock, in the reminiscences of pioneers, and in brief and uncritical eulogies in such subsidized publications as Bancroft's *The Chronicles of the Builders*.

Yet the influence of the four was so great that during the years they controlled the bonanza mines they were almost continuously in the public eye. From the early seventies until well into the nineties there was hardly an issue of an important West Coast newspaper that did not contain reference to some phase of their activities. Moreover, most of this was prejudiced in viewpoint and heated in tone, for the partners' operations closely affected many thousands in all walks of life. That they were able to exert so decisive an influence on the region's economy is of course an indication of the caliber of the men themselves. Three of the four were "strong" characters, typical of the group that shouldered their way to the top all over America during the final third of the past century. They were men of consuming ambition, resourceful, acquisitive, and uncommonly able, and, like most of their class, relentless in their opposition to whatever stood in the way of their drive toward wealth and power.

In their attitude toward the Silver Kings, citizens of the Coast were long divided into two camps. Those who shared, or hoped to share, in their enormously profitable enterprises looked on them as instruments by which the entire West was to enjoy an era of sustained and universal prosperity. Another group took an exactly opposite view: these could see in the firm's operations only a series of shrewd maneuvers by which the capital of the region was drained off from legitimate channels of investment and poured into mining stocks, creating great fortunes for a few while it impoverished tens of thousands. Numerically, those who held the latter view were before long in the majority, for the early popularity of the four declined as their field of operations broadened and their methods came to be understood. From the middle seventies on, fewer than half a dozen of the Coast's newspapers consistently supported the policies of the firm; all others were given over to frequent and violent denunciations.

Little of this mass of material is of interest to present day readers, yet this record of forgotten controversies is important for the light it throws on the characters, aims, and business ethics of the four. These biographical studies have, therefore, been chiefly based on contemporary accounts of their activities as they are preserved in the files of Virginia City, San Francisco, and Sacramento newspapers from 1873 to the end of the century. However, other sources of information are not entirely lacking. Western magazines of the period contain occasional references to the activities of the group, as do numerous books and an imposing array of pamphlets. The latter are mainly official reports put out by the managers of the bonanza mines and designed to justify their methods and confound their critics, with a sprinkling of counterblasts sponsored by their opponents. There is also a considerable bulk of manuscript material: official records of the mines and the business correspondence of the controlling partners, plus certain dictated statements gathered by agents of the historian Bancroft and preserved in the Bancroft Library. It is from these sources, pieced out by personal recollections of the few Comstock pioneers whose memories run back sixty years and beyond, and by certain family reminiscences passed on to the descendants of participants, that this record of the lives and times of the Silver Kings has been compiled.

Acknowledgments to individuals and institutions, and a listing of sources, will be found at the end of the volume.

SILVER KINGS

Part One

The Setting

1

THE sixties and seventies of the last century were uncommonly eventful decades, yet throughout that period American newspaper-readers were daily invited to put aside more weighty matters and to regale themselves with news of one small Western mining community. Nevada's Comstock Lode was discovered in 1859 and for twenty years it enjoyed an ever widening renown. As time passed, its silver mines became a sort of national anodyne, a sure avenue of escape into a land where every dream came true and every illusion had the substance of reality. All over America millions believed that there, granted the opportunity and a bit of luck, one's visions of wealth and power and prestige would surely materialize. The nation had never had a more satisfactory wishing well.

Writers have been describing the lode for well over eighty years, always in terms of superlatives. It has been called the largest and richest mining strike in history, "the most stupendous treasure trove of precious metals ever to dazzle the eye of man." One Western editor likened it to Aladdin's cave; another was sure that if the productions of all the mines of antiquity were gathered together, their total would not equal a normal month's output of the

Comstock. Elsewhere than on the Pacific slope such statements were sometimes put down as bombast, yet they were only mild exaggerations: the lode had a way of making almost any extravagance seem moderate. First and last the mines yielded close to four hundred million dollars in silver and gold. They made enormous fortunes for half a dozen men, besides creating a score of mere millionaires and putting hundreds in possession of nest-eggs that ranged from a hundred thousand dollars upwards.

These formidable wealth-producing properties were concentrated in a small area: the lode was less than two miles long and only a few hundred feet wide at its broadest point. Its leading town, Virginia City, never had more than twenty-five thousand inhabitants, and even during its active years population sometimes dropped to half that figure. But its influence was ever out of proportion to its size. For fifteen years men and women all over the West daily felt its impact, sometimes remotely and at second hand, often directly, as an unseen force that arbitrarily determined the rise and fall of their personal fortunes.

A city that wielded an influence overshadowing that of places ten times its size was naturally much in the public eye. Leading journals regularly sent correspondents to observe and describe the fantastic happenings on the lode. One of the most observant arrived in 1875, charged with explaining the phenomenon to readers of Mr. Greeley's *Tribune*. The New Yorker found the region totally unlike anything he had seen on his world-wide travels. He explained that the great ore bodies lay beneath the shoulder of a large and undecorative mountain and that the mountain itself loomed above as scarred and desolate a region as he ever hoped to see. It was a spot where few men would willingly have chosen to live, yet the journalist found there a modern, solidly built city, from which arose, twenty-four hours a day, seven days a week, a continuous humming roar of activity. He presently identified the roar: it came from hundreds of stamps in the mills of the lower town, ceaselessly rising and falling as they reduced to powder the famous Comstock ore. Overlaying this monotone was a medley of other sounds, the

concerted scrape of miner's boots over the plank sidewalks as shifts changed, the blasts of scores of whistles,
all pitched to different keys and all active, the periodical
jolting blasts in the underground stopes. Until they had
become habituated to this clatter, strangers found sleep
impossible. For the first three nights the *Tribune*'s man
lay awake until dawn.

It was not alone Virginia's lack of nocturnal quiet that
stirred the visitor's interest. He walked the length of C
Street, passing block after block of brick-and-stone business houses. Like others before him, he wondered why
the residents had built so substantially on so insecure an
economic foundation. The lode's ore deposits were of
course of unknown depth and might at any time yield
up the last of their millable quartz. By their nature
mining towns were ephemeral places, thrown up to serve
a temporary need and to be casually abandoned when
their usefulness ended; yet here was one that had clearly
been designed to last a century.

The place abounded in other paradoxes. With rare ex-
ceptions all male citizens wore the rough garb of day-
laborers; all patronized the same bars, ate at the same
restaurants, and speculated in the same stocks at the same
brokerage offices. Impossible to tell who were the four-
dollar-a-day miners and who the owners of bonanzas currently paying their million a month in dividends. In most
mine or mill towns of the seventies the typical resident
lived in a squalid shack, ate coarse food in inadequate
quantities, and existed on the ragged edge of want. Not
so his Virginia City compatriot. Close observation convinced the *Tribune* reporter that to the last man (and
woman) Virginia's citizens had the tastes of Sybarites. The
town's merchants catered exclusively to a luxury trade.
Stores were piled high with quality merchandise, all in
brisk demand; only inferior goods remained on the shelves.
All this and more found its way into the visitor's dis-
patches as he piled detail on surprising detail. In a narrow
window of a C Street jewelry store he saw an array of
diamonds that would have done credit to a shop on the
rue de la Paix. Only in size and appointments were the

town's leading restaurants inferior to New York's best; in the variety and quality of their food and in the skill of its preparation they were unexcelled elsewhere on the continent, and this went too for their well-stocked wine cellars.

The fact that this city of luxury-lovers stood in the midst of thousands of square miles of appalling desolation heightened the dramatic effect: everywhere the visitor was drawn up by startling incongruities. He visited the quarters of the Washoe Club and admired its lounge and bar and cardroom; he reported that except for inferior paintings and bronzes the place compared favorably with the most luxurious men's clubs of New York or Boston. After a dinner prepared by the club's admirable chef, he stood long before one of the windows of the lounge, thoughtfully regarding the jagged mountains, pale and ghostly in the moonlight, ridge succeeding sterile ridge as far as his eye could carry. City of contrasts!

But this was in 1875, when the Comstock was at the apex of its prosperity. It had not always been so. Sixteen years had passed since the first claims had been staked out at the head of the canyons furrowing Sun Mountain. Much had happened.

The story of the lode's discovery and early development is a long record of bad luck, bad judgment, and general ineptness. In the summer of 1849 and through the early fifties, tens of thousands of gold-hunters had hurried through the Carson Valley, hell-bent for California, never suspecting that a few miles off the trail lay wealth far greater than they were likely to find on the other side of the Sierra. The history of the lode was a series of such ironies. As early as 1850, west-bound Argonauts had found traces of gold beside the streams flowing into the Carson River, but the yield was small and this hot, parched land held few attractions to eyes that remembered the green meadows of home. For close to ten years Gold Canyon and near-by Six Mile Creek had remained "poor men's bonanzas," giving up a meager living to a succession of prospectors too unenterprising to move on to more lucrative diggings. All were gold miners, familiar with the technique of placer operations, but with so little curiosity that none had tried to identify the heavy, bluish sand that clogged their rockers: this they cursed and shoveled aside.

Not until the summer of 1859 did someone think to send specimens of the curious "blue stuff" across the mountains for analysis. A Grass Valley assayer applied routine tests, doubted the accuracy of his results, and, with heightened interest, ran the tests a second time. No question then remained. The bothersome blue substance was an exceedingly rich silver sulphide, mixed with gold: it assayed close to four thousand dollars a ton. Another of the lode's ironies presently came to light. Two years earlier Ethan and Hosea Grosh, brothers, had wandered into the area and made the same discovery, identifying an outcropping near the head of one of the canyons as silver-bearing quartz and, with such rudimentary equipment as they could improvise, accurately assaying its value. The young pair, sons of a Philadelphia clergyman, prudently said nothing of the discovery. Their placer claim yielded enough gold to support them while they laid plans to develop the silver ledge. Their further history is brief and tragic. The younger, Hosea, injured his foot with a pick; the wound became infected and a month later he died. The survivor operated their placer claim through the weeks of late fall. Then, having panned enough gold to pay the cost of his brother's illness and funeral, he and a companion set off for California, where he hoped to raise capital to build a mill in which to reduce the silver ore. But their delayed start brought on a second catastrophe. It was dangerously late in the season when the pair headed across the mountains. Before they had reached the summit they were caught in a series of violent storms; for four days and nights they struggled through blinding snow and on the fifth day stumbled upon a snowbound settlement high on the west slope of the Sierra. Delirious from exhaustion and with his hands and feet frozen, the last Grosh brother maintained his hold on life for twelve days longer; then he, too, died, taking with him the secret of the silver ledge.

The next to stumble on the lode were men of a different caliber from Hosea and Ethan Grosh, and in the end they were only slightly more fortunate. Naïve and unenterprising, their ambition dulled by successive failures, this hard-bitten group was poorly equipped for the responsibilities and temptations of riches. The twin canyons on the east slope of Sun Mountain had been worked and reworked since the early fifties, and with a progressively smaller return. After eight years the poor man's bonanza was playing out. Placers that had once averaged five dollars a day now yielded hardly enough to provide the barest necessities, and Saturday night sprees in the sunbaked settlements of the valley had been abandoned.

Then, when the area seemed no longer capable of supporting even this niggardly hand-to-mouth existence, the outlook suddenly brightened. In the spring of '59, prospectors came in contact with the outer fringes of the long-illusive lode. James Finney ("Old Virginny"), Alex Henderson, and several others made a mild strike near the head of Gold Canyon. An outcropping of reddish rock having engaged their interest, they ran a few experimental panfuls, first pounding the decomposed quartz into small pieces with hammers. The result was far better than they had hoped; they went to work in earnest, and within a week their earnings had jumped to eight, ten, then to twenty dollars a day. By then every placer lower down the canyon had been abandoned and their owners had staked out new claims adjacent to the red ledge. Late comers, finding everything in the vicinity pre-empted, passed over the canyon's upper rim and entered the head of Six Mile Canyon, where they relocated claims that had been casually worked the year before. Here luck continued bad until two prospectors, Peter O'Riley and Patrick McLaughlin, commenced deepening the mouth of a tiny spring, hoping to increase the flow of water into their rocker. Some vagrant impulse caused them to toss into their rocker a few shovelfuls of sand removed from the spring. When the lighter material had been washed away, the pair stared goggle-eyed into the rocker: its bottom was covered with a film of finely granulated gold.

For half a day O'Riley and McLaughlin worked their small bonanza; then Henry Comstock ("Old Pancake"), boastful and arrogant and rapacious, rode over the divide and into camp; he was mounted on a scrawny mule, his long legs scraping the sagebrush. The two incautiously admitted that they had run on a bit of luck and proudly displayed the evidence: half an inch of pale yellow gold in the bottom of a tin can. This was enough for Old Pancake. Greedy and loquacious, by sheer noise and bluster he overbore the objections of the discoverers and persuaded them to share their claim with him and one Manny Penrod, basing his argument on the shaky ground that the latter were owners of the spring. The four thereupon staked out claims up and down the canyon, each taking three hundred feet, plus another three hundred permitted them by right of discovery: a total of fifteen hundred feet. They placed no particularly high value on their holdings; they were content to work the small but lucrative pocket beside the spring. It proved to be by far the richest strike yet made in the area. The four men daily washed out several hundred dollars in gold, notwithstanding increasing quantities of blue sand that hampered their operations. Nearly two months passed before a sample was sent over the mountains for the historic assay that ended the lean early years of the Washoe.

Californians who had advance knowledge of the assays tried hard to keep the information secret until they could cross the mountains and buy the claims from their unsuspecting owners. But of all secrets none is so difficult to keep as that of a mining strike. Within a day or two after the first group had slipped unobtrusively out of Grass Valley, the trails over the Sierra were dotted with men from the California diggings, all mysteriously in possession of the facts and hot on the trail of the leaders. They were followed by others, first scores, then hundreds as the eastward rush over the mountains got under way. Through the fall of '59 and until early snows blocked the upper passes, the migration continued, while sprawling camps

sprang up at the heads of the canyons and hundreds of
stone mounds marking claim boundaries were erected on
the barren canyon-sides.

Meantime the lode was witnessing the final irony of its
pre-boom era. The owners of the original claims were be-
sieged by eager strangers offering what seemed fantastically
extravagant sums for their property. Finney and O'Riley
and Comstock and the others did not long refuse: these
newcomers were clearly bent on squandering their abundant dollars and it would have been uncivil to disappoint
them. One by one the veterans of the region's lean years
unloaded their holdings. McLaughlin was first: he sold
for $3,500 his quarter interest in a property that was
producing $400 a day from surface workings with crude
equipment. Manny Penrod held out for a few days longer
and received two and a half times as much, while Henry
Comstock topped that figure, realizing $11,000 for a
property that had cost him only half an hour of arguments
and threats. But the real hero of this exploit was Pat
O'Riley: long after the other three had pocketed their gains
he continued to stand firm—to be rewarded at last with an
offer that strained credulity: a whopping $40,000. Holders
of adjacent claims joined the carnival of selling: Gould,
Curry, Hale, Norcross, Best, Belcher—each gave his name
to mines that later became famous all over the land, but
the millions they produced enriched others.

What did the pioneer group do with their windfalls?
The lode was named for Old Pancake Comstock, and its
chief city for Old Virginny Finney; the distinction profited
neither of them. Comstock invested his $11,000 in a Car-
son City supply store, went broke, and drifted north into
Montana. A year or two later he committed suicide.
Finney squandered his winnings and was killed by falling
off a horse. When Alvah Gould sold, for less than $500,
his half interest in the Gould and Curry, he boasted of
having duped the credulous Californians; but his claim
yielded fifteen millions, and Gould ended his days operating a peanut stand in Reno. McLaughlin became a forty-
dollar-a-month cook, and O'Riley having lost his $40,000
in speculation, went insane; both died paupers. Irony

enough. Not one of the original owners held on to a dollar of his preposterously small return. First and last, the lode yielded hundreds of millions, but it all flowed into the pockets of far shrewder men than Finney, Comstock, O'Riley, McLaughlin, and their fellows.

2

THE first exploiters of the lode left behind a record of confusion, waste, and chicanery rather worse than that of most frontier mining camps. A web of boundary disputes clogged the courts and periodically brought operations to a standstill; the judiciary was weak and venal (a judge was considered reprehensibly lax only if he sold out to *both* sides), elections were decided by open bribery, and desperadoes from all over the West swaggered unmolested through the streets and bars, robbing and cheating and killing with impunity.

But the ore was rich and close to the surface and the men in control were intent on making a quick clean-up and a quick getaway. Somehow the work of skimming off the first easy profits was accomplished. Quartz was scooped up from the open cuts, from horizontal tunnels into the canyon-sides, or from shallow shafts that needed no equipment except hand-operated windlasses for raising the ore-buckets. By then, however, it had grown clear that this was no flash-camp, to be stripped and abandoned in a few months. Its rich ore bodies continued downward, no one could say how far. This meant long-range operations, the establishment of both mines and camps on a semi-permanent basis. Before the end of the first year some semblance of order had begun to grow out of chaos. Lawlessness was curbed and steps were taken to protect the thousands who continued to stream into the expanding towns. At the same time mining methods were undergoing equally drastic changes. The surface workings were presently exhausted, and as shafts deepened, more formal equipment and more complicated techniques were called for: power-driven hoisting apparatus, timbering to support the stopes and drifts and to line the shafts, ways of providing air to the lower workings.

Methods of coping with all these problems had to be improvised as the need arose. Horses or, frequently, jackasses—the ubiquitous "Washoe canaries" of the early Comstock—powered the windlasses, and when these in turn proved unable to lift the ore from the lengthening shafts, little fifteen-horsepower engines were manufactured in San Francisco and set up beside the mine-heads. Timbering presented a problem less easily surmounted, for the Comstock ore was mainly black sulphuret, a difficult substance to handle because it crumbled easily and tended to cave. The usual method of timbering, long in use throughout the world, was to support the roofs of stopes and tunnels by wooden pillars extending from floor to ceiling. But when this technique was introduced into the Comstock (from the quartz mines of California), it speedily proved unworkable. As the soft ore was removed, the rock above settled, splintering the heaviest timbers; cave-ins became so frequent that operations were often brought to a complete stop. In the summer of 1860, miners in the Ophir (the mine discovered a year earlier by McLaughlin and O'Riley) hit a vein of exceedingly rich ore that steadily broadened as they followed it downward. At the 175-foot level the deposit was sixty-five feet wide: how to extract so large a mass of brittle, unstable ore defied the ingenuity of the engineers. The situation was ironical; the owners had tapped a veritable treasure-trove only to meet defeat in successive efforts to find a method of removing it. "The Ophir Company began to wish themselves less fortunate, as their miners narrowly escaped burial day after day in their attempts to stope out the ore."

At this juncture one of the company's managers had an inspiration. In a quartz-mining district of California lived one Philip Deidesheimer, a young German engineer who had displayed resourcefulness in coping with the problems of deep mining. Deidesheimer was summoned over the mountains; he inspected the Ophir ore body, spent several weeks conducting a series of experiments, and in the end hit on what proved an ideal solution. This was the device that came to be known as square-set timbering: a series of interlocking rectangular frames, built of heavy timbers and designed to be placed in tiers one above another, and so to fill the excavated space from floor to roof. Simple as the method was, it remained in use in all the Comstock mines as long as operations continued. The Deidesheimer square-sets made it possible to remove with convenience and safety ore bodies of an extent never before known in mining operations: vast underground caverns hundreds of feet from wall to wall and from floor to ceiling. In 1875 a visitor to the underground workings of one of the leading mines thus described the scene:

"Cribs of timber were piled in successive stages from basement to dome four hundred feet above, and everywhere men were at work . . . climbing up to their assigned stopes with swinging lanterns or flickering candles, picking and drilling at the crumbling ore, or pushing lines of loaded cars to the stations at the shaft. Flashes of exploding powder were blazing from the rent faces of the stopes; blasts of gas and smoke filled the connecting drifts; muffled roars echoed along the dark galleries, and at all hours a hail of rock fragments might be heard rattling to the floor of the level, and massive lumps of ore falling heavily on the slanting pile at the foot of the breast. Half naked men . . . were shoveling ore and pushing cars; others, standing on the slippery piles, were guiding the power-drills which churned holes in the ore with incessant thumps, or cleaving the softer sulphurets with steel picks swung lightly by muscular arms. . . ."

All this was made possible by the square-set technique, yet Deidesheimer received little monetary return from his immensely useful device. He remained for years on the lode as mine superintendent or consultant, amassed a considerable fortune, lost it in one of the periodical stockmarket declines, and died poor.

But Comstock mining presented other difficulties, few of which were so easily overcome. Some remained to plague the owners as long as operations continued, and in each case the problem grew in urgency with each foot of downward progress. A major task was that of providing an adequate air supply. In the shallow early-day workings, ventilation had presented no problem, but as the shafts deepened and the underground drifts pushed outward hundreds of feet, the air at the faces of the cuts grew unbearably foul. In the summer of 1860, great canvas air-traps were rigged up at the mouths of the shafts; these revolved to capture the winds of the breezy town and funnel them through processed cloth pipes to the ends of the drifts. But the device was practicable only in workings two hundred feet or less from the surface. As the miners penetrated deeper—to five hundred feet, a thousand, two thousand, eventually to below three thousand—far more elaborate—and expensive—ventilating systems had to be installed. These were of slow development; meantime the miners worked with lowered efficiency and under conditions of acute discomfort. "Adits were cut for hundreds of feet without any ventilating shaft, and men worked with dogged persistence at the end of the drifts, breathing an atmosphere so foul that candles flickered and burned with a faint blue flame."

The problem was further complicated by the fact that the temperature of the rock increased with each foot of downward progress, rising to above 120 degrees at twenty-two hundred feet. Nor was this all. In the deeper levels streams of water were encountered so hot that steam filled the drifts, obscuring the faces of the cuts. Temperature on occasion rose to 140 degrees, well beyond the endurance even of picked miners who by long training had become inured to working in heat so intense that it stifled casual visitors.

Steadily more complicated measures had to be taken to combat bad air and high temperatures. All along the lode mines were joined by connecting drifts designed to promote air circulation from one to another; at the same time ventilating shafts were sunk at intervals, giving the long and winding drifts more direct connection with the surface. From the late 1860's on, powerful air-pumps, known as Root blowers, were installed in all the mines. These pumped compressed air through an intricate system of pipes, some as large as twenty inches in diameter, extending down the shafts and through thousands of feet of tunnels to the remotest workings. The longer blowers forced nine hundred cubic feet of air a minute through the ventilating pipes, yet conditions in the lower levels continued difficult in the extreme. There men worked in ever shorter shifts, naked except for breechcloths and shoes. Tons of ice were daily sent down the shafts: "half-fainting men chewed fragments greedily to cool their parched throats, and carried lumps in their clenched hands . . . iced water in the tanks was drunk in extraordinary quantity." In the summer of 1878 the daily ice allotment in one mine was ninety-five pounds for each man; more than two million pounds were used that year. Yet the heat, hovering around 130 degrees at the faces of the drifts, was so oppressive that shifts had to be shortened to half an hour, then to fifteen minutes. Had it not been for the introduction of power-driven Burleigh drills, the work would have had to stop entirely; to swing a pick or operate a hand-drill would have been beyond human endurance. As it was, four men failed to accomplish as much as one working in the cooler levels nearer the surface.

Through the late 1870's Comstock newspapers made almost daily reference to the extreme heat of the deep workings. In July 1877, miners sinking a shaft in the Savage encountered water so hot (157 degrees) that they worked in clouds of stifling vapor, their pick-handles so hot they were obliged to use gloves; cloths repeatedly dipped in ice-water were wrapped about the drills. Two years later the temperature in a gallery of the Yellow Jacket reached and remained at 137 degrees, and at the two-thousand-foot level of the Crown Point it rose to 150 degrees—"a place for salamanders rather than men." When water of 170 degrees Fahrenheit was encountered in the Yellow Jacket, a local paper announced, not without pride, that the Comstock had won still another distinction. Not only were its mines the world's richest; they were incomparably the hottest.

Exposed to such temperatures and breathing the stagnant air, men spent forty-five minutes of each hour beneath the nearest air-vent, going forward to their stations for successive brief periods and returning bathed in sweat

and often bent over with cramps. The pain of these
"stomach knots" was intense; workmen so stricken were
hurried to the surface and given rigorous massage treatment until the perspiration began to flow, whereupon
they returned to their posts, seemingly as well as ever.
There were occasional deaths, but on the whole the miners
—picked men all—came through the ordeal well. Usually
they spent not more than a week on the deepest parts of
the mines; they were then transferred to workings nearer
the surface, whereupon they rapidly put on the weight
they had sweated off in the inferno-like areas below.

The Sutro Tunnel, designed to drain the mines and to
simplify the problem of removing the ore from the deeper
levels, was begun in 1869. While it was building, not
alone the men but the normally docile Washoe canaries
were subjected to the ordeal of extreme heat and foul air.
As the four-mile bore neared completion, conditions became no less severe than in the mines themselves. The
face of the tunnel was then more than two miles from the
nearest ventilating shaft, and the wiry little mules that
pulled the work trains were with difficulty forced into its
far reaches. They would stop at points where jets of air
from the distant Root blowers were entering the tunnel,
and no amount of persuasion could induce them to go
farther. "More than once a rationally-obstinate mule thrust
his head into the end of the canvas air-pipe and was
literally torn away by main strength; as the miners, when
other means failed, tied his tail to two other mules in his
train and forced them to haul back their companion,
snorting viciously and slipping with stiff legs over the wet
floor. . . ."

But heat and bad air were not the only problems, or
even the most difficult. It was the floods of water gushing
into the lower workings that hastened the abandonment
of deep mining on the lode. Washoe engineers always
maintained that, given ore of sufficient richness, means
could be devised to operate at any depth; the only question was: Will it pay? But experience eventually proved
that there were mechanical limits to the volume of water
that could be raised from depths of three thousand feet

and beyond. As the 1870's ended, that limit was being approached the length of the lode. Above fifteen hundred feet, keeping the mines dry presented no insuperable problems, but when the shafts penetrated below two thousand feet the difficulties multiplied. In 1875 so large a volume of water was encountered in the Hale & Norcross and Savage that their powerful pumps were unable to cope with it and the lower workings were flooded to a depth of 450 feet. New and still larger pumps were installed, but despite their capacity of ten million gallons a month the pumping-out process proved tediously slow: after thirty months of continuous operation, the water level had fallen only fifty feet. By 1880 the combined shaft of the Consolidated Virginia and California had pumps with a capacity of 640 gallons a minute, operated by an engine developing 480 horsepower. Even more massive equipment was presently installed at other mine-heads: engines of six hundred horsepower operated pumps capable of hoisting a hundred thousand gallons an hour from depths of 2,800 feet. Yet this powerful apparatus, working continuously at full capacity, was barely able to keep pace with the torrents of water draining into the mines. By then many were ready to admit that deep mining had about reached its farthest limit. Only surpassingly rich new ore bodies—none of which were encountered—would justify the expense of further increasing the number and size of the Cornish pumps.

The Sutro Tunnel was broken through in 1878, after thirteen years of Herculean effort, and only then was the water brought under control. The tunnel, with its lateral extensions north and south, tapped the lode at the 1,650-foot level and it was necessary only to pump from the bottoms of the shafts to that point. But the long delay in completing the project had rendered it comparatively useless. By then the last of the great ore bodies had been worked out and—no others of comparable size having been discovered—operations began the decline that was to end a few years later in an almost complete stoppage.

During the years when the lode was in its heyday the machines of the Comstock were an unfailing source of pride to the mechanically minded. The size and power and ingenuity of its power-operated equipment had—as the Washoe press never tired of boasting—no counterpart elsewhere in the world. Not only were the appliances for ventilating the mines and keeping them dry the most efficient ever devised; not less ingenious were the methods of handling the ore. To move the vast quantity of quartz from the depths of the mountain (seven billion tons were extracted during the first two decades), to convey it to and through the mills, and to carry off the tailings to the immense dumps required a high order of engineering and mechanical skill. So did the bringing of an adequate water supply over twenty miles of rugged desert from the Sierra foothills; so too was the building of the Virginia & Truckee Railroad connecting the silver towns with the Carson Valley, a road that climbed two thousand feet in fifteen miles, much of it up the sides of winding, precipitous canyons.

But to the eyes of natives and visitors alike, the machination of the Comstock reached its apex in the high-speed cages that ceaselessly traveled up and down the shafts, plunging straight down (sometimes to a depth of more than half a mile) so fast that the intermediate stations flashed past like the lighted windows of an express train, and on the return trips lifting six-ton loads of ore or waste rock with as little apparent effort as though they carried "a cargo of feathers." Suspended from ribbon-like cables of woven steel, the three-decker cages lunged up and down the shafts at a pace that, to the uninitiated, seemed reckless in the extreme; yet they were under such perfect control that the operators at the mine-heads were able to stop them at stations three thousand feet below at the exact point desired, never an inch too high or too low. To the admiring 1870's this was the ultimate perfection of mechanical ingenuity.

3

MANY leading mines and mills were close to the center of the town, only a short walk from C Street and the Virginia

& Truckee station. The uncovering of the big bonanza in 1873 had fired the imagination of the whole country, and during the next half-dozen years a steady stream of visitors arrived, all eager to see the fabulous treasure-trove. Run-of-the-mill tourists were sent below in charge of underlings, but when persons of importance appeared, the owners themselves took them in tow. On their return to the surface, all were interviewed by reporters from the *Territorial Enterprise* and the *Evening Chronicle* in Virginia City, and the *Evening News* over the divide at Gold Hill; few failed to mention the heat of the lower levels. John A. Logan, former Civil War general and then Senator from Illinois, wiped rivulets of sweat from his face and observed that the silver dollar was worth all its hundred cents. Robert Ingersoll confessed that an hour in the steaming underground passages had shaken his well-publicized agnosticism: possibly there might be a hell after all. Statesmen, preachers, titled foreigners, authors, lecturers, actors crowded one upon the other. Residents grew used to the sight of private cars coupled to the end of the morning train from Reno, and ceased to be curious about what eminent personages the town was harboring. After 1876, visitors were put up in style at the new International, five stories high and boasting the only hydraulic elevator between Chicago and the Coast, and boasting too a cuisine and wine cellar equal to Delmonico's in New York.

Each visitor received a welcome befitting his importance. Generals Sherman and Sheridan, James G. Blaine, Henry Ward Beecher, Presidents Harrison and Hayes, and a dozen others were met at the depot, paraded through the streets behind uniformed drill teams, serenaded by the combined Virginia City and Gold Hill bands, taken on a tour of the mines, and tendered a banquet in the marble-floored dining-room of the International. These celebrations reached their climax during General Grant's visit in 1879. He and his party were taken on a two-hour tour of the bonanza mines; when they reached the surface the usually taciturn general remarked: "That's as close to hell as I ever want to get!" Later, from a balcony of the International, Grant reviewed the town's firemen, Civil War veterans, drill teams, and a contingent of ragged Piutes decked out in war-paint. At the banquet that followed, Grant regarded Wells Drury, local newspaperman, whose diminutive figure was resplendent in the uniform of a local marching club. "Young fellow," Grant observed dryly, "I never had so fine a uniform all the time I was general of the armies."

Visitors to the big bonanza followed a fixed routine. From the Consolidated Virginia office they passed into a large, carpeted room where they exchanged their clothes for outfits better adapted to the humid underground workings. The garments were provided by the mine's managers: heavy shoes, cotton shirts and breeches, felt hats, and, for the long, swift ride in the cages, thick woolen coats. Adjoining this chamber was a bathroom where the returning visitor might enjoy a cooling tub before reassuming his everyday garb. A similar but smaller room was provided for the ladies, in which hung rows of roomy smocks of brown alpaca, woolen skirts, and stout shoes, topped off by shapeless felt hats of the same sort provided for the men. Although these outfits failed to enhance the alluring qualities of feminine visitors, they served their purpose of protecting them from the mud and grime of the lower workings.

But a visit to the underground stopes and galleries was only part of the entertainment provided for visitors; not all the Comstock's wonders were below the surface. An instructive half day could be spent following the course of the ore from the time it issued from the shafts until the refined metal, cast in heavy ingots, was wheeled into the bullion room and stacked like cordwood to await shipment to Carson City or San Francisco. The huge California mill, completed in 1879, with its eighty stamps, its batteries of amalgamating pans, agitators, and settlers, was hailed as the most complete and efficient ore-reducing plant in mining history; it was but one of a score of mills whose tall stacks day and night poured plumes of wood-smoke into the desert air.

The fortunes of town and mines were inseparably linked. Business boomed while production remained high, and trading in bonanza stocks was brisk. During slack periods hundreds of miners tramped C Street with empty pockets, the crowds in the bars thinned out, and merchants eyed their overloaded shelves and revived trade by slashing prices. But in good times or bad the Comstocker lived well. As early as 1866 the miners had organized, and fixed the minimum wage below ground at four dollars for an eight-hour shift—compared to five dollars a week paid for similar work in England, and $1.65 a week in Saxony. Moreover, they managed to maintain that scale as long as the lode remained active, successfully defeating periodical drives of the owners to reduce payrolls in slack times.

Drawing wages that made him the envy of his fellows the world over, the Washoe miner spent freely. Nothing but the best suited him, in food, in clothing, and in entertainment. His living-quarters, however, left much to be desired. Only in the area above C Street were comfortable, well-cared-for residences to be found. There mineowners and superintendents, the town's merchants, and professional men had built ornate little cottages, with prim wooden fences surrounding their steep gardens. Elsewhere domestic architecture was strictly utilitarian. On the slanting ground of the lower town, extending more than a mile to the north and south, were acres of wooden shacks built wall to wall, huddled close about the mills and hoisting works or at the edges of the immense dumps. The arid climate and stony soil, plus high water-rates, discouraged gardens. "One walks for blocks," wrote a visitor in the 1880's, "without seeing a plant or shrub, or rarely even a blade of grass." A few houses showed signs of once having been whitewashed; the great majority had never known a painter's brush and their rough wooden sides had been bleached a uniform gray by the dry, dusty summers. Inside, the tiny rooms were partitioned with cloth and paper, their outer walls poor protection against the winter snows and the year-round Washoe zephyrs— violent winds that sometimes ripped off the roofs of the jerry-built shacks and sent them fluttering down the canyons.

Between this unprepossessing district and the homes of the prosperous were the business center and the scores of hotels and lodging-houses that sheltered the town's uncommonly high percentage of bachelors. Several of the C Street hotels were comfortable, well-operated establishments, and of course every inhabitant considered the International the most luxurious hostelry between Chicago and the Coast. No such claim was made on behalf of the rooming-houses: scores of angular, barracks-like boxes, two or three stories high, with lines of cubicles opening off narrow hallways. Here heat was provided by cast-iron stoves, illumination by candles or kerosene lamps. Many of the rooms were without outside windows; transoms opening into hallways provided whatever light and air they got. Few had bathrooms, and the toilets were in the back yards: the Comstock was always lamentably lax in the matter of plumbing. For these luxuries the patrons paid from forty to sixty dollars a month, including meals. This was during comparatively active periods; in slack times rates were sharply reduced.

Prosperous citizens did not find life insupportable in the barren town: they lived in comfort and with a degree of luxury. Many were "Washoe widowers," who put up at the International or the better boarding-houses while their wives and children remained "down below"—the Comstock's name for San Francisco and its environs. Others installed their families in cottages high on the side of Mount Davidson. For recreation they frequented the Crystal on C Street, the most luxurious of the town's numberless bars. The Crystal was the "millionaires' saloon"; its restaurant was said to rival even the dining-room of the International, while on the floor above were the quarters of the Washoe Club, "surpassing in luxury and in the perfection of its appointments any gentlemen's club in Western America."

The town's workmen had no Washoe Club. Their clubs were the saloons that occupied, on an average, every second building on both sides of C Street for three quarters of a mile. The miners crowded them day and night, mainly because there were few other places to go. True, the

Miners' Union had a substantial brick building on the block above, with a library of several thousand volumes, and Piper's Opera House was a regular stopping-place for theatrical troupes passing from coast to coast. These, besides touring lecturers or musicians and Saturday-night boxing or wrestling bouts, were the sum of the town's amusements. It was meager fare. The saloon being the only resource for the great majority, the consumption of spirits was high. One friendly critic of Comstock mores stated that, in good times and bad, drink was the curse of the lode, adding that many consumed a quart of whisky a day, in numberless small drinks, and continued year after year. One authority calculated that the hundred saloons remaining in 1880—when the lode was already on the down grade—dispensed seventy-five thousand gallons of hard liquor that year, and twice that volume of wine and beer. This was a per capita consumption of twenty-two and a half gallons per year, one third of which was whisky. At the prevailing rate of "a bit a drink," $900,-000 was expended "quenching the thirst of twenty thousand people; yet 1880 was called a dry year in comparison with 1876."

Curiously, gambling was much less prevalent here than in other frontier towns, perhaps because trading in mining stocks was almost universal, and the hazards of that speculation—to say nothing of its expense—left little time or money for such conventional games of chance as faro, roulette, or three-card monte. Even such inveterate gamblers as the Chinese preferred to risk their savings in the brokerage houses on C Street. As a consequence, the town's Oriental quarter—three crowded blocks on the flat below the railroad depot—had far fewer fan-tan houses than the Little Cantons of other Western cities. It had, however, quite as many opium dives, and rather more than its share of prostitutes.

In this it did not differ from the rest of the town, for during the heyday of the lode Virginia's prostitutes were notorious all over the West. The yield of the mines, the efficiency of the mills, and the luxury of its hotels and eating-places were unfailing sources of civic pride; but citizens boasted too of a red-light district superior to any other from Denver to the Coast, both in size and in the variety and amiability of its inmates. Visitors of note, having been shown through the mines and mills and entertained at the Washoe Club, were as a matter of course piloted down the steep grade to the double row of white cottages that lined D Street for two crowded blocks. For it was a tradition of the town that after an evening in the C Street bars or a show at Piper's Opera House convivial groups turned by common consent toward "the line." Recent writers have delighted in romanticizing the Comstock's prostitutes; this is in contrast to the more realistic early-day viewpoint. In reporting frequent violent deaths on D Street, the town's reporters usually disposed of such routine assignments with a single sentence. One reads: "A woman known as Grace Fanshaw, age about twenty-five, residing at 26 South D Street, committed suicide last night by drinking laudanum during a fit of despondency brought on by blighted love, acute alcoholism and bad investments."

Even Julia Bulette, long the darling of the fiction-writers, won the gratitude of her contemporaries mainly because she helped relieve the boredom in the early camp, where diversions were few. She has been more written about than any other Comstock woman, not even excepting Eilley Orrum, the boarding-house keeper whose tiny Gold Hill bonanza gave her a season of high prosperity, and who later won added renown as the "Washoe Seeress." Julia, who, in the words of one writer, "caressed Sun Mountain with a gentle touch of splendor," reached Virginia City when that chaotic cluster of shacks was making a rapid transition from camp to town; and for two years she was close to the center of every happening. Of her early history little is known. One account states that she was born in Liverpool and that her real name was Smith; but whatever her background, her Comstock period was surely her most triumphant. Except for bands of Piute squaws and a few gaunt frontier women, she was the miners' only symbol of the gentle and civilizing sex. They made the most of her, and she of them. Her establishment was an oasis of elegance in a community of tents, cabins, bars, and cheerless rooming-houses. She occupied a place of honor in the Fourth of July parade of 1861; she was patron and mascot of one of the volunteer fire companies; she addressed a mass meeting in support of the Sanitary Fund (designed to ease the lot of wounded Union soldiers) and, like others of the town's leaders, bid in the fund's historic sack of flour and turned it back to be auctioned off again. The boom of 1863 raised her to affluence; thereafter she daily drove through the streets in a handsome carriage, the doors of which bore the Bulette crest: four aces surmounted by a lion couchant. Then, at the height of her notoriety, she was found strangled one morning in her widely known bed, with her jewels missing. The entire lode went into mourning; mills shut down and miners remained above ground the day of her funeral. Thousands followed the Virginia City band and uniformed fire companies to the cemetery, saw her buried with pomp and dignity, and marched back to town to the tune of *The Girl I Left Behind Me*. Nearly a year later her murderer incautiously tried to peddle some of his loot, and Julia posthumously provided the lode with a second holiday. Again mines and business houses were closed while John Millian was ceremoniously hanged from a gallows set up in the natural amphitheater north of town. By then the Bulette legend was firmly established; her stature has grown with the years. Only once was her supremacy challenged. Several years later one of the ladies of D Street met the morning train from Reno in an open carriage, graciously welcomed a clergyman newly called to a local parish and paraded him the length of C Street before depositing him, beaming but puzzled at the cheering crowds, at the door of his parsonage.

4

THE ceaseless noise and activity of the Washoe towns, the nervous tension compounded of instability, recklessness, and the gambler's atmosphere of impending fortune, attracted the adventurous and daring from all over the West and fed the excitement their natures craved. It was an environment in which a man's inner character quickly revealed itself. The strong were toughened by its challenges and shouldered their way to the top, the wily or vicious speedily found their level, and those with hidden weaknesses seldom long withstood the lode's abundant temptations. The Comstock—"no nursery for tender consciences" —regarded these processes with unconcern; it passed no judgments, set up no rules designed to protect the sheep from the wolves, to shield the weak from the consequences of their folly. Strangers from more conventional places were often shocked by what seemed to them a complete lack of ethics, business or personal. Thomas Starr King, San Francisco's crusading preacher, returned from a visit in 1863 and pronounced Virginia "a city of gopher holes, Ophir holes, and loafer holes." Another visitor called it "a city of stovepipes and single men's wives"; and a third wrote: "I have seen more rascality, great and small, in my brief forty days in this wilderness of sagebrush, sharpers and prostitutes, than in thirteen years' experience in our not squeamishly moral state of California. . . . God help me! I never saw such a land." But the maligned lode was not without defenders. "Frontier towns," stated one, "differ from others only because here men do openly and in broad daylight what the conventions of older communities require them to do by stealth."

The acres of neglected graves on the hillsides north of Virginia reveal how many lives ended before they had well begun, by violence, by recurring epidemics; many no doubt died because they could not withstand the temptations of the teeming, wide-open towns. But there were also those who, seasoned by their years on the Comstock, went on to make their marks in the larger world beyond. The most conspicuous example is, of course, Mark Twain, but the lode never took Mark to its heart, and even today mention of his name is likely to bring a baneful gleam to the eyes of doddering old-timers. "Sure, Mark was around here once. Can't say he ever lived here, exactly; just stopped off a couple of months, then went below and never came back. Took the night stage, I understand, sort of eased out of town. Seems there was a little matter of a board-bill." You mention another journalist, Dan De Quille, Twain's friend and mentor on the *Enterprise,* and get a different reaction. "Dandy Quille? What you might call a striking figure. Skinny as a lamp-post and pretty near as tall; wore a long cape and a big wide black hat. A real striking figure." You ask: "Ever read his stories in the *Enterprise?"* The ancient points a bony finger down the street: you regard the old *Enterprise* office, a narrow brick building, its walls tilting rakishly to the south. "Must've seen him come out of that door a thousand times. Had a desk just inside that far window. He was a heavy drinker, but queer. Once he wrote a book." "That's right," you prompt; *"The History of the Big Bonanza."* "Some such name. Got Dan into a pot of trouble. Quit his job and started peddling his book. Rented a buck-board and drove all over the country: Gold Hill, Silver City, Dayton, all the way to Carson. Whenever a fellow bought a book Dan bought *him* a drink. Pretty soon he'd get feeling generous and start passing books out free. Wasn't long before they was gone and he owed the company six hundred dollars. Had to go back working for the paper. Every kid in town knew Dandy Quille; his long black cape kept getting greener and seedier-looking year after year. Must have seen him come out of that door a thousand times. . . ."

When the Comstock came on lean years, Dan De Quille remained behind long after his fellow newspapermen had moved on: C. C. Goodwin to edit the *Salt Lake Tribune,* Arthur McEwen to become a Hearst editor and to publish in his shortlived weekly *Letter* vitriolic attacks on the Comstock's leaders; the two Davis brothers, one of whom, Sam, long published the Carson City *Appeal,* while Bob became a well-known figure in New York journalism. The list is lengthy: Edward W. Townsend, popular for his "Chimmy Fadden" stories; Charles Michelson, like McEwen a Hearst editor, and later publicist for the Democratic Party during the triumphant Roosevelt regime; Joe Goodman, proprietor of the *Enterprise,* who years later

voiced the nostalgia of a generation of Comstock veterans
in the verses that began:

> In youth when I did love, did love
> 　(To quote the sexton's homely ditty)
> I lived six thousand feet above
> 　Sea level, in Virginia City;
> The site was bleak, the houses small
> 　The narrow streets unpaved and slanting,
> But now it seems to me of all
> 　The spots on earth the most enchanting.

Goodman's partner on the *Enterprise* was Rollin Daggett, short, fat, and whimsical, with a strain of Iroquois blood in his veins. Daggett later abandoned journalism for politics, served a term in Congress, and was appointed Minister to Hawaii, where his most memorable feat of diplomacy was to teach King Kalakaua to play stud poker. The problematical rewards of Nevada politics tempted others from the lode's editorial rooms. One was Tom Fitch, owner of the *Gold Hill News,* whose platform eloquence was such that his name on the list of speakers assured an overflow crowd at any political rally, regardless of whose candidacy he was currently supporting. But Fitch had more luck electing others than himself. He managed to get one term in Congress, but his ambition to go to the Senate remained unrealized. Once the prize seemed within his grasp, but the Republican caucus made a last-minute switch and chose another candidate. Fitch stood up and briefly addressed the assemblage: "I know now exactly how Lazarus felt. I too have been licked by dogs."

In fifteen years the Comstock sent four adopted sons to the Senate: Stewart, Sharon, Fair, and Jones. None of this group appreciably raised the average of statesmanship within that body, but all contributed to its growing renown as a millionaires' club. The office was never cheaply won: half a million was not considered an excessive price to pay to control the legislature in a campaign year. "Wasn't he elected honest?" demanded the manager of a successful candidate. "Didn't every man get his five dollars?" The cost of votes was often higher. William Sharon and John P. Jones fought tooth and nail for the prize in 1873; both were owners of bonanza mines and the spending was prodigious. Sharon was defeated; but four years later he returned to the lists, and this time the "overmastering weight of his sock" permitted him to carry off the plum. Part of the contents of his sock went to buy the *Enterprise,* the politics of which thereupon made a complete about-face. "You have fastened yourself upon the vitals of the state like a hyena," it had saluted Sharon at the opening of his campaign in 1872. Four years later it was telling its subscribers: "The present prosperity of Western Nevada is more due to Mr. Sharon than to any ten men. . . ."

The ablest of the Comstock senators was William M. Stewart, whose long service at Washington began when Nevada entered the Union in 1865 and lasted, with one or two breaks, until after the turn of the century. Stewart, one of the legal lights who had hurried to the lode soon after its discovery, was a huge blond giant, so austere in his manner and bearing that he was said to "move like a cathedral." Innumerable stories were told of him. In the early sixties, while the lode was enmeshed in a snarl of boundary disputes, his fees averaged $125,000 a year. Once while he was arguing a case the frequent interruptions of an opposing attorney aroused his ire. He glared at the offender, a small but wily attorney named Baldwin. "You little shrimp," he roared, "if you interrupt me again, I'll eat you!" Baldwin retorted blandly: "If you do, Mr. Stewart, you'll have more brains in your belly than you ever had in your head!" During one of his campaigns a speaker stated that Stewart "towers among men like the Colossus of Rhodes." An unfriendly paper quoted the remark and added: "and he has as much brass in his composition."

Lawsuits clogged the courts during the entire two decades of the lode's activity, but the town's attorneys reaped their richest harvest in the early and middle sixties. In six years the twelve leading mines figured in 245 actions, all expensive in time and money. There were months-long periods when operations were completely suspended while owners and lawyers struggled to untangle the involved litigation. One famous suit was between the Chollar and the Potosi, two bordering properties that struck it rich in 1861. The contest lasted until 1865, when the two mines combined to form the Chollar-Potosi; the expense of the protracted litigation was $1,300,000. Others were almost as costly. Ophir and the Burning Moscow settled their boundary dispute only after an expenditure of $1,-070,000. One authority estimated that between 1860 and 1865 legal fees aggregated nine million dollars, one-fifth the total output of the lode in those years.

These were serious battles, with many millions at stake, but Comstock litigation had also its lighter side. Once a Storey County sheriff, instructed to assemble a panel of jurors, issued subpœnas to every cross-eyed citizen in town, and followed with a panel of giants, not one of whom stood less than six feet six inches high. Even such sober occasions as coroner's inquests were not exempt from the lode's raffish humor, as when a jury, sitting on the case of a miner killed by a piece of falling ore, rendered a verdict that the victim had "died of quartz on the brain." The legal gentry worked hard and played hard, and the attorney who complained that he was slowly starving to death was guilty of only a mild exaggeration: his plaint was that he had no appetite for breakfast, no time for lunch, and was usually too drunk to eat his dinner.

For years Washoe residents were known all over the Coast as accomplished tipplers; it was a well-earned distinction. When the camp was founded in 1859, the first commercial enterprise to be set up was a bar: two planks supported by whisky kegs, with a strip of canvas overhead to shield patrons from the fierce desert sun. It enjoyed a brisk trade. Competitors soon appeared, their patronage the heavier because water from the few feeble springs was believed—erroneously—to contain strychnine and hence to be unsafe to drink without first being liberally diluted with Sazarac whisky. During the first two years the camps on both sides of the divide had five saloons to every establishment dealing in other commodities; later this proportion grew less, but to the end the ratio remained high.

Actual drunkenness, however, was curiously rare; even on Saturday nights, traditionally the Comstock's time for conviviality, those in the crowded bars remained capable of locomotion and for the most part orderly. The Comstock miner carried his liquor well, and a number of ingenious theories were advanced to explain the phenomenon. One held that the altitude was responsible: men swore that in the dry, light air of Mount Davidson one could consume without deleterious effect a quantity of spirits that in San Francisco, six thousand feet nearer sea level, would have sent one reeling into the nearest gutter. A more likely explanation is that by long habit the town's tipplers had built up a formidable resistance to alcohol and an immunity to the outward signs of intoxication. The man who drank intermittently throughout the day—such was the custom of the Comstock— could consume a volume of intoxicants that, had he crowded it into the social evening hours, would have put him under the table. Another deterrent to unseemly excesses was the strictly enforced rule barring miners who showed any evidence of intoxication from going below ground. But there were occasions when these self-imposed restraints were cheerfully discarded and the entire male population went on extended community busts. One such was in 1865 when news of Lee's surrender reached the Comstock. For three days no newspapers were published on either side of the divide; their staffs were busy celebrating the glorious victory. Besides, who among the subscribers would have been able to read them?

5

BY THE MIDDLE sixties the silver towns were in the trough of their second serious depression. In six years the mines had produced in excess of fifty million dollars, but inept and extravagant management, faulty milling methods, and costly litigation had consumed every dollar of profits and much besides. Moreover, the rich ore bodies comparatively near the surface were nearing exhaustion and exploratory shafts sunk below the five-hundred-foot mark had uniformly proved barren. Business was at a standstill on both sides of the divide. Merchants, a third of their customers gone and the rest jobless and broke, stripped the stocks from their shelves and hauled them off to one or another of the booming new camps farther east. Mines were shutting down the length of the lode while their managers strove to raise new capital, and when stockholders refused to pay the successive assessments, their forfeited stock was put up as security for loans— at steadily increasing interest rates that presently reached a ruinous twelve per cent a month. A spirit of pessimism had succeeded the early sanguine hopes. Many were convinced that the Comstock was well past its peak and that another year or two would see the final end of operations.

At this juncture a potent new force began to make itself felt. In San Francisco, William Chapman Ralston, most resourceful and daring of the Coast's financiers, had organized the Bank of California and was casting about for a qualified man to manage the branch he planned to establish at Virginia City. His choice fell on William Sharon, a precise, dandified little man of forty-four, whose surface geniality concealed a devious and crafty nature. Arriving in the fall of 1864, when the affairs of the lode had reached a hopeless impasse, with its residents "sitting helplessly on a third of a billion dollars' worth of treasure," Sharon was shrewd enough to realize that here was an opportunity such as gamblers dream of. Through the door of the agency's new office at C and Taylor streets came the harassed managers of virtually every mine on the lode, of most of the mills, besides hard-pressed merchants, sawmill-owners, and trucking contractors. Each in turn was admitted behind the rail and ushered into the manager's office. A small but smil-

ing Santa Claus, Sharon passed out the bank's funds with
an amiable unconcern that delighted the needy borrowers. San Francisco, queen city of the Coast, had graciously come to the rescue of the impoverished villages below
Mount Davidson. The money she supplied, through genial
Mr. Sharon—not at the former usurious interest rate but
at a conservative five per cent a month—broke the log-
jam of inaction, speeded litigation, put idle crews back
to work above and below ground, rehabilitated mills, and
caused the welcome clatter of stamps once more to echo
against the mountainside.

For months Sharon was the benevolent patron of the
lode, the magician who at a wave of his golden wand
had lifted the Comstock out of the doldrums. The honeymoon was lamentably brief. Borrowers were presently
again passing behind the railing, anxious to renew their
notes and perhaps to increase their size to complete development work already in progress. But now the small
figure behind the manager's desk bore less resemblance
to Santa Claus; he greeted visitors with the formality of a
conscientious employee concerned for the safety of the
bank's investments. Each loan was closely scrutinized; it
was renewed only if additional security was forthcoming.
Notes that failed to meet the suddenly rigid requirements
were called; if they were not paid promptly, foreclosure
proceedings began. During the first months of 1865 Sharon's brief season of popularity vanished; his office became
"Sharon's sweat room" as the bank one by one took over
many of the lode's most desirable properties. It had been
a hazardous gamble on the part of the Ralston-Sharon
group, but their San Francisco bank had become the
Coast's wealthiest financial house by taking just such
chances, and again Ralston's good luck held. As mines
came under control of the new owners and operations
were speeded up, a series of rich new ore bodies were
uncovered, mills went into around-the-clock operation,
and the renewed flow of dividends sent prices soaring
on the long-stagnant market.

By 1867 the Comstock was in the grip of a new and

greater boom, and this time the major share of the profits flowed into the hands of the bank group. Sharon had meantime been consolidating his position as King of the Comstock by extending control over subsidiary sources of profit: mills, timber, water, fuel, machinery, and much more. Not only did the dapper little Crœsus aspire to gather in the mines and their sources of supply; he planned a further step: that of controlling the flow of traffic between the silver towns and the outer world. From the beginning this had been carried, at very high cost, in stages and huge freight-wagons laboriously drawn up the steep grades by multiple teams of horses or mules. In 1869 Sharon began the construction of the Virginia & Truckee Railroad; when it was completed three years later, his ambition to make himself complete master of the Comstock seemed on the point of being realized.

Meantime he had been extending his control over those properties that still remained in other hands. One of the most valuable of these was the Hale & Norcross, an actively producing mine, the chief owner of which was Charles L. Low. With much caution Sharon set about picking up shares, aiming at securing a majority of the stock and so of electing his own trustees at the forthcoming annual meeting, in March 1868. But such stealthy raids had by then been so often carried out that speculators at both Virginia City and San Francisco had grown adept at smelling them out. For all Sharon's cunning, suspicions were aroused that someone was planning a corner in Hale & Norcross. The consequence was that those who owned shares not yet gathered in made the most of their position. Hale & Norcross shares rose from below $300 at the beginning of January to $2,925 a month later. But that was only the beginning. With both Low and Sharon bidding for the crucial few shares that would swing the election, the offering price approached astronomical heights: $4,100 on February 11, $7,100 four days later. The race was so close that even at these figures shares were eagerly sought for. One broker, learning that a miner, snowbound in a mountain village in Plumas

County, owned a single share, traveled night and day, through snow and ice, by stagecoach and otherwise, only to discover that some other person had preceded him and obtained the stock. A San Francisco banker had on deposit three shares that belonged to a man whose whereabouts was unknown. So much pressure was brought to bear that the banker turned the stock over to one of the contending groups, thereby giving them the coveted majority. But before the day of the meeting the missing owner appeared and reclaimed his stock, thereby throwing the issue again in doubt. The "Hale & Norcross corner" kept the Coast in turmoil for weeks, with both sides buying recklessly without regard to the intrinsic worth of the stocks. As the election approached, bids of $10,000 a share were made, with no takers. Sharon eventually won, but only after a very heavy outlay. The exploit proved costly, for although he assumed control in March, the mine's ore body pinched out soon afterward. During the remainder of the year production fell off sharply and the value of the stock declined steadily, reaching $41.50 by September.

It was at this point in the checkered history of the Hale & Norcross that two new figures entered the picture. Both had recently attained a minor prominence on the Comstock, and one—John W. Mackay—was the largest owner of a small but profitable Gold Hill mine, the Kentuck. The other was James Graham Fair, whose mining experience, like that of Mackay, had been gained in California's Mother Lode. Both were thoroughly familiar with the Hale & Norcross (a year or two earlier Fair had served for a few months as its assistant superintendent), and both were convinced that despite its current poor production record the mine's prospects were good. The two agreed that an attempt to wrest its control from Sharon would be a good gamble. Accordingly, for the second time in two years a raid on the Hale & Norcross got under way, this time with Sharon and the "Bank crowd" as prospective victims and with two comparatively obscure operators engineering the coup. It was a daring scheme considering the fact that Fair was almost entirely

without capital and Mackay's resources—his profits from
the Kentuck—were small by comparison with those of
Sharon and his backers. But there were circumstances favorable to the success of their plot. Soon after Sharon had
taken control, dividends had ceased and a series of assessments were levied. Not wishing to pay the latter out of his
own pocket, Sharon had prudently sold most of his stock,
knowing that he could buy it back at favorable prices
should he get advance intimation that the current exploration work had uncovered promising new ore. Assessments,
plus low production, had as always depressed the value of
the stock, and this of course minimized the risk the amateur speculators were taking. Even if Mackay and Fair
failed to gain control, they were convinced that whatever
stock they bought was worth the prevailing low prices.

They planned their campaign with a prudent skill that
would have done credit to far more experienced operators.
Both early recognized that their coup would have to be
carried out on the floor of the San Francisco Mining Exchange and that it would be necessary to have an able and
discreet broker to conduct their operations there. Their
choice settled on James C. Flood, who with his partner,
William S. O'Brien, had recently closed their Washington
Street saloon and set themselves up as traders in Comstock stocks. The four men entered into an oral agreement
to buy up enough Hale & Norcross stock to give them
control. Mackay agreed to take a three-eighth interest;
Flood and O'Brien together obligated themselves to pay
for a like proportion, and Fair assumed responsibility for
the remaining two-eighths. The venture taxed the resources
of all four. It is said that Flood and O'Brien borrowed
fifty thousand dollars to finance their share of the purchases, and that to make up his quota Fair was obliged to
give his partners promissory notes, secured by future earnings and by his salary as superintendent. Only Mackay
had the cash in hand.

Quietly Flood set to work, operating with such skill that
for weeks the San Francisco brokers, usually alert for
signs of abnormal trading, were unaware that anything
unusual was going on. Not until February 1869, less than

a month before the stockholders' meeting, did word of the raid reach the public: the *Gold Hill News* on February 27 printed a paragraph stating that "as J. G. Fair and J. W. Mackay, of Virginia City, own over four hundred shares of Hale & Norcross stock, they will be likely to control the election of officers in March." The prediction proved correct. Sharon for once had been caught napping; when he awoke to his danger and entered the market, the battle was already lost. Firmly in control, the Fair-Mackay-Flood-O'Brien group voted out Sharon's trustees and installed their own. It was the first major defeat Sharon had suffered during his five-year reign as King of the Comstock. The exploit won for the new firm the lasting enmity of the powerful bank crowd, and a series of fierce battles followed. Sharon, shrewd and able, was enraged that a group that he considered rank amateurs, operating on a shoestring, had so neatly outwitted him; the "scrawny little Midas" vowed vengeance.

What happened next did not contribute to Sharon's peace of mind. Flood became president (succeeding Sharon) and O'Brien and Mackay were elected trustees. The new board dismissed the former superintendent and installed Fair in his place. An $80,000 assessment had been leveled by the old management; this was canceled and the funds already collected were returned to the stockholders. More gratifying still was the next development. Hardly had the Mackay-Fair group taken charge when promising new ore-bodies were uncovered; these, with rigid economy in operation, speedily put the mine on a paying basis. During the rest of 1869, dividends of almost $200,000 were paid; the next year, Fair having located another and richer deposit, they passed the $500,000 mark. Thereafter production fell off as the high-grade ore was exhausted; by 1872, dividends had fallen to a mere $80,000, and the next year assessments were resumed.

Elated by the success of their first venture, the four amateur operators looked about for another property that could be profitably exploited. They presently found it. Their ultimate success exceeded their wildest hopes; in less than three years, through their discovery and development of the big bonanza, "incomparably the richest strike of precious metals in mining history," they had made themselves undisputed masters of the Comstock, their names household words all over the West.

Part Two

Mackay

1

MACKAY was the youngest and ablest member of what presently became known as the bonanza firm, and he survived his three partners by periods that ranged from eight to twenty-four years.

Until the infirmities of age came upon him he took pride in the fact that his physical strength exceeded that of most far younger men. In later years he delighted to recall his experiences in the crude mining camps on both sides of the Sierra, where he had lived simply and vigorously, wielding shovel or ax from daylight to dark and nightly falling into his bunk in a state of pleasant exhaustion. The austerities of youth are usually attractive only in retrospect, but Mackay seems from the beginning to have taken pleasure in bending his back to whatever hard physical tasks presented themselves. Later, when growing responsibilities demanded that he lay aside his workman's tools and spend long hours behind a desk, he was at pains to keep himself fit. His partners might by easy living grow soft and develop paunches: he kept his weight down and his muscles hard. Long before the physical-culture fad had become popular he faithfully followed its precepts, and it was not time wasted. He retained the figure and bearing of an athlete far beyond the period when most of his contemporaries had resigned themselves to a sedentary and physically unenterprising old age. One evening in London, when he was close to seventy, he entertained a group in the office of his Commercial Cable Company by locking hands one by one with each man present (some of whom were less than half his age), elbows on desk, and by sustained pressure forcing their forearms backward until their hands touched the desk. He explained that this was a trick he had learned on the Yuba River half a century earlier: it was just a matter of knowing how and from what angle to exert pressure.

All his life he exerted pressure to keep himself in good physical trim. At Virginia City in the middle sixties he was one of the faithful who gathered nightly at Bill Davis's gymnasium on South C Street. There, stripped to the waist, he went through three bruising rounds with whatever opponent presented himself. Mackay was a slow but tenacious boxer who made up in aggressiveness what he lacked in skill. Of all forms of exercise this was his favorite: it developed co-ordination of hand and eye, put a premium on coolness under fire, and gave him needed practice in controlling his never stable temper. He regarded the sport so highly that some years after the bonanza firm opened its bank in San Francisco, Mackay had a basement room fitted up as a gymnasium and invited employees to relax there after business hours. One of those who most frequently made use of it was a brash young Irishman named Corbett. Corbett developed so much boxing skill that soon he was defeating the best amateurs in the city. Mackay was pleased when the nineteen-year-old clerk made himself kingpin of the city's light heavyweights; his interest waned, however, when he presently learned that the youth had turned professional. For a young man qualified to hold a clerkship in the Nevada Bank to embark on a career as a professional fighter violated his lively sense of the appropriate. A year or two later Corbett, then twenty-one, was on his way to New Orleans for his first important fight, with Jake Kilrain, who had recently lost the heavyweight title to John L.

Sullivan after a titanic, bare-knuckle slugging match that had lasted seventy-five rounds. At a way-station en route, Corbett, decked out in cap and sweater, was sprinting up and down beside the track when a west-bound train pulled in. Mackay was among the passengers; he recognized his former clerk and demanded to know what he was doing there. Corbett answered proudly that he was on his way to New Orleans to fight the great Kilrain. "I hope he gives you a damn good licking," said Mackay shortly, and climbed back into his car.

But Corbett defeated the aging Kilrain and in 1892 won the championship by knocking out Sullivan. Mackay thereupon relented, and from then onward the new champ had no more ardent supporter. In the fall of 1894 the papers announced that Corbett was setting off for London to play the lead in a melodrama called *Gentleman Jack*. A few days before he sailed, Mackay wrote asking him to call; Corbett went to the mining man's Fifth Avenue apartment, where Mackay informed him that prize fighters were not highly regarded in England and that he would be ignored in polite circles unless he was properly introduced. He added: "I want to give you letters to some of my friends over there to show them that a man can be both a pugilist and a gentleman." Later Mackay cabled his son Clarence, asking him to keep an eye on the boxer. Clarence responded by sending an enormous floral piece over the footlights of the Drury Lane Theatre the night *Gentleman Jack* opened; later he came back-stage, bringing with him a young friend, the Duke of Teck. Thanks to this introduction, Corbett, far from finding himself a social pariah, became a favorite of the young bloods of the town. Before each of his subsequent fights Corbett found in his dressing-room a message from the mining man wishing him luck. When he risked—and lost—his title to Bob Fitzsimmons at Carson City in 1897, Mackay, then in London, invited a group of friends to the cable company's office to hear a blow-by-blow description of the battle; it was the first time such news had been telegraphed half around the world.

Mackay had almost no formal education, and after he

had lifted himself out of the ranks of day-laborers he tried hard to master the polite accomplishments. An acquaintance tells of hunting him up at his Virginia City quarters late at night and finding him, after sixteen hours spent overseeing the affairs of the world's richest group of mines, plodding patiently through a textbook of elementary English grammar. These studies could not have been particularly fruitful, for in later years Coast newspapers delighted to quote his complacent references to "me and Fair." But he had a natural dignity and an easy adaptability that far outweighed his lack of schooling. In the middle 1890's a young San Franciscan who had known Mackay on the Comstock met him on an overland train and was invited into his compartment. J. B. Levison still recalls his surprise at the unlettered millionaire's choice of reading matter; lying on the car seat was an open copy of the *North American Review,* then the most erudite of American periodicals.

Mackay stuttered badly all through his childhood and well into his twenties. Later he overcame the handicap— or perhaps he merely outgrew it—but by then his habit of speaking slowly and carefully was firmly established; to the end he practiced a cautious economy of words that impressed the public fully as much as his extravagances in other directions. From the middle seventies onward he made the Palace Hotel his headquarters when he was in San Francisco. One day a stranger stopped at the desk and asked to see the mining man. "Mr. Mackay? He just stepped into the bar with some other gentlemen," said the clerk. "But how will I recognize him?" asked the visitor. "He'll be the one who says nothing and pays the bill." The stranger went in, regarded the group at the bar for a few moments, then stepped forward and unerringly tapped Mackay on the shoulder.

Because his wife preferred to live in Europe and to educate their two sons there, Mackay's home for many years was a series of hotel rooms, first at Virginia City, then in New York and San Francisco. Once a year he crossed the Atlantic and spent a few weeks with his family, then headed west again, always with relief. His wife's social successes pleased him and he uncomplainingly footed the bills, but the guests he encountered in her Paris or London drawing-rooms left him cold. He had a convenient understanding with Dick Dey, his San Francisco business manager; on receipt of a certain code word Dey would dispatch a cable summoning him back to America on urgent business. One night in London, James D. Phelan, who was soon to be San Francisco's mayor, caught sight of Mackay's tall figure in the dining-room of the Carlton. "He was at the head of a table entertaining a large and brilliant social company, with Mrs. Mackay. He called me to his side as I was leaving the room to say how bored he was and that he wished he were as young as I, and in California again."

This was during almost the last year of his life; earlier such functions had aroused not only boredom but resentment. On his visits to the huge house he had purchased for his wife in Paris he took a malicious pleasure in regaling guests with tales of his boyhood in Dublin, when there had seldom been enough to eat, and family, cows, and pigs had amiably shared a common room. The pigs in the living-room may have been imaginary, but Mackay disliked nearly all his wife's friends, and in their presence it pleased him to play the part of uncouth miner, important only because of his millions. He well knew that stories of his Western crudities were current among the hard-up members of the Paris American colony and the decayed fringes of French aristocracy who made up the bulk of Mrs. Mackay's circle. He repaid their toleration with a robust contempt for all things east of Sandy Hook. Although for more than a decade he yearly visited Paris, he stubbornly refused to learn a word of French; on his afternoon walks along the Champs-Élysées or through the Bois he took his son Willie along to conduct necessary conversations with the natives. The barbarian's prejudices extended even to French wines and French cooking. A slug of bourbon was the only apéritif he permitted himself, and he sometimes took a glass of champagne with his dessert; during the meal itself he refused to touch a drop. Each time his wife changed her admirable chef he personally instructed the newcomer on how to prepare his favorite dish: corned beef and cabbage.

For his time and station his tastes were singularly temperate. He ate and drank sparingly, smoked cigars in moderation. For a time his favorite relaxation was an evening of high-stake poker. He played cards as he boxed, seriously and methodically, keeping his opponent under constant pressure. But that was before the lid had been pried off the big bonanza and before he discovered the fascination of large-scale operations on the Mining Exchange. With his profits sometimes running as high as $800,000 a month, the lesser gambling of the card table lost its appeal. Once in the back room of the Washoe Club he threw down his cards in disgust. "I don't care whether I win or lose," he lamented. "When you can't enjoy winning at poker, there's no fun left in anything." He wandered off, the picture of dejection. But he continued to find solace in keeping himself physically fit, although as time passed he had to abandon boxing and foot-racing and other violent exercise. He enjoyed walking, and he used elevators only when he could not avoid them (he refused to enter the lifts in his Paris and London houses on the logical grounds that they consumed too much time). In his last years he took up billiards, some say at the urging of his friend of the early Comstock, Sam Clemens.

He had two other lasting enthusiasms: music and the drama. During the summer after his family moved to Paris he spent each Sunday afternoon in the parlor of a Virginia City neighbor, listening with delight while two young girls, Minnie Phol and Lou Newmeyer, sang the sedate ballads of the day, accompanying themselves on a cottage organ. Years later in New York he was one of the group that helped Maurice Grau to establish the Metropolitan, thus beginning a family tradition—carried on by his son Clarence—of sponsoring opera and opera singers. When the Comstock was in its heyday, the great of the theatrical world stopped off on their way to and from the Coast to appear in Piper's Opera House: McCullough, Barrett, Edwin Booth, Jefferson, O'Neill, Melville, Menken, Modjeska, Patti, Lotta Crabtree, and scores of others.

Mackay saw them all, at first frugally from a gallery seat, later from a box, from which he could have stepped onto the stage. Visitors to the sagging, barnlike structure are still shown "Mackay's box." John Piper could never bring himself to bargain with artists over the size of their fees, and when this weakness periodically got him into hot water, Mackay became his financial backer. The arrangement was one designed to delight the soul of any impresario: when an engagement returned a profit it went to Piper; when there was a deficit Mackay shouldered it. But Mackay must have considered it money well spent, for it led to acquaintance with many of the great of the theater, and all these friendships persisted. After Mackay died, Dick Dey revealed that the mining man had come to the aid of numerous members of the improvident profession by helping them over periods of financial stress. He loaned Lawrence Barrett $25,000, Billy Florence $15,000, John McCullough an unspecified sum—and, Dey emphasized, every cent was repaid. This had not invariably been so with those who followed more stable professions. In San Francisco in the summer of '78 Mackay learned that a fellow guest at the Palace Hotel, an actor named Henry Montague (who had played opposite Adelaide Neilson) was desperately ill with consumption. Mackay unobtrusively paid his hotel and doctor's bills and, after he died, shipped his body to his family in the East.

His generosity to the sick actor and the secrecy with which it had been extended were typical. Rich men who made a too ostentatious display of their wealth aroused his scorn, and he often went to extraordinary lengths to avoid anything that would make him personally conspicuous. When the newspapers of the middle seventies began referring to him grandly as a "bonanza king," the title revolted him. "Makes me nothing but a damn millionaire with a swelled head," he snorted, and urged his acquaintances of the press to avoid such nonsense in the future. Once a New York journal polled the nation's rich men with the question: "Does wealth bring happiness?" Mackay's answer was an explosive "No." Perhaps he was thinking of the poker games he could no longer enjoy, of his wife and sons in permanent voluntary exile, and of the hordes of strangers who constantly made demands on his time and attention, destroying his privacy. No, wealth did not bring happiness, not when it was counted in tens of millions. He once remarked plaintively to Robert L. Fulton: "The fellow who has $200,000 and tries to make more is only borrowing trouble." Two hundred thousand then seemed to him about right; earlier he had set a more modest goal. While he was working the Yuba River placers in California he once announced that if he ever got hold of $25,000 he would throw down his tools and spend the rest of his days loafing.

2

HE WAS entirely without snobbishness, and it irked him that his present great wealth set him apart from friends who had shared the carefree poverty of his beginnings. On visits to San Francisco he complained that the strangers who jammed his Nevada Block office and lay in wait for him at his hotel kept away the old-timers he really wanted to see. "Even old Jack O'Brien won't come to see me any more," he once told Dey. O'Brien had been his closest friend of the California days; the two had together tramped over the Sierra in 1859, heading for Nevada diggings. He fought long and stubbornly against the barrier his multiple millions imposed between his old life and his new. In the end he recognized that it had been a losing battle, but he held out far longer than most very rich men. His wife (who had made the transition from poverty to wealth without visible struggle) continued to urge on him the convenience and social correctness of a valet. He scornfully rejected the suggestion: such fripperies were for the "bums and parasites" who frequented their Paris dinner parties; besides, what would the boys on the Comstock think? But the servant who looked after his comfort on visits to Paris made himself so unobtrusively useful that in the end Mackay took him back across the Atlantic. It was not an altogether happy assignment for the young Frenchman. Mackay refused to permit him to help him dress, or to draw his bath, or to shave him, all proper duties for a well-trained valet.

For years Mackay followed the conventional method by which the rich man of his day rid himself of bothersome strangers: he lent them money. Hence the chronically improvident, the panhandlers and purveyors of hard-luck stories—and even on occasion someone who was in genuine need—kept close tab on his movements and constituted a welcoming committee on his visits to San Francisco. This gentry had seldom had a more open-handed benefactor. Mackay drew the line at answering begging letters from strangers, but aside from that his bounty had no discernible limits. Newspaper notices of his arrival were a signal for a gathering of the supplicants. "He never came," stated Dey, "but there was a crowd of small borrowers stretching all the way from the entrance here [Mackay's office was at the corner of Pine and Montgomery streets] to the entrance of the Palace Hotel. He reckoned that it used to cost him fifty dollars to walk from the Nevada Block to the Palace, and he always carried the price with him, in gold. . . ." This was for the small fry; the more expensive borrowers sought him out in his office.

He well knew that he was often imposed on, but he had neither time nor inclination to check each story and there was always a chance that some borrower's need was real and pressing. Even in instances when he had obviously been imposed on he was more often amused than resentful. Once a premature explosion in one of the stopes of the Consolidated Virginia cost the life of a miner, and Mackay volunteered to pay his funeral expenses. The undertaker presented an exorbitant bill: six hundred dollars. Mackay commented that the victim's legs had been blown off by the blast. "If he had been whole I suppose the undertaker would have charged me a thousand." Normally he was neither surprised nor concerned when men he had helped forgot their obligation as soon as the emergency had passed: one expected to be bilked a good part of the time. But his Irish temper was unpredictable and there were occasions when he would stop creditors on the street and publicly demand payment in full. Such episodes puzzled his associates; those thus singled out were sometimes old friends who were in dire straits. Why he should suddenly decide to press these men for payment, while making no effort to collect the debts of scores of less needy creditors, was a mystery never explained.

All his life he had enjoyed magnificent health, and his contacts with the medical profession were few. That was fortunate, for there is no record that he ever paid a doctor's bill without kicking like a steer. Once in the early 1890's he was stricken with appendicitis; he was rushed to a San Francisco hospital and operated on. During his convalescence a friend was curious to know what sort of operation he had had. "I don't know," Mackay returned gloomily. "Judging by the size of his bill, the doctor must have removed my entire insides." Only a few months later, in February 1893, an old man named Rippey, who held Mackay responsible for losses sustained in mining speculation years before, followed the millionaire into an alley in the rear of the Lick House and, from a distance of ten feet, fired a pistol ball into his back. Mackay was helped into a hack and driven to the Palace, where two surgeons, Keeley and Morse, probed for the bullet, Mackay meantime refusing an anesthetic. The wound was not dangerous and in a few weeks he was up and about again. In due time the physicians presented their bills, and when Mackay learned their size—Keeley's fee was $7,000, Morse's $3,000—he flatly refused to pay. The doctors, equally stubborn, filed suit to collect, but before the case came to trial Mackay was called east on business and an out-of-court settlement was reached. Keeley scaled down his bill to $3,000 and Morse to $1,500.

Yet he was constantly passing out far larger sums without seeming to give the matter a second thought. In 1899 James Phelan conceived the plan of erecting in Union Square a monument commemorating Dewey's victory at Manila Bay. Mackay happened to be in town and Phelan called at his Nevada Block office, hoping for a modest contribution; within five minutes he was outside again with a check for five thousand dollars in his pocket. That, however, was in the nature of a novelty: Mackay's philanthropies were nearly all personal, and he often went to extraordinary lengths to avoid possible embarrassment to their recipients. Thus he issued orders to his office staff that routine payments to pensioners must always be in cash: this was to spare them the necessity of having to cash checks that might be recognized as charity by bank tellers. When he expected a needy friend to call, he would sometimes seal some currency in an envelope and place it on a table; then as the guest was about to leave, he would casually direct attention to it and ask him to take it along. A young law student, son of an old-time employee, received one such envelope; when he opened it outside Mackay's door he found five hundred-dollar bills. Even more tactful was his handling of an emergency at Virginia City in the late seventies. An acquaintance had left town suddenly, and investigation disclosed that he had embezzled several hundred dollars from his employer. Mackay went to see the fugitive's wife. The missing cash, he suggested, might be found in her husband's clothes: had she searched through them? She had. Well, why not make a second, more careful search? She went into the bedroom and returned presently to report that she had found nothing. Mackay professed to be deeply puzzled: he was sure his friend had not stolen the money. As he was leaving he nodded toward an old coat hanging in the hall: had she overlooked that? After the door had closed she explored its pockets—and found the amount of coin missing, and a substantial sum besides.

He imposed one condition on recipients of his bounty: his donations must always be anonymous. Sam Davis recalled that once on his reporter's round at Virginia he examined an account book at the Sisters' Hospital, thinking it was open for inspection. There he found that Mackay's name was down for a monthly contribution of five hundred dollars, but when he proposed making a public announcement of the gift, the sisters urged him to say nothing: Mr. Mackay had made it clear that if the news got out, the monthly payments would stop. Similarly during one of the slack periods on the Comstock, when most of the mines were shut down, Mackay secretly authorized a Virginia City grocer to supply provisions to any customer who was unable to pay. That winter Mackay's grocery bill averaged three thousand dollars a month. The great fire of October 1875, which wiped out the entire central part of the town, made even heavier demands on his purse. While the fire was at its height, one of Father Manogue's parishioners lamented that Virginia's beautiful little church, St. Mary's of the Mountains, was in ruins. Mackay was furiously busy directing efforts to heap sand and rock over the mouth of the great Consolidated Virginia shaft. He paused long enough to assure the speaker that if the fire could be kept from the mine's lower workings he would gladly rebuild "twenty churches." St. Mary's of the Mountains was duly rebuilt, largely with Mackay's help; it remains today the chief ornament of the decaying town.

Mackay's own house on Howard Street went up in the general holocaust and he moved into the upper story of the Gould & Curry office, just beyond the burned area. A day or two later he encountered an old friend, James McCullough, and finding that he was homeless, Mackay insisted that he share his own cramped quarters: for weeks the two occupied improvised bunks at opposite ends of the room. Hundreds of the homeless camped on the bare mountainside, putting up such shelter as they could to protect them from the raw winds of late fall. McCullough was delegated to circulate among dispossessed families and to pass out orders on Breed & Crosby, wood and coal dealers, entitling them to as much fuel as they needed. Mackay made his customary admonition: the source of this bounty must not under any circumstances be revealed. During this emergency his philanthropy found yet another outlet. H. M. Yerrington, superintendent of the Virginia & Truckee Railroad, was authorized to provide transportation for all who wished to leave the shattered town. Two thousand were thus sent down the mountain at Mackay's expense, most of them to towns in the Carson Valley, some as far afield as California.

His passion for anonymity in these matters was not shared by every Comstock capitalist, and the well-publicized philanthropies of some of his associates aroused his scorn. Once in San Francisco he encountered the editor of the *Chronicle,* Dennis McCarthy, and informed him gravely that he had sensational news. In some excitement McCarthy inquired what the world-shaking information might be. Mackay replied gravely: "Fair has given a box of apples to the Orphans' Home at Carson and wants a two-column write-up."

On the day in 1902 when news of Mackay's death reached San Francisco, Dick Dey granted an interview, in which he revealed that a considerable group of Comstock pioneers had been receiving a monthly dole from Mackay; his passing would be sad news indeed to these pensioners. Dey added some revealing details. The dead man had outstanding more than a million dollars in personal debts, all bad. One owed $400,000, another $200,000, a third $150,000. All three men were living and in comfortable circumstances. Every loan then on the books had been made during the last two decades of Mackay's life; earlier obligations had long since been written off. "I sat with him in this very office one Sunday afternoon about twenty years ago," Dey continued, "and saw him tear up notes amounting to more than $1,000,000. 'That fellow's broke,' he'd say, and rip! and into the waste-basket would go paper that stood for anything from $500 to $50,000. 'That fellow's dead, Dey, can't collect from him, so here goes.' ... 'Now this fellow may get on his feet one of these days and if he does he'll remember the amount, but in the meantime I might as well get the evidence out of the way so he won't be pressed in case anything happens to me....'"

During his lifetime he accomplished the formidable feat of distributing in the form of individual gifts (often thinly disguised as loans) not less than five million dollars. In the end he was by no means sure that the aid he had passed out so lavishly and in so many directions had not done more harm than good. In the late nineties he confessed: "I want to help people; I like to do it; but when I look back and see the result of trying, I'm ready to swear I'll never give or lend another friend a dollar. . . . It takes the backbone out of a man to have money given to him. . . ." Such periods of pessimism may have been responsible for certain odd behavior that intermittently puzzled those about him. From time to time and for no discernible reason he would turn misanthrope, shutting himself up in office or hotel room, denying himself to old friends, and treating those he could not avoid with a brusqueness calculated to alienate them for life. The mood would pass as suddenly as it had come upon him and the next time he met these acquaintances he would behave with his customary affability.

Like most men of moods and crotchets, he was likely to take violent offense for trivial reasons (or for no reason at all) and to preserve his good humor in the face of far greater provocation. One sure way to arouse his resentment was to be late for an engagement; those who failed to appear promptly were required to make a new appointment, which might be many days in the future; if they were late a second time Mackay crossed them permanently off his list. Another of his oddities was a marked hostility to Englishmen—a circumstance that might have been a compensating reaction to his wife's pronounced and undiscriminating admiration for all things British. At an annual meeting of the Consolidated Virginia stockholders in January 1877 one James White, ex-member of the British Parliament, showed up and spoke briefly and mildly on behalf of the corporation's English shareholders. Mackay's response was so personal and abusive that the entire local press was moved to protest. "Mr. White," stated the *Post,* "will return to England with no exalted idea of American hospitality and American mining men."

More violent still was his encounter with W. C. Bonynge, another Englishman. The two were acquaintances of long standing; during the seventies Bonynge's brokerage office in San Francisco had executed many commissions both for Mackay's personal account and for the bonanza firm. Having prospered, the Englishman in the middle eighties returned to London, where he moved in select social circles. One of his handsome daughters married Viscount Deerhurst, and both she and her mother were presented at Queen Victoria's sedate court. Mr. Bonynge had, in the *Call's* words, "done himself proud." By then Mackay's family had likewise taken up residence in London, where they frequently met the Bonynges.

In view of these common interests it might be supposed that when the two men met at San Francisco one day in 1891, they would have greeted each other with mutual pleasure. Such was far from the case. One day Mackay, having business with I. W. Hellman, president of the Nevada Bank, stepped into the latter's office, which adjoined his own. Hellman was entertaining a visitor; the visitor was Bonynge. At sight of them, Mackay's ruddy face turned several shades darker; he strode to the Englishman's side and ordered him to stand up and defend himself. A moment later the two elderly capitalists—Mackay was sixty, Bonynge a year or two older—were slugging it out toe to toe. It required half a dozen clerks, summoned by Hellman, to separate the pair and send them off in separate hacks to their hotels. Next morning's newspapers carried heavily ironic accounts of the battle. The Nevada Bank, stated one, hadn't seen such spirited boxing since Jim Corbett had given up his clerkship and turned professional.

Each man presently gave his version of the origin of the quarrel: it had grown out of a bitter social rivalry between their families in London. Soon after Bonynge's wife and daughter had been presented at court, a story had appeared in a London weekly questioning Bonynge's claim that he had served with distinction in the Crimean War (he was supposed to have taken part in the gallant charge of Balaklava) and hinting that his financial and social standing in California had been less eminent than he had given his London friends to understand. Rightly or not, Bonynge suspected that the ammunition for this attack had been supplied by the Mackays. "Here if ever was a case of the pot feuding with the kettle," stated the

San Francisco Call, "and Kettle Bonynge was not slow to accept the challenge." In any event, soon after there appeared in another paper—the January 1, 1891, issue of *Truth*—an article citing convincing evidence that the Mackay family tree was some degrees less than aristocratic. That Bonynge was responsible for this counterblast Mackay had no doubt at all. "He published articles about me and my family," he told the reporters, "and I made up my mind to give him a hiding the first time we met. I don't regret it." Bonynge's chief regret was that Mackay's assault had taken him by surprise; he had not been given the time to get his guard up. Except for that unethical first blow Mackay had done him no damage. As for the *Truth* article, the Englishman insisted that it contained nothing of a spiteful or scandalous nature, and all facts could easily be verified. True, it had pointed out that the Mackays had not always enjoyed unlimited wealth, but what of it? Was there anything disgraceful about honest poverty? The debate continued for days, and in his "Prattle" column in the *Examiner,* Ambrose Bierce commemorated the encounter with a mock-heroic ode. But it was not one of Bierce's best efforts. The public rapidly lost interest.

3

UNLIKE most men who rise from rags to riches, Mackay in his later years failed to supply interviewers with reminiscences of his early struggles, and details of his childhood are consequently meager. A few stray facts are known. He was born at Dublin on November 28, 1831. When he was nine, his family migrated to New York, where his Scotch-Irish father died within two years and John left school and went to work to help support his mother and younger sister.

Little more than that is definitely known of Mackay's first dozen years. Writers who touch on that period have had to overcome the lack of documentation by drawing on their imaginations. One account has him shining shoes on the New York sidewalks. Another states that he worked in a grocery store, but this might have been a case of confusing Mackay with his future partner Flood, whose first job was that of delivery boy for a New York grocer. Another and more elaborate theory is that he became a newsboy and that while he was hawking the *Herald* on Bowery street corners he conceived so strong an admiration for James Gordon Bennett that half a century later he went into partnership with the publisher's son and founded the Mackay-Bennett Cable Company, forerunner of the Postal Telegraph. One of Mackay's few references to this period has a touch of Irish sentimentality. When the Postal's new building was built on lower Broadway, Mackay chose for his private office an eighth-floor room that looked out over City Hall Square and into Franklin Street. He explained that from its windows he could see the site of the house where he had lived as a child.

When he was sixteen he was apprenticed to William H. Webb, builder of many of the side-wheel steamers of the forties and later. During his four years in Webb's shipyard he acquired the skill in the use of tools that served him well when he reached the Comstock a dozen years later. On the day he completed his apprenticeship one of the steamers he had helped build was put in commission and Mackay accompanied her on her maiden voyage to California. This vessel might have been the 2,000-ton *Golden Gate,* which entered the Panama-San Francisco run in November 1851. At any event, Mackay was twenty when he reached California late in that year. This was well beyond the time when any but the uncommonly lucky could pick up easy fortunes in the diggings, but mining fascinated the ex-shipbuilder and for the next eight years he knocked about the towns and camps of the Sierra foothills, mostly on the north fork of the Yuba in the neighborhood of Downieville. There he gained nothing beyond a bare livelihood, but again he stored up experiences that were to prove useful later on. He was far from regarding these years as wasted. Life in the placer camps involved no hardships for the husky young Irishman: long hours of exhausting work in the ice-cold creek-beds constituted a challenge in the overcoming of which he took a constant delight, and all his life he remembered this stay in the Sierra canyons as the happiest period of his life. There he had found the austere Elysium his fancy preferred, with good-fellowship and no responsibilities, where one worked only enough to supply one's need for food and clothing and shelter: who would ask more?

He was still contentedly working the Yuba diggings in the fall of '59 while news of rich silver strikes in Nevada Territory was racing from camp to camp. The fever spread the length of the Mother Lode, while thousands waited impatiently through the winter; then when spring thaws cleared the snow-blocked passes, the concerted rush began. Mackay and his friend Jack O'Brien shouldered their light packs and joined the stampede. When they reached the divide above Virginia City, O'Brien fished a fifty-cent piece out of his pocket—it was the last of their joint capital—and hurled it back down the canyon, whereupon they turned and tramped penniless into camp. Reminded of this episode years later, Mackay commented: "Jack has been doing that all his life."

During the next two years Mackay repeated on the windy shoulder of Mount Davidson the program he had followed in California. He became a pick-and-shovel man at four dollars a day. Then, when the first shafts began to be sunk, he graduated into timber work and his pay jumped to six dollars. He was a sound artisan, sober and reliable, but thus far there had been nothing to indicate that he would presently lift himself above the ranks of skilled laborers. Not until he was thirty did signs of latent ambition begin to manifest themselves. In the spring of 1861 he quit his job as timberman and, putting to use his knowledge of construction techniques, set himself up as a contractor. His first assignment was to run a tunnel for the owners of an unproductive mine called the Union, at the northern end of the lode. Evidently this job was creditably done, for others followed. At that period it was customary for contractors to take part of their compensation—sometimes all of it—in the stock of the mines they were helping develop. Most of the shares Mackay thus acquired were worthless, but not all. By 1863 he was part owner of four small claims that either were actively producing or contained promising leads. He was on his way to realizing his ambition to accumulate twenty-five thousand dollars and retire, but his next venture put an end to that plan.

With another shoestring operator, J. M. Walker, he bought control of a considerable property near the geographical center of the lode and together they set about developing it. This mine was the Bullion—a name that its successive owners found to be singularly inappropriate: over the decades some five million dollars were expended probing its barren depths, without uncovering a ton of millable ore. It must have been soon after Mackay had lost his savings in the Bullion that Mark Twain, then a reporter on the *Enterprise,* suggested that the two swap jobs. Mackay rejected the offer, remarking: "No, I won't trade, Sam. I've never swindled anybody and I don't intend to start now."

He continued speculating modestly in this claim or that, and a year or two later came his first stroke of luck. Again in partnership with Walker he got control of the Kentuck, a narrow mine—it occupied only one hundred feet of the lode—over the divide in Gold Canyon. The Kentuck was not a highly regarded property. Two years earlier it had yielded a considerable quantity of low-grade ore, but the deposit had pinched out and further exploration had encountered only country rock. But it adjoined the Crown Point, and the Crown Point was returning a handsome profit to its owners. Mackay considered the Kentuck's prospects good enough to warrant gambling sixty thousand dollars to finance its further exploration. He and Walker borrowed that sum—at the prevailing interest rate of three per cent a month—from James Phelan, father of the future San Francisco mayor. The development of the Kentuck swallowed up the sixty thousand dollars and as much more as the partners could raise, and still no new ore was found. Meantime their note had become due and the partners, afraid Phelan would refuse to extend it, were forced to drastic measures. Mackay hunted up the capitalist and, protesting violently that they were paying an outrageously high interest rate, demanded that it be reduced. Phelan listened to his tirade, then banged his fist on the table and announced angrily that the note would be renewed at three per cent or not at all. Mackay continued the argument for some time longer, then meekly signed. He returned in triumph to Walker: the ruse had gained them a three-month reprieve.

This proved time enough; before the note was again due the Kentuck had hit a small but rich bonanza, and Mackay was enjoying his first real prosperity. The Kentuck produced, first and last, not much less than five million dollars, of which more than a million and a quarter was paid in dividends. Three quarters of this production was in the three years from '66 to '69, and during most of that period Mackay was the mine's chief owner, Walker having sold out (for $600,000) in 1867. Mackay now had far more than $25,000, but the strong wine of success brought visions, not of retirement, but of new and still more lucrative enterprises. It was at this turning-point in his career that he allied himself with James G. Fair and so set in motion the chain of circumstances that soon after led to the formation of the bonanza firm.

4

DURING the early period of their acquaintance Mackay was a frequent guest at Fair's cottage on A Street, high on the shoulder of Mount Davidson. There Fair's amiable wife (the former Theresa Rooney of Angels Camp) made the stranger welcome and so cemented a friendship that was to prove highly useful to her later on. The domestic instinct was ever strong in Mackay—who, ironically enough, was fated to live nearly all his life in hotels or boarding-houses—and these pleasant evenings at his friend's fireside must have accentuated his loneliness. At any rate he was a frequent guest of the Fairs during the early months of 1866, and presently he had a still more compelling reason to frequent the A Street cottage. About that time hospitable Mrs. Fair began inviting for supper and an evening of talk and music not only her husband's bachelor friend but a neighbor from across the street, a young woman who worked hard and had few diversions. She was a Mrs. Bryant, whose physician husband had unfortunately taken to drink and deserted her, and who supported herself and her young daughter by doing "fancy work" for one of the C Street drygoods stores. Theresa Fair later stated that she had invited Mackay to her house because he was lonely and Mrs. Bryant because she looked as though she needed a substantial, home-cooked meal. But the hostess was Irish and therefore a born matchmaker, and the probabilities are that she envisioned a romance between her two lonely and personable guests. Planned or not, the romance duly materialized; the pair were married before the summer ended.

Marie Hungerford Bryant, petite and blue-eyed and pretty, was then only twenty-three (Mackay was thirty-six), but she had already had experiences more varied than befall most women in a lifetime. Born in Brooklyn in 1843, she had come west ten years later with her mother and her younger sister. The journey was made by water, via Panama, and during the passage the mother had added to the slender family resources by serving as nursemaid to the children of the more prosperous passengers. The father, Daniel E. Hungerford, met them at the San Francisco dock, and the reunited family traveled by river steamer and stage to Downieville, a placer-mining center high in the Sierra foothills. There for the next several years they led a precarious existence. By then lean times had come to gold towns, and money was everywhere scarce, but the Hungerfords fared rather worse than most. For although Daniel Hungerford had served with some distinction in the Mexican War (he had attained the rank of captain), he was completely unable to cope with the problems of civilian life. When his family joined him, this veteran of Buena Vista and Cerro Gordo was Downieville's barber, his income so small that his wife had to hire out as a nurse to the town's ailing citizens. This brought her in contact with the county physician, a young man named

Edmund Bryant, a native of New York and a cousin of William Cullen Bryant. Although he was still in his early twenties, Dr. Bryant seemed on his way to becoming a distinguished surgeon. He had reached Downieville in 1857, four years after the arrival of Mrs. Hungerford and her two daughters. Existing records of the town reveal that three years later, on January 1, 1860, he married Marie Louise Antoinette, elder of the two Hungerford children. Bryant was twenty-three, his bride sixteen.

One of the first results of this union was an improvement in the Hungerford fortunes: the bride's father put away his razor and shears and became steward of the county hospital at Downieville. Soon there were other changes. News of the Nevada silver strike had reached Downieville some months before Dr. Bryant's marriage; many of the town's miners had already left for the new diggings and others planned to follow in the spring. The doctor and his father-in-law did not join in these first waves; both remained behind at Downieville, probably with reluctance, for reports seeping back across the Sierra told of ever richer strikes.

The opportunity to join the migration came from an unexpected quarter. In the late spring of 1860 the Indians of western Nevada, mostly warlike Piutes, resenting the large influx of whites into their territory, went on the warpath and, having lured into ambush a detachment of settlers sent to put them down, routed them with heavy losses. This "Battle of Pyramid Lake" alarmed the entire Coast, and companies of volunteers were organized on both sides of the Sierra. One was raised at Downieville, and both Hungerford and Bryant were active in its organization, the former becoming its captain, the latter company surgeon. The Indians were duly met and dispersed and a few months later a regular army post was established at Fort Churchill to prevent further outbreaks. Neither Captain Hungerford nor his son-in-law recrossed the mountains. Hungerford settled in Virginia City and Dr. Bryant opened a sort of health resort at Steamboat Springs (so called from jets of steam rising from natural hot springs), a dozen miles to the north.

There for a time the Bryants prospered. A daughter, Eva, was born in 1861 and a second, Marie, a year later. Then disaster struck: the young physician fell victim to alcohol and drugs and presently the little family was broken up. Mrs. Bryant and her daughters went to live with the Hungerfords at Virginia and the doctor drifted back to California. The pair met again only once. In 1866, only a few months before her marriage to Mackay, Mrs. Bryant learned that the doctor was desperately ill in the town of La Porte, in northern California; she joined him there and nursed him until he died. Meantime their younger daughter, Marie, had died and been buried in one of Virginia City's barren cemeteries. Many years later the former Mrs. Bryant, then living in London, bought a plot in a San Francisco cemetery and had the bodies of father and daughter transferred there.

After the breakup of her marriage the nineteen-year-old mother had a difficult time supporting herself and her remaining child. She got no help from her father, for at the onset of the Civil War Captain Hungerford had hurried to San Francisco, intent on recruiting a regiment of volunteers and leading them against the Rebels. San Francisco directories of the period reveal that Mrs. Hungerford lived on California Street near Dupont, where she placed advertisements in the newspapers, offering private lessons in conversational French. Up at Virginia City young Mrs. Bryant was also teaching French, at a recently established academy for the daughters of the town's first families; in addition she did "piece-work" sewing for fashionable lady customers of Rosener Brothers' store. Her combined income from these two sources could not have been large. She and her surviving daughter lived in a furnished room in A Street, in such genteel poverty that kind Mrs. Fair made a point of inviting her to supper several times a week.

Thus the young widow met Mackay at a time when her fortunes were at a low ebb, and when Mackay's prospects were correspondingly bright. Prosperity and romance having come to him at about the same time, it is not surprising that his double good fortune caused him for once to depart from his habitual reserve. The marriage was performed in the parlor of Fair's cottage, with Father (later Bishop) Manogue, the town's popular priest, officiating, and with Jim and Theresa Fair as witnesses. In his newly expansive mood the bridegroom dispatched a case of champagne to each of the Comstock newspapers: the *Enterprise*, and *Daily Trespass* in Virginia City, and the *News* over the divide at Gold Hill, and next day all three journals carried enthusiastic but somewhat confused accounts of the ceremony.

Now a man of family, Mackay bought a lot high on the mountainside at Howard and Taylor streets and built a two-story cottage, with gabled roof and neat picket fence, rather more modest in style than its neighbors. There he installed his bride, his young stepdaughter, Eva Bryant, and his mother-in-law, and it was there in 1869 that Mrs. H. H. Mathews, who was later to write a tartly realistic account of domestic life on the Comstock, went to work as a seamstress for the ladies of the house. Mrs. Mathews's wages were one dollar a day plus meals. She remained long enough to observe that when the wind blew (which was most of the time), air currents raced inside the Mackay partitions, causing the cloth-and-paper walls of the sitting-room alternately to billow outward and recede in a most disconcerting fashion. She quit her job at the end of a week—not because of this eerie phenomenon, but because she was not permitted to sit with the family at supper, the ladies explaining that it would not be seemly for Mr. Mackay to eat with the "hired help."

Mackay's mounting prosperity permitted his wife to indulge a growing taste for travel, and year by year her absences from home grew longer and more frequent. The Comstock held unpleasant memories for her, and besides it was noisy and windy and crude. She was often "down below," and it was there, in August 1870, that their first child was born. He was named John, after his father, but all his life he was known as Willie. Soon after Willie's birth the entire family set off on a European tour—proof enough that the Mackays had entered the select circle of the rich. The junket is said to have been engineered by

Mrs. Hungerford, who was eager to renew acquaintance with her childhood friends in France and perhaps to impress them with her wealthy and generous son-in-law. At any rate the party was large: Mackay himself, his wife, his stepdaughter, Eva (whom he presently adopted), his son, Mr. and Mrs. Hungerford and their daughter Ada, and Alice O'Grady, who went along as nursemaid to the infant Willie.

This European trip marked the real beginning of one of the notable careers in American social history. Marie Hungerford Mackay was twenty-eight when she first set foot on foreign soil, and the Brooklyn-born girl had already had an uncommonly varied career. It had been a life of contrasts sufficiently violent to shake the confidence of most young women of her time and place; her it affected not at all. Whatever might happen, whether good luck or bad, she took in stride, her self-assurance unshaken. In later years many recalled that during her Downieville childhood she had borne herself "like a princess," her manner always serene and aloof, seemingly remote from her raw frontier surroundings. Later, as Dr. Bryant's bride, the sixteen-year-old girl had behaved with a cool dignity—suitable to the wife of the town's leading physician—that impressed matrons twice her age. At Virginia City during her widowhood she bore adversity with a casual unconcern. A quarter of a century later one of the Rosener brothers remembered that on her daily calls at their C Street store to pick up the sewing by which she supported herself, she had carried herself "like a queen in calico."

The party returned from Europe in the fall of 1873 and Mackay hurried back to Virginia City. His wife and family remained behind in San Francisco. After Paris, the crudities of the mining town, its noise and dust and confusion, attracted her even less than before. Besides, social life on the Comstock was severely limited, whereas the Coast metropolis offered cosmopolitan diversions not far inferior to those of the French capital, and Mrs. Mackay was already captured by the sedately glittering functions of the era and eager to share in them.

As a setting for her entry into San Francisco's society, she purchased, for thirty thousand dollars, a three-story wooden residence at 805 O'Farrell Street. This she proceeded to furnish in the ornate French style fashionable at the time, and it was there that a second son, Clarence Hungerford Mackay, was born in 1874. Mrs. Mackay remained in the O'Farrell Street house less than three years; she had never felt fully at home there, and its purchase came to be regarded as a mistake in judgment. The neighborhood was one of moderately prosperous tradesmen and professional men; it was quiet and respectable, but quite without social distinction, not to be compared with the windy hilltop a few blocks to the northeast where a group of immense new mansions were going up. It has been said that had Mrs. Mackay established herself on Nob Hill she would have contentedly remained in San Francisco the rest of her life, but that of course is pure speculation. In any event, she turned her eyes elsewhere—and not in the direction of Nob Hill. By then the bonanza firm's mines were coming into full production, and the management of these fabulous properties demanded Mackay's full attention. He was so seldom with his family that they might have been separated by half the earth's circumference. Perhaps that fact was pointed out to him by his wife, for when she suggested returning to Europe he apparently offered no strong objections. So in 1876 the O'Farrell Street house was sold; Mackay saw his family off for Paris and returned to Virginia City. The Howard Street cottage having been destroyed (along with most of the town) in the 1875 fire, he lived for many months in the Gould & Curry office, then took up quarters on the top floor of the International Hotel when that ornament of the town was completed in 1877.

Although he probably did not know it at the time, he had permanently joined the ranks of the Washoe widowers. Having established herself in Europe, Mrs. Mackay showed a growing reluctance to return: only once in the next quarter century did she recross the Atlantic, and then for the briefest of stays. In the beginning, however, there was nothing to indicate that she planned a permanent exile. She had expected to remain in Paris only a year or two, visiting her parents (who had remained behind when the Mackays had returned from their first European tour) and putting her daughter and two sons in charge of French governesses. Before she boarded the steamer at New York she had paid a sentimental visit to the mother of her first husband, whose surviving son, Dr. William Cullen Bryant (cousin of the poet), was a prominent New York physician. Her connection with this distinguished family was always a source of pride to her. Some years later, when she commissioned Tiffany & Company to make an elaborate silver service for her Paris house (the silver came from the Comstock) she personally chose the decorative motif: each piece was embossed with the poet's head in bas-relief, his hair falling about his shoulders.

In Paris the group—Mrs. Mackay, the three children, and the two nursemaids—put up at a hotel while she began a search for more suitable quarters. This was not a task to be lightly undertaken, for by then the extraordinary richness of the Nevada mines had made them almost as renowned in France as they were at home, and the wife of the man who was becoming known as the King of the Comstock had no wish to attract attention by a mere vulgar display of money. Washoe profits had already sent abroad too many brash emissaries to bring discredit to America in general and the Far West in particular. There had been, for example, the illiterate ex-teamster Sandy Bowers, and his wife, the incredible Eilley. Many in Paris still remembered their visit fifteen years earlier, when they had casually scattered twenty thousand American dollars among the shopkeepers in a single day, then had hurried off to the American legation and informed the ambassador that Mr. and Mrs. Bowers, of Carson City, Utah Territory, wished to meet the Emperor Napoleon and his Empress Eugénie, and could Mr. Ambassador arrange to get them an invite to one of their balls? Marie Mackay, daughter of an army officer and wife of a multimillionaire, was above such antics, and she had besides her sagacious, French-born mother to advise her. Parisians must be

made to understand that not all wives of Comstock plutocrats were cast in the same mold as Eilley Orrum Bowers.

The house she eventually chose was one of the most desirable in the city, a four-story stone mansion at number 9
rue Tilsit. With its grounds the big French Renaissance
structure occupied an entire square off the Champs-
Élysées, adjacent to the Arc de Triomphe. So substantial
a property in so desirable a location naturally commanded
no trifling sum: more than a million francs went into its
purchase, and another quarter of a million was spent for
its furnishings. With this bold step the daughter of the
Downieville barber launched her campaign to win a
place in the inner circle of French society, for the mansion
provided a setting appropriate to the elaborate entertain-
ments she planned. All that was now lacking were guests.

But the social life of Paris was lamentably conservative,
and even a handsome house and a bottomless purse were
not in themselves enough to unlock its doors. Those were
mistaken, however, who imagined that the rich and comely
American woman faced a long struggle. She moved into
the rue Tilsit house late in 1876. Less than a year later
came one of those fortunate happenings of which social
climbers dream. At one stroke it established her as one of
the leading hostesses of the Continent, easily the most
conspicuous figure in the American colony of the French
capital.

Oddly enough, she owed this piece of good luck to that
most impractical of mortals, Colonel Hungerford.

5

THE picturesque colonel deserves a word in passing. He
and his wife had then been living in Paris about four
years, pensioners of their now absurdly rich son-in-law.
Westerners returning home from European jaunts reported
that the old soldier was much in evidence, his tall figure
and white goatee conspicuous in the Paris bars and cafés
where Americans forgathered. Such news interested thousands all over the Pacific Coast, for the rags-to-riches

story of the Hungerfords had fascinated a whole generation of Californians.

He was born in upstate New York about 1800, the youngest of seven sons. One of the hobbies of his later years was genealogy, and he assiduously traced his family back to a certain warlike Sir Robert de Hungerford, Knight of the Shire of Wilts, who had made sanguinary history in fourteenth-century England. That military prowess had for so long been a family trait must have delighted him; but in the intervening centuries the Hungerfords had come on hard times, and Daniel's parents were so poor that he had had to go to work while he was hardly more than a child. At fifteen he was "deputy inspector of beef and pork" for the town of Waterford, New York; prior to that he had attended the near-by Saratoga Academy, and although his stay there must have been brief, he yet found time to organize the students into a military company and to install himself as their captain. This exploit was typical. His consuming interest in all things military developed early and lasted as long as he lived. At a reunion of Mexican War veterans at San Francisco in the early 1860's he jocularly remarked that he had been born to the sound of martial music and had cut his eye-teeth on the scabbard of a cavalry saber. He moved about a great deal during his youth; wherever he found himself he rounded up a band of recruits and set about instructing them in the manual of arms. His subsequent history can best be told in terms of his military affiliations. By 1842 he was a captain in the New York state militia. Four years later came the great adventure of the Mexican War, his one contact with the actual smoke of battle. Back from Mexico, a veteran of Vera Cruz, Cerro Gordo, and Chapultepec, he endured for two years the humdrum life of Brooklyn—even then a distressingly unmilitary environment—then set off for California.

As others have done before him and since, he presently discovered that an aptitude for military life does not invariably presage a like success in the duller pursuits of peace. In San Francisco he drifted from job to job: unloading ships in the bay, clerking in a store, becoming successively a butcher, an auctioneer, and a miner. By 1851 he had opened his barber shop in Downieville, where one can imagine him, while he plied razor and shears, regaling his customers with the inside story of the Mexican campaigns. In Downieville he of course set about organizing a military company: the result was the Sierra Guard, Captain Daniel E. Hungerford commanding, said to have been the first fully trained and uniformed volunteer military organization in California. Soon the Sierra Guard was taken into the state militia, and not long afterward the Indian uprising beyond the mountains sent the company hurrying off to Nevada. But the Piute War fizzled out and the Sierra Guard saw no action.

Meantime mounting tensions in the East were making it clearer that warfare on a larger scale could not long be delayed. Hungerford, then living at Virginia City, offered his services to the authorities both in Washington and in his home state of New York. Before a reply could be received, word of the firing on Sumter reached Nevada. That same night Hungerford boarded a stage for San Francisco, where he caught the first available steamer for the scene of battle. Less than a month later he was encamped in a meadow outside Washington, a lieutenant colonel in the 36th New York Volunteer Infantry. There followed a solid year of drilling, of waiting for arms and equipment, of moving from camp to camp. The doughty colonel fumed and fretted. At last, finding further inaction unendurable, and at odds with his commander, General Couch, he resigned his commission and returned to San Francisco.

He had conceived a bold plan: to recruit a regiment of California volunteers and to lead them on a flank attack against the Rebels by way of Texas. But California's cautious Governor Stanford failed to warm to this scheme, and after months of fruitless interviews, of addressing rallies and circulating petitions, Hungerford acknowledged defeat and set off for Virginia City. There he was more successful: Nevada granted the authority her sister state had withheld, and the work of recruiting got under way. Eight companies—two of cavalry and six of infantry—

were organized, and their training and equipping began; then, for reasons now obscure, the whole project was abandoned. One can imagine how shattering this blow must have been to the warlike colonel. With the greatest conflict of the century raging and his country in dire peril (largely through lack of just such leadership as he might have supplied), a perverse fate denied him the privilege of striking a single blow in her defense. He lived through the Civil War without once hearing the clash of a saber, the whine of a solitary Minié ball, the jarring boom of a single mortar.

Perhaps it was to compensate for this disappointment that Hungerford became involved in an intrigue designed to rescue the sister nation to the south from the yoke of foreign oppressors. A quixotic plot to force Maximilian I from his unstable throne was secretly hatched in San Francisco, a ship was chartered, and arms and ammunition smuggled aboard. Meanwhile Hungerford and his confederates were assembling a band of adventurers for this desperate mission. But again the colonel saw his dreams of military glory shattered. At the last moment the French consul got wind of what was afoot; he tipped off the authorities, and Hungerford and twenty others were lodged in the city jail. They were eventually turned loose with a reprimand, after promising never again to use American soil to plot the overthrow of a friendly government. But Hungerford's interest in Mexico (scene of his one great campaign) was not shaken by this fiasco. Presently we find him living at La Paz, on the Lower California peninsula. There he was known as the "Doctor Americano"—a flair for medicine had somehow been added to his many accomplishments—and engaged in certain intrigues the nature of which remains shrouded in mystery to this day.

During much of this period the colonel's wife and daughters shared the fate usual among the dependents of men engaged in righting the wrongs of the world; they supported themselves as best they could. Then, in 1867, had come his elder daughter's marriage to the affluent Mr. Mackay, and immediately the colonel's run of bad luck came to an end. European travel, pilgrimages to the battle-fields of Mexico, a flat in Paris in which to display his military trophies and to entertain old comrades-in-arms—all this, thanks to a liberal and increasingly wealthy son-in-law, was now possible. He made the most of them, for prosperity no less than military glory was necessary to his complete content. His later years were singularly pleasant, for now he had leisure to review his eventful past, and ample funds to indulge the pleasures most appropriate to an old warhorse: talk and toddy. Through the middle and late seventies and well into the eighties he remained one of the most picturesque of the minor celebrities of Paris. To thousands of Frenchmen he was the embodiment of the American martial spirit, a striking figure at his daughter's social functions and during his daily promenades along the boulevards. All accounts agree that he looked the part: tall and straight as a ramrod, with keen blue eyes beneath shaggy brows and with the stiff, purposeful stride suggestive of the parade ground. He habitually dressed in a long blue frock coat and broad-brimmed felt hat (like those worn by Union generals during the war) and carried a gold-headed cane, which he wielded with "all the . . . éclat of a cavalry officer leading a charge against the enemy's center." One admiring interviewer wrote that he "might have posed for a statue of Mars himself," and another, deceived perhaps by his white mane and goatee, reported that he was a product of the deep South, scion of a famous New Orleans family. It was a natural mistake.

Above the mantel of his Paris drawing-room were the swords he had carried in the Mexican and Piute campaigns; his military medals and commissions and citations adorned its walls. To these appropriate quarters he delighted to invite whatever American military figures chanced to visit Paris; there over successive toddies the campaigns of two wars were refought, the errors expiated, and the glorious victories suitably toasted. Perhaps it was after one such evening that his wife returned to find Hungerford far gone in his cups. The cook was missing and Mrs. Hungerford wanted to know what had become of her. "She was drunk," returned the colonel severely. "I dismissed her." "You're drunk yourself," charged his wife. "That may be, m'dear," was the dignified retort, "but I won't have two people drunk in the house at the same time."

To prove that he was not yet ready for the shelf, the colonel returned to the United States in 1878 and went into a "railroad promotion" in Texas. This experience was brief, however, and a year later he was back in Paris presiding over a reunion of Mexican War veterans. Ten years later, when he was well past eighty, he went to live in Rome with his daughter Ada, who had married an Italian, Count Telfener. There the window of his study in the Castle Ada—purchased for the Count and his bride by the ever generous Mackay—overlooked the Campagna. To a study of the campaigns of that ancient battleground the old man devoted his final months, and it was there, in the summer of 1890, that he died. Almost forty years later the doughty colonel's name reappeared briefly in American newspapers. When Clarence Hungerford Mackay died, in 1938, his will bequeathed "the sword and medals of the testator's grandfather, Daniel E. Hungerford," to Clarence's son, and urged on him the careful preservation of these priceless heirlooms.

6

ONE of the chief ironies of Colonel Hungerford's life was the fact that his greatest victory was won, not on the battlefield, but in one of the hard-fought campaigns of his daughter's drawing-room.

It was soon after Mrs. Mackay moved into her rue Tilsit house that the colonel executed the most brilliant coup of his career. As a proper military man, he delighted to keep tab on his old comrades-in-arms, and so he had been following closely the round-the-world progress of the most distinguished soldier of them all, General Grant. Fresh from four years in the White House, Grant had set off, in 1877, on a world tour. His itinerary included a visit to the French capital, and it was this happy circumstance that inspired Colonel Hungerford with his great idea. What more fitting than that during the general's stay in Paris he should be entertained by the daughter of one who had borne arms with him in the Mexican War? The fact that Grant and Hungerford had never met was a minor detail: both had helped humble the arrogant Mexicans, Grant as a lieutenant and Hungerford as a captain. This connection seemed sufficient not only to the colonel but to his daughter. Patriotism no less than expediency demanded that the hero be suitably welcomed to France; besides, what better occasion could be imagined to mark her introduction to Parisian society? "Mrs. Mackay," stated one of her admirers, "decided that, although on foreign soil, her father's renowned comrade-in-arms should be welcomed by such a scene of dazzling brilliancy that all the glories of the Empire could not excel. . . ." An invitation was accordingly cabled to Grant and in due time came a gracious reply: the General would be delighted during his stay in Paris to accept the hospitality of Mrs. Mackay.

How great was that lady's joy may be judged by the scope of the preparations that promptly got under way. During the next few days an army of artisans converged on the rue Tilsit. The entire lower floor of the mansion was redecorated, with the American national colors predominant; in carrying out this motif every stick of furniture was carted off and reupholstered in red, white, and blue satin. Meantime a pavilion was rushed to completion in the garden, with tapestry-covered walls and clusters of gas-lamps, and one wall of the drawing-room was torn out to permit joining this with the temporary pavilion to form one vast chamber. Parisians looked on it with wonder and awe. This was their first experience with wealthy American hostesses in their lavishly expansive moods. Criticism was heard in some quarters. Members of the American colony were quite understandably disturbed that this newcomer from a barbarous place called Nevada had captured the most illustrious American to come to Paris since the days of Franklin, and followers of Blanqui and Thiers chose to consider so prodigious an expenditure for so trifling a purpose an affront to a city that had recently endured the privations of a siege and the bloodshed of the Commune.

Crowds gathered daily to watch the show, and gendarmes were assigned to keep them moving past the tall iron fence. Some were startled by certain devices Mrs. Mackay had caused to be placed on standards about the garden: huge American eagles in shields. A few hissed and hurled imprecations, but this was due to a misunderstanding: a populace that six years earlier had watched the banners of a victorious enemy carried down the Champs-Élysées could not readily distinguish between American and Germanic eagles. The newspapers duly made the distinction clear. There were daily stories in the French press, one of which—later stoutly denied—related that in her zeal to honor her countryman Mrs. Mackay had petitioned the authorities to decorate the Arc de Triomphe. Told that her plea had been rejected, she is said to have tossed her pretty head and announced loftily: "Very well, I'll buy their old arch and decorate it myself!" This tale made the rounds of the world's newspapers. As much as the Grant reception itself, it was responsible for making Mrs. Mackay's name a household word on both sides of the Atlantic.

Of the great event, one of Grant's early biographers, William Ralston Balch, wrote this first-hand account:

"Later in the day [November 21, 1877] he attended a fete, consisting of dinner and ball, given by Mrs. Mackay, wife of Bonanza Mackay, at her splendid mansion in rue Tilsit. It was the greatest sensational event of the season and for the time being overshadowed in importance, as far as the American colony and fashionable society were concerned, the existing political crisis.

"The covers were for twenty-four, and the guests were General Grant and family and the members of the American legation and consulate and their families. There were no unofficial Americans present at the dinner. The menu was inscribed on small silver tablets. . . . After the dinner a grand reception and ball took place, at which three hundred guests were present. Among the guests were the Marquis de Lafayette, M. M. de Rochambeau, and others. . . .

"The American colony was largely represented and the number of beautiful women was very remarkable. The ladies' costumes displayed extraordinary taste, elegance and richness. The dancing commenced early and continued until four o'clock in the morning. . . ."

The guest of honor retired early, but not so early as to deprive Colonel Hungerford of an opportunity to exchange with his fellow campaigner reminiscences of the glorious day at Chapultepec.

The Grant reception, that happy combination of luck and enterprise, gave Mrs. Mackay a degree of social prestige she could not otherwise have won without years of skillful maneuvering. Thereafter she had no doubt in what direction her destiny lay. She aspired to draw to her Paris home not alone the great figures of the aristocracy and statesmanship and finance, but also leaders in the arts: musicians, singers, painters, littérateurs—for was she not herself an accomplished pianist and related by her first marriage to a distinguished American poet? To many this seemed an uncommonly ambitious program. But to set against her lack of cosmopolitan background or experience, she had certain manifest advantages: a husband who was the chief owner of a group of mines that were currently producing above a million dollars a month and that had still untapped resources, believed to be virtually inexhaustible, a consuming desire for social advancement, a fluent command of the French language, beauty, a poised and gracious manner, boundless self-confidence, and a saving strain of hard common sense. She was the first fabulously rich American woman to exile herself in Europe and to entertain on a scale of prodigal magnificence. She succeeded far better than most of her later imitators.

For the next quarter century her social triumphs were staple reading for millions all over America. It was a period when lives of rich countrymen who moved in the upper circles of European society held a singular fascination for staunch democrats from Maine to California. Paris and London correspondents regularly cabled accounts of her receptions and appended lists of her more distinguished guests. Thus John Mackay in his hotel room at San Francisco or Virginia City was often privileged to read that his wife had entertained such renowned figures as Isabella, the exiled Queen of Spain, or Marshal Marie Edmé de MacMahon, survivor of the rout at Sedan and currently President of the Third French Republic.

When other news failed, Paris correspondents could always acceptably fill a half-column with a description of the Mackay jewels—"the finest collection outside the royal treasuries." The prize of her collection was a necklace of sapphires, "with a pendant gem the size of a pigeon's egg, set in large diamonds." This had been assembled for her, at a cost of $300,000 by the jeweler Boucheron, and its public exhibition had been one of the highlights of the Paris Exposition of 1878. Lesser items were two sets of pearls, each consisting of necklace, bracelets and diadem. One necklace was particularly noteworthy: five rows of pearls of graduated sizes, "the lower row the size of the largest huckleberries and the uppermost row bigger than a large pea." More striking still was a diamond bracelet "that encircles the arm above the elbow five times; it is formed of a single row of very large diamonds, three hundred in number. . . ." One writer estimated that the collection had cost well over a million dollars, and went on to explain that its owner was not in the habit of wearing all her jewels simultaneously; it was in fact her custom to appear at dinners and balls, and even at the opera, with the greater part of her collection safely at home in her jewel casket. Years later her famous sapphire necklace reappeared in the news. In San Francisco, when William Rippey shot Mackay and then fired a bullet into his own head, he carried in his pocket a rambling note that accused the mining magnate of having spent for his wife's sapphires "a sum sufficient to assure a comfortable old age for five hundred of his indigent countrymen."

The marriage of Mackay's adopted daughter, Eva, filled the social columns all over the land during the early months of 1885. The groom was Ferdinand Julian Colonna, Prince of Galarto, a member of the Neapolitan branch of this important Italian family. Mackay crossed the Atlantic for the event, and so staid a publication as the London *Pall Mall Gazette* reported that the miner (whom it referred to grandly as "the Big Bonanza") appeared to be "perfectly at home among the princes representing the oldest houses in Italy . . . and just as free from arrogance as his amiable and pretty wife." Rounding out his catalogue of the Mackay family, the reporter described the bride as "small, slim and artless" and added that the two Mackay sons, Willie and Clarence, wore impeccable cutaway jackets and had "striking Irish faces." This international marriage was widely heralded as a genuine romance, not one of the sordid alliances by which a title was bartered for a million or two of sound American dollars. Only a few years later, however, the pair quarreled and separated; a divorce suit followed, the details of which for many months claimed public attention on both sides of the Atlantic.

Meantime Mrs. Mackay's growing fame was still further enhanced when Ludovic Halévy, popular French writer of his day, published a novel called *L'Abbé Constantin*. The book, which sprang into immediate popularity, concerned a young, beautiful, and immensely rich American woman who, tiring of Paris, had closed her mansion there and retired to the provinces to enjoy the pleasures of rural life in a château which her husband had bought for her at a cost of two million francs. For many years *L'Abbé Constantin* was a favorite reading text in elementary French in American schools; few of the thousands who read it had any intimation that the story is other than fanciful. When it was first published, however, many recognized that the author had drawn one of its chief characters from life. The parallel was too exact to admit any doubt. The generous and gracious Madame Scott of the novel inevitably suggested Mrs. Mackay, who had become celebrated all over France for her lavish social functions and her open-handed benefactions. Madame Scott was young, she was immensely rich, she was a Catholic; moreover, she had a younger, unmarried sister, and she had recently moved into a huge house in the most fashionable part of Paris. In the book, when news reached the village of Lizotte that this famous lady had bought the near-by château, a son of the former owner exclaims:

"Madame Scott!"

"Do you know her?" demands his mother.

"Do I know her? If only I did! Not at all. But I was at a ball at her house about six weeks ago."

"A ball at her house, and you do not know her—what sort of woman is she, then?"

"Charming, exquisite, a dream, a marvel."

"And there is a Monsieur Scott?"

"Certainly; a tall, fair man. He was at the ball. He was pointed out to me. He bowed to the right and left at random. He did not enjoy himself, I assure you. He looked at us and seemed to be saying to himself: 'Who are all these people? What do they come to my house for?' We went to see Madame Scott and Miss Percival, Madame Scott's sister, and it was worth the trouble."

Further details came out, the current gossip in Paris about this fabulous family from America.

"This great fortune is quite new. It is said that ten years ago Madame Scott was begging in the streets of New York.

"They have, somewhere in America, a silver mine; an actual, a real mine, a silver mine in which there is money. Oh, you will see the splendor that will shine! We will all look like poor people. It is claimed that they have a hundred thousand francs a day to spend. . . ."

The story is a genteel little romance. The Abbé Constantin, for many years curé of the village, sees in the coming of this rich and worldly woman—who is an American and of course a heretic—the end of the simple, devout life of his parishioners, and the end too of his pleasant weekly dinners at the château. Nothing of the sort happens: Madame Scott and her sister prove to be not only gracious and liberal; they are also devout Catholics. Far from finding his influence at an end, the old man enters into a sort of priestly millennium, with a limitless supply of francs to distribute to the deserving poor and with dinners at the château more delicious and bountiful than ever before. Finally he has the climactic delight of seeing his ward, a most estimable young man, engaged to the charming Miss Percival, heiress to uncounted dollars. It is a light-hearted fable throughout, and Madame Scott is its gracious and beautiful heroine. There is no record that Mrs. Mackay ever denied that this character might indeed have been drawn from life.

Her long and acrimonious quarrel with Jean Louis Ernest Meissonier, which entertained two continents during the middle eighties, must have been far less pleasing to her than Halévy's innocuous novel. Meissonier, "a vain and peppery little man, lording it over Paris and sure of his own immortality," was then at the apex of his fame as France's most popular painter. Having made his reputation with huge historical canvases commemorating the victories of Napoleon I, he had turned to the more lucrative field of portrait-painting. His studio on the Parc Monceau was daily crowded with wealthy patrons, all eager to have their likenesses done by the master, and there in due course appeared Mrs. Mackay. But her portrait, a meticulously executed work showing the subject seated, a richly embroidered fabric draped about her shoulders, proved unsatisfactory to the sitter and she suggested certain alterations. These the painter would not bring himself to make. If his client refused to accept the portrait he would, he stated, send it to the fall salon and sell it for far more than the eighty thousand francs she had agreed to pay for it.

News of this impasse got into the newspapers, and public opinion was sharply divided. One pro-Mackay critic wrote: "Admirable though it is as a work of art, the picture is a gross caricature of the fair sitter, who is a handsome, refined-looking woman, and not the vulgar washerwoman masquerading in a medieval costume that Meissonier has represented her to be." On the other hand, the French were incensed that a mere rich American should presume to reject the work of the nation's most celebrated artist. The debate went on for weeks, with journalists on both sides of the Atlantic joining in. At the height of the excitement Mrs. Mackay paid Meissonier in full and carried off the portrait; thereupon she invited a group of friends to the rue Tilsit and in their presence dramatically consigned it to the flames. Far from ending the matter, this exploit elevated what had been a private quarrel into something approximating an international crisis. All over two continents the public hotly debated a delicate question of ethics: did the ownership of a work of art give one the privilege of destroying it? Opinions differed in America and England, but in France the reaction was both unanimous and violent. The abuse of the Paris press was so vituperative that at length the lady shook the dust of the boulevards from her heels and moved lock and stock to London. She publicly announced that she was permanently closing her rue Tilsit house and taking up residence in England. When she was asked to explain this move, she announced blandly that, on the whole, she believed the British were more sincere and trustworthy than the French.

In London she set about duplicating the social successes she had enjoyed on the far side of the Channel. As a setting for her campaign she bought one of the most imposing residences in the city. Descriptions of No. 6 Carlton House Terrace were cabled across the Atlantic, of the "colossal dimensions" of its public rooms—library and dining-room on the main floor and drawing-room and ballroom above, the latter reached by a magnificent marble staircase that had cost the original owner, the Duke of Leinster, three hundred thousand dollars. By any standard the London mansion was an impressive property and the type of hospitality its new owner dispensed was in keeping. American newspapers described a formal dinner held there in July 1886 honoring the Prince of Wales, at which event an even hundred guests filled the huge dining-room. Afterward the *New York World*'s account continues, the title-studded crowd ascended to the ballroom, where they were entertained by twenty Russian choir singers, two artistes from the Comédie Française and—for, after all, the hostess was Brooklyn-born—by an American baritone, Edward Oudin. The dispatch concludes with this description of the ballroom décor: "The balcony was shut in from the street by mirrors and draperies, and in each of the recesses . . . was placed a column formed by great, super-imposed blocks of ice surrounded with palms and white, feathery ferns. Behind each column was a ruby-tinted lamp that shone through the crystal blocks of ice with a soft and roseate glow. . . ."

Reprinting this bit, the *San Francisco Call* captioned it: "Magnificent Mrs. Mackay." The irony of the heading was not displeasing to many of the lady's former acquaintances on the Coast. There were some who rejoiced in her triumphs: to them, little Miss Hungerford's phenomenal rise was Cinderella's story come to life. Others were not above the human vice of envy. Reading the effusions of the society reporters—"The whole affair passed off brilliantly, Mrs. Mackay being a hostess beyond compare . . ." "She is an honor to her sex and to her countrymen abroad . . ." —old-time friends on both sides of the Sierra shook their heads in unbelief. Could this indeed be the Mamie Hungerford they had known, daughter of Downieville's barber and widow of young Dr. Bryant, who had died prematurely of drink and drugs? A credit to her sex indeed! If she wished to deserve the praise, let her close her preposterous London mansion and hurry back and rescue her husband from the hotel rooms that had been his home for years and give him the companionship and comfort that were his right. If she must squander the Mackay millions, let them be spent in the country that had produced them.

Thus, accounts of her European successes were critically read on the West Coast, and any misstatement, any attempt to romanticize her early background, was promptly detected and exposed. One story out of London made casual reference to the fact that she had been graduated with honors from a California academy for young ladies, the Benicia Convent. At once the convent's records were searched without bringing to light any indication that she had ever been enrolled there. Another account stated that Colonel Hungerford had been a "leading chemist" in Downieville—and dozens came happily forward to testify that his scissors had often clipped their hair. When news reached the Coast in 1889 that Mrs. Mackay had sued the proprietor of the Manchester *Examiner* for libel because his paper had stated that her mother had pieced out the family income by washing clothes for the miners, letters arguing the question pro and con blossomed in the California journals. The editor of a mining-town weekly, the *Sierra Tribune,* came to the defense of his fellow journalist across the water. Scores of old-timers, he stated, clearly remembered when Mrs. Hungerford had lived in a cabin between Downieville and a camp called Port Wine, where she had been happy to earn an honest dollar by washing shirts and jeans of the Argonauts. "Why should Mrs. Mackay feel bad?" he inquired. "She was glad enough to eat the bread and butter earned by her mother in playing the kitchen piano."

Some of the stories of her humble beginnings were obvious fabrications, invented by the spiteful and envious at home and abroad. A member of the American colony in Paris, resenting her social success, is said to have originated the myth—still sometimes encountered—that she operated a boarding-house in Virginia City and that Mackay met her when he began taking his meals there. Another story had it that their acquaintance began when the destitute widow sought out the miner and asked alms to keep her children from starvation; yet another stated that she was a cook in the family of one of Mackay's friends, presumably Fair. These and other tales (including some far less flattering) presently became so numerous that in 1891 a writer in the *Alta California* came to her defense: "All the ridiculous stories that have appeared respecting her in the papers are pure invention. She never wanted to illuminate the Arc de Triomphe, for instance, and never offered to buy it. . . ." And at Virginia City Sam Rosener announced: "She never had to worry where her next meal was coming from. She was an expert with a needle and her hand embroidery was so fine our customers were always asking for more. We gave her as much work as she could do and paid her liberally. . . ." During that period she had also taught French in a Comstock girls' school.

Years later, word reached Mackay that his elder son Willie had been showing marked attention to a schoolteacher: his informant thought perhaps the boy might marry her. Mackay was undisturbed. "Why not?" he demanded. "I married one."

Mrs. Mackay had been so long in the public eye that when, in the spring of 1893, it became known that she was returning to her native land, curiosity was high across the nation. The drama of her return was heightened by the fact that her husband lay in his hotel room in San Francisco, victim of Rippey's bullet and thought to be critically wounded. Her long journey to his side was heralded as a "race of death" and thousands followed its progress. By the time her steamer reached New York, however, Mackay's physicians had pronounced him out of danger, and the tension relaxed. None the less, wife and sons hurried direct from the pier to Jersey City, where a private car, the Corsair, waited to begin the dash across the continent. But there were delays along the way and a full week passed before the party reached the Coast. A crowd of friends, newspaper reporters, and the merely curious, gathered at Oakland pier and watched while the lady, looking chic and surprisingly youthful, tripped down the steps of the Corsair, her pet Skye terrier, Jacques, under one arm. The *Call*'s reporter made note of the fact that "her dress was French, her hat was French, and her smile was French," and listened while she explained the reason for their slow transcontinental passage: "Regular trains hauled our car. . . . I do not like the jolting of a special engine pulling one car."

During the ferry ride she graciously permitted the interview to continue. Yes, she had had daily reports of Mr. Mackay's condition all the way across the continent. When had she last seen him? About two years before, when he had spent several weeks in London. This was her first visit to the United States in seventeen years and of course she had observed many changes. Her plans? They would depend on Mr. Mackay's condition, and his wishes. Was she planning to establish a home in California? She thought that unlikely: she already had a place in London and another in Paris; what use would she have for still another? Then came a more delicate question: Had her long residence abroad made her a stranger in her native land? Her reply was emphatic. "Wrap me in an American flag," she exclaimed dramatically, "and you will see that it belongs there!" The reporters turned their attention to the two Mackay sons, one in his early twenties, the other seventeen, and concluded that their London topcoats and broad English accents gave them the air of having been wrapped, not in the Stars and Stripes, but in the Union Jack.

The party hurried to the Palace Hotel, then up to the third-floor sickroom. Mackay had so far recovered that a night or two later he was able to accompany the visitors on a tour of Chinatown, where his wife exclaimed like any tourist over the picturesque sights of the quarter and found only the smells annoying. Acquaintances who sought her out were greeted with unassuming cordiality, and one friend of the distant Downieville days announced as he left the Palace suite: "Mrs. Mackay is a very grand lady, but she's still as sweet and charming as when she was only little Marie Hungerford." Only one untoward incident marred this triumphant return: Willie fell victim to a toothache and, while applying a powerful drug to ease the pain, inadvertently swallowed a drop or two and became violently ill. Within a few days, however, he had so far recovered that he was able to cross with his family to Oakland pier and begin the long journey back to London.

It was Mrs. Mackay's last American visit for nearly ten years. When next she crossed the Atlantic it was to supervise the sealing of her husband's body in the family vault at the Greenwood Cemetery in Brooklyn. A few years later she closed the Carlton House Terrace mansion and went to live with her son Clarence at Roslyn, Long Island. There she remained for more than twenty years, living quietly, seldom venturing outside the gates of the estate. She died there as recently as 1928, at the age of eighty-five, her years of social successes in Europe all but forgotten by the world.

7

WHAT John Mackay, a reticent man of simple tastes,
thought of the pomp with which his wife had surrounded
herself and of the ceaseless glare of notoriety in which
she lived was never fully known. For well over two
decades the two lived on opposite sides of the Atlantic,
yet few suggested that their married life was other than
congenial. During most of that period Mackay made annual visits, first to Paris, then to London, where he passed
a few weeks with his family before turning west again to
take up the task of producing the income his wife spent
with so expert a hand.

He was assuredly one of the most generous of husbands.
Not only did he support his lady in regal magnificence;
her entire family signally benefited by his ever open purse.
Toward his picturesque and garrulous father-in-law he was
a model of forbearance. The gallant colonel's hours-long
monologues must have bored him almost to distraction,
and he is said to have once referred to that estimable gentleman as "that God-damned old windbag." Yet he was
careful not to permit the ladies to see his annoyance and
he continued to support the old man in luxury as long as
he lived. During the involved marital troubles of Eva Bryant Mackay Colonna he stood by her staunchly, and in
the end secured her freedom from her Italian husband by
paying over a very large number of American dollars. It
is probable that this expenditure gave him a certain satisfaction, for the custom of marrying off rich American girls
to impoverished holders of foreign titles seemed to him
the height of folly. He was far from sharing his wife's
admiration for members—any members—of the European
aristocracy, and he made little attempt to conceal his dis-
taste for the hangers-on who frequented her Paris and
London houses. On his annual visits he associated with
these amiable loafers only when his duty as host made it
imperative, escaping at the earliest opportunity, usually
to a hotel where visiting American acquaintances were
stopping. There, in shirt-sleeves and with a bottle of

whisky and siphon handy, he played poker by the hour, returning home only when he was sure the last guest had departed.

In America he lived simply and his personal expenses were small. "When he comes to New York," stated the *World* in 1893, "he slips off the train with a gripsack in one hand and an umbrella in the other and walks to his hotel." For some years he stopped at the Hoffman House, owned by Edward S. Stokes. Later, when Stokes, following his customary bent, swindled Mackay in a business deal, the mining man transferred his headquarters to the Windsor. The *World*'s account adds that he never telegraphed ahead for accommodations, taking without complaint whatever quarters were assigned to him, usually a single room for which he paid five dollars a night. In Virginia City he for years occupied a corner room on the top floor of the International. That famous old hotel remained in operation for many years after Virginia's other glories had faded. In 1903 a visitor to the disintegrating town was met at the station by its current owner, an ancient Chinese named Charley Young, who carried the visitor's bag up the hill, stepped behind the mahogany counter, opened the huge brass-bound register and presented a rusty pen. The rates? Four bits for rooms on the first two floors, two bits for those above. The celebrated hydraulic elevators had long since ceased to function and tariffs were fixed by the number of stairs guests were required to climb. The newcomer examined the spacious chamber into which he was ushered: its carpet faded and threadbare, its immense walnut bed and marble-topped dresser, its Nottingham lace curtains hanging in shreds from ornate gilt poles; probably it was just such a room as Mackay had occupied a quarter century earlier. Downstairs again, the 1903 guest studied two deep furrows worn into the marble flagging of the lobby, one leading from the doorway to the dining-room, the other to the bar. Fire destroyed the historic old building in 1914.

By then all the men the mines had enriched (and more whom they had impoverished) had long since deserted the Comstock. Mackay continued to list Virginia City as his legal residence, but that was mere sentiment; there is no record that he visited the place during his last twenty years. After he died, a probate court appraiser made an inventory of his Comstock property: its total value was $305. Items included a lot valued at $10; a one-story frame building, $50; a Diebold Norris & Co. safe, $150; a black walnut desk, $10; a letter-press stand, fifty cents; one-eighth cord nut-pine wood, $1; eighteen burlap ore sacks, no value.

His interests had long since veered in other directions, but none of his later ventures was as lucrative as his Comstock investments. In 1879 an inventor interested him in a new type of explosive, more powerful than dynamite and said to be impossible to explode except by percussion caps. Mackay invested half a million dollars in a plant at Oakland, California, and began the large-scale manufacture of Eureka Safety Powder. One of his friends became agent for the product in Arizona Territory and spent several months giving graphic proof of the product's safety before mineowners and others. During his demonstrations sticks of the explosives were stamped on, run over by ore-cars, and pounded with sledge-hammers. On his way back to San Francisco, his pockets bulging with orders, the agent picked up a newspaper and learned that the product was far less safe than he had been led to believe: on the previous day something had gone wrong during the manufacturing process and the Oakland factory had been blown sky-high. Both Mackay and his star salesman retired precipitously from the powder business.

Perhaps as a result of this fiasco, Mackay planned a two-year tour of the world, then abandoned it when the Nevada legislature appointed him representative of the Silver State at one of the periodical Paris expositions. In 1881 he received a second public honor. President Arthur named him a special ambassador to the coronation of Alexander III, and he and his wife set off for Moscow, where both were presented at the Russian court and took part in the brilliant functions that ushered in that Czarist regime. Two years later he was projected into world-wide notoriety when a mathematically minded reporter calculated that Mackay's income exceeded ten thousand dollars a day. He published his findings in a London newspaper, the story was promptly reprinted in a dozen languages, and for months Mackay was deluged with thousands of letters, their writers all eager to enjoy his income for periods that ranged from five minutes to ten years. One Scottish lady asked for five hundred pounds to permit her to spend the winter in Italy; a German student demanded that Mackay finance the publication of his treatise on economics, which advocated the seizure of large private fortunes and their distribution to deserving students; an American tourist urged that Mackay subsidize a boarding-house in Paris at which homesick Yankees could obtain proper American food, well cooked and cheap. Hoping to stem this flood, Mackay announced that his daily income was not the advertised ten thousand dollars but a beggarly twenty-nine hundred; moreover, he served notice that all begging letters would be destroyed unread. His mail continued heavy for many months, then slowly tapered off. It is said that only one of the many thousands of pleas bore fruit: residents of the city of Nancy petitioned him to erect a statue of Jeanne d'Arc on the square where, in 1429, Jeanne had offered prayers to her patron, St. Lorraine. The statue duly materialized, but only after a long delay. The handsome equestrian figure was not installed and dedicated until 1895.

Production of the bonanza mines declined sharply after 1878, and during the next few years much time and money were spent in an unsuccessful search for other rich ore bodies. By 1883 Mackay had grown convinced that the lode had only "poor man's pudding" to offer; he accordingly sold his remaining Comstock stocks and prepared to devote himself permanently to rest and travel and to indulging his taste for poker, billiards, and the theater. But a life given over to such frivolities early proved insupportable, and he was presently considering a number of business ventures: the building and operation of a fleet of trans-Atlantic steamers, an underground street-car line in New York. When these projects were abandoned his interest centered on a third: transocean cables. With a wife and family on the far side of the Atlantic, Mackay was painfully aware of the high tolls charged by the company —controlled by Jay Gould—that then enjoyed a monopolistic control of the business: its rate was seventy-five cents a word.

The reasons why Mackay entered the cable business— a field remote from his previous experience—are obscure; one version states that the impulse came from James Gordon Bennett, for whom Mackay had admiration second only to that he entertained for General Grant. As owner of the *New York Herald,* Bennett had of course ample reason to want to bring about a reduction in cable rates. The two joined forces and, in 1883, organized the Commercial Cable Company, designed to lay and operate cables from New York to London, and the Continent. Mackay put up seventy per cent of the capital and became the corporation's president; Bennett supplied twenty per cent, and a group of their friends took the remainder. Within a year, a specially fitted steamer, the *Mackay-Bennett,* was busy laying the first cable. It was put in operation in 1884 and immediately proved useful to the *Herald's* owner by giving that paper an advantage both in cost and speed over its competitors in the transmission of European news. It was less successful, however, in other directions, for it was soon clear that if the new concern hoped to do a general commercial business it must have access to telegraph lines within the United States. The Western Union, by far the largest of American telegraph companies, refused to relay messages coming over the Mackay-Bennett cable, and Mackay started the involved and financially hazardous project of buying up smaller companies and consolidating them into a system that could offer effective competition to the Western Union. His first step was the purchase of the Postal Telegraph Company, then a struggling concern that offered but feeble competition to its dominant rival, and with this as a nucleus he proceeded to take over a number of small independent companies.

Meantime the Commercial Cable Company was having other troubles. Shortly before the first Mackay-Bennett cable was put in operation, its Gould-owned rival dropped the trans-Atlantic rate from seventy-five to fifty cents a word. Mackay countered by inaugurating a forty-cent rate; Gould met the cut. Two years later Gould began war in earnest, lowering the word rate to twelve cents, and again Mackay followed suit. This rate held for a year and a half, with both companies losing heavily. At last Gould gave in, and in September 1888 the two companies boosted the toll to twenty-five cents a word. At the time he announced the end of the rate war, Gould added ruefully: "There's no beating John Mackay. If he needs another million or two he goes to his silver mine and digs it up." This was highly inaccurate; Mackay's silver mines had ceased to pay dividends nearly a decade earlier. While the rate war was in progress, Jim Fair—whose opinion of the financial astuteness of his partner was never high— went about San Francisco cheerfully predicting that Mackay would sink his last dollar to the bottom of the Atlantic.

There were times when Fair's prophecy seemed likely to prove accurate. The building up of a nation-wide telegraph system, while at the same time he was extending his cable lines throughout the world—all in the face of bitter competition—proved a heavy drain even on his abundant resources. By 1888 domestic rate wars instituted by the Western Union had proved so costly that Mackay was willing to admit defeat. "I don't care a damn about the money I've put in," he wrote his friend Stokes. "I just want to get out. . . ." Again: "The best thing to do is to sell out the whole plant to the Western Union, ticker and all." This correspondence became public two years later when Mackay sued Stokes for $375,000, money he claimed to have advanced the latter and which Stokes had neither returned nor accounted for. The suit dragged through the courts for several years; the ultimate decision was in Stokes's favor.

Meantime his patchwork telegraph system had been extended to a point where it could boast an almost national coverage and so could offer fairly effective competition to the Western Union. No longer faced with staggering annual deficits, Mackay lost his earlier desire to sell out. His final years were devoted to building up a world-wide communications system and to putting it on a sound financial basis. From his headquarters in the Postal Telegraph's sixteen-story building at 253 Broadway he made periodical tours of the country, keeping watch over hundreds of domestic branches and agencies, and twice a year crossing the Atlantic to visit the offices of the Commercial Cable Company.

On his frequent treks to the West Coast old acquaintances began to observe that at last he was beginning to show signs of strain. His traditional quiet affability seemed sometimes a trifle forced, and his temper grew progressively less stable. To the cronies who gathered nightly in his Palace Hotel room he recalled with nostalgic pleasure the days when he had worked his placer claims on the Yuba, content if they yielded enough to supply his simple needs and to finance an occasional Saturday night spree in the nearest town. He was no longer sure that an immense fortune was worth the constant effort needed to conserve and administer it.

One afternoon in October 1895 he chanced to be in the San Francisco office of his cable company when a message from Paris was placed before him: his elder son, twenty-five-year-old Willie, was dangerously ill. Mackay cabled for details, but before his inquiry could be delivered, two other messages arrived. One warned him to prepare for the worst; the other stated that the young man was dead.

Mackay remained at the cable office all night and gradually news of the tragedy filtered through. The young man had rented a château outside Paris; after luncheon one day his two companions had suggested a steeplechase race. Three horses were saddled—Mackay's mount was a spirited, half-broken colt—and the sport began. On the second round of the course one of the riders came upon Mackay lying unconscious on the ground; the exact cause of the accident was never learned. He was carried to the château, where he regained consciousness briefly, then lapsed into a coma and died. No member of his family was present. His mother was visiting in Normandy, his brother was at school in England, his half-sister, Princess Colonna, although she was in Paris, could not be located.

The young man was buried with the pomp of a prince. The house on the rue Tilsit, closed for years, was reopened. "Its entire front . . . was covered with mourning draperies, the lamps before the mansion were lighted and covered with crepe, and street traffic was entirely suspended in the vicinity of the Arc de Triomphe. . . ." A hundred thousand francs were expended to drape the nave and aisles of the Church of St. Ferdinand des Ternes, where High Mass was said, "with full vocal and orchestral accompaniment, several leading operatic artists assisting in the choir. . . ." Later the mile-long funeral procession passed through the Paris streets to the Chapel of St. Augustine, "where the body was placed, constantly watched over by nuns, until it is shipped to America. . . ."

Symbols of mourning were visible too across the United States. In New York five thousand yards of crepe converted the entrance of the Postal Telegraph building into a somber black arch, set off with white rosettes. The *World,* which had been campaigning against exorbitant cable rates, remarked tartly: "It is such a decoration as is made when some great public man is dead." Work was speeded up on the intricate Mackay mausoleum, already taking shape at Greenwood Cemetery. Before it was finished, young Mackay's body was brought across the Atlantic on the French liner *Lorraine* (one end of its main salon had been partitioned off and converted into a chapel) and again placed in a temporary vault. Meantime the construction of the Greenwood tomb was closely followed all over the land. An interested nation learned that this was to be "incomparably the handsomest mausoleum in the world," that its cost was $250,000, and that its chief ornaments were symbolical bronze statuary groups at each of its four corners: Mercy crowning Hope, Religion consoling Grief, Faith arousing Youth, and Peace—which was evidently doing nothing in particular.

Mackay had long planned to turn over to his elder son the management of his properties, and the latter had been carefully trained for the responsibility. Faced by this emergency, the surviving son, twenty-year-old Clarence Hungerford Mackay, stepped into the breach, applying himself to learning the details of the vast business he would some day head. It was an uncommonly intricate task, for the Mackay cable companies were pushing out over large areas of the earth's surface, and in the domestic field the Postal Telegraph system was still expanding. Through the late nineties, Clarence applied himself industriously, for that conscientious young man had come to realize that he might soon be called upon to shoulder the full burden. By way of announcing his accession to power in the family enterprises, his father, in 1899, purchased a fifty-room Louis XIII mansion, Harbor Hills, at Roslyn, Long Island, and presented it as a wedding gift to Clarence and his bride, the former Katherine Duer, of New York.

Mackay celebrated his seventieth birthday toward the end of 1901 and prepared to retire when his final major job was finished: the laying of the first trans-Pacific cable to its eastern terminus at Manila. He had been warned that the time to step down was at hand, for the vitality that had sustained him for seven decades had begun to fail. As the century closed, Dr. John Gallwey, San Francisco heart specialist, advised a general slowing down, but a man of Mackay's large affairs could not immediately follow that advice to the full. Projects already launched and in the critical stages of their planning had to be carried through. The ailing man remained in harness, sparing himself as much as possible and looking forward in a few months to the leisure he had not known since childhood.

Through the early months of 1902 he remained in New York directing the laying of the final section of the Philippine cable, and in June business of the Commercial Cable Company took him to London. On July 17 a message over the company's line informed the public that the old man had suffered a sunstroke while at luncheon in his London office: he was thought not to be seriously ill. Two days later his condition grew worse and three physicians were summoned to Carlton House Terrace. Their diagnosis caused alarm; cables were dispatched to the sick man's son in New York and his stepdaughter in Paris. Both arrived too late: Princess Colonna by an hour, Clarence by four days. Mackay died during the evening of July 20, 1902, of heart failure brought on by pneumonia.

The passing of the last surviving member of the once potent bonanza firm was front-page news all over the world. In London a procession of carriages stopped before 8 Carlton House Terrace while messages of condolence were ceremoniously presented and inquiries made after the welfare of the widow. On the far side of the Atlantic the dead man's accomplishments were reviewed in column-long obituaries that sketched his recent rise in the communications field, made much of his wife's social successes, told again the story of Princess Colonna's marriage and divorce, and—except on the West Coast—devoted curiously little space to his fabulous Comstock winnings, fountainhead of the wealth that had made all the rest possible. Crepe appeared on the doors of the Postal Telegraph offices from coast to coast, and at noon on July 23 the wires of every Mackay-controlled company went dead for five minutes.

Mackay's death gave editors all over the land an opportunity to describe again the Greenwood mausoleum and to point out that thus far only two of that handsome structure's twenty-four niches were occupied: by the bodies of Willie and Colonel Hungerford. Not until four months later was the bonanza king's body sealed in its appointed place. His widow's strength would not permit an immediate crossing of the Atlantic; his body was embalmed and placed in a London vault pending her return to health.

Estimates of the size of the Mackay estate ranged from thirty millions upward to sixty. The *New York Tribune's* guess was fifty millions. In San Francisco Dick Dey countered the inevitable question by remarking. "I don't suppose he knew within twenty millions what he was worth." Dey rattled off the names of some of the enterprises in which the dead man had been interested: he was president of the Commercial Cable Company, the Postal Telegraph Company, and the Pacific Commercial

Cable Company; vice-president of a sugar refinery in Yonkers (of which a fellow San Franciscan, Gus Spreckels, was president); director of the Canadian Pacific railroads and of the Nevada Bank in San Francisco; part owner of an elevator-manufacturing concern in New York and of copper and gold mines in California, Idaho, and Alaska. In addition, he owned real estate in San Francisco and New York and had extensive holdings of land in other parts of California.

Significantly, in listings of Mackay's assets, no mention was made of his once immense Virginia City holdings. The great bonanza mines had ceased to pay dividends almost a quarter century earlier, and all operations had long since been suspended. The great mills and hoisting works had been stripped of whatever was worth salvaging and the shells of the huge buildings were falling to ruin. Underground, the miles of shafts and galleries and stopes, once as familiar to Mackay as the mines' surface buildings— and far more exciting—were sealed and silent as the Greenwood tomb, the entire lower works flooded, the area above the 1,650-foot level, drained by the Sutro Tunnel, a fantastic labyrinth of debris: choked tunnels, caved-in stopes, timbers telescoped into grotesque shapes by the pressures of tens of millions of tons of slowly settling earth. In silence and darkness, beneath Mount Davidson as in the niche at Greenwood, the earth was patiently reclaiming its own.

Part Three

Fair

1

"A master mechanic . . . a perfect judge of any kind of machinery . . . one of the shrewdest of the financiers . . . and from early childhood more interested in the affairs of James G. Fair than in any other soul on earth. . . ."

THIS quotation is from the recollections of a Comstock editor who had known Fair very well; others have written in like vein. All those who had first-hand knowledge of the man and his methods agreed that he was an uncommonly able mine superintendent, a skilled practitioner of the arts of accumulation, and a man who, having amassed a huge fortune, dedicated his declining years to nurturing, protecting, and increasing it. Having paid him these tributes, acquaintances usually proceeded, with noticeably heightened pleasure, to a catalogue of his less endearing traits. Of all the Comstock's conspicuous figures, Fair was easily the least admired, a fact of which he was aware and which he regarded with complete indifference. The good opinion of his fellows he valued so little that at no stage of his career did he exert himself to deserve it. He aimed rather to please himself, and in that he succeeded even better than most. "To the last his self-approval was perfect," wrote one commentator. Others have expressed the same thought in different words, including Fair himself, who once remarked: "I've always built my success on other men's failures."

The public was far from sharing his self-complacency. "Since James G. Fair died last week," wrote Arthur McEwen in 1894, "his name has been on everyone's lips. I have yet to hear a good word spoken of him." Fair's death brought forth few of the encomiums that commonly accompany the passing of a multimillionaire. "In a small back room at the Lick House," began the *Examiner's* obituary, "the embalming poison in his veins, the ice upon his chest, lies all that is mortal of James G. Fair, the man who spent the years of his life accumulating from twenty to forty million dollars." Other Coast papers reported his death in similar fashion, their column-long parting salutes describing him variously as gross, dull, greedy, grasping, mean, and malignant. Tributes to his solid accomplishments were not wholly lacking, but such praise was directed where it most clearly belonged: to his mastery of the art of hoarding dollars and of causing them to multiply. "If fortune had given him birth in the servants' hall," stated a writer in 1894, "he would have died steward of the estate, or its mortgagee." Another wrote that he had sacrificed family, friends, and honor to gratify his money-making instinct, and that he had never shown any sign that the decision had caused him a moment's regret. Yet few of the men who penned these candid appraisals could conceal a certain grudging admiration. The week Fair died, Arthur McEwen filled two pages of his weekly *Letter* with savage abuse, of which the following are examples: "Never did I meet a man of good intelligence who had dealings with him of any sort who did not detest him. . . . The common estimate of Fair, though spoken freely— the utterance obviously hearty satisfaction to the profane —is not printable." But when he reached the final paragraph McEwen was constrained to add: "Yet he was a stout warrior. I saw him a few days ago, smoking the one daily cigar his physician allowed him. . . . His front was bold and calm as he walked the streets with the end not a week away. . . ."

In 1888 the California historian Hubert Howe Bancroft, angling to add Fair's name to the list of sponsors of his profitable series of Western biographies, *The Chronicles of the Builders,* sent one of his assistants to interview the mining magnate. The notes of this interview assay Fair's qualities with even-handed candor. The scribe, George Morrison, found him "a very cool man . . . no conscience to trouble him, no sentiment." He described Fair's geniality, his boundless egoism, his sly belittlement of the accomplishments of his ex-partners, with the obvious intent of throwing his own abilities into bolder relief. Morrison reported to Bancroft that Fair would pay well to have his life-story included in the series, but he warned that it would need to be carefully written so as to make clear that in every phase of the bonanza firm's activities Fair was always right and his associates invariably wrong. Of course the published sketch closely followed these suggestions. *The Chronicles of the Builders* was a vanity publication, and any man who paid the high admittance fee did so in the knowledge that he would go down to posterity exactly as he wished to be. That Fair permitted himself this expensive and obviously worthless luxury must have puzzled his acquaintances; he had always been at pains to make known his scorn of the virtues others professed to admire. The explanation must be that the old man really believed he merited whatever praise his hired biographer chose to heap on him. "An appeal to his vanity was the only thing that ever opened Fair's purse-strings," stated one of the Comstock historians. He parted with fifteen thousand dollars for the Bancroft sketch. It was one of the few bad bargains he ever made—twenty-five pages of evasions, flattery, and platitudinous generalities.

This was regrettable, for Fair had qualities that deserved a far more realistic exploration of his singular personality. Much was written about him during his lifetime and later; it is mostly uncritical abuse. For years a variety of "Fair stories" were in circulation in San Francisco and Virginia City, all bearing on his egocentric obsession, his exclusive concern with whatever forwarded his own ends. He himself was mainly responsible for the harsh judgments the public passed on him. He took pleasure in advertising to the world traits of character that other men would have been at pains to conceal. If he bested another in a business deal, half the town knew it next morning, and the more outrageous the trick, the greater his pride in telling of it. In 1879, on orders of his physician, he resigned as superintendent of the world's richest mine and made a leisurely tour of the world. Not wishing to set off alone on so extended a trip, he invited a Virginia City friend to accompany him. The latter accepted with pleasure, the more so because he assumed that he was to be Fair's guest. That impression lasted throughout the voyage; not until they returned to Virginia City did Fair present him with an itemized bill for half their joint expenses—its total exceeded six thousand dollars.

His exploits might—and often did—violate every canon of fairness and justice; Fair was unconcerned. If he conducted himself with shrewdness and so overcame a duller opponent he was first to make the story known. Once his partners wanted to increase the pay of an able and hardworking employee. Fair vetoed the plan, explaining: "A hungry hound hunts best." He chose his victims where he found them; members of his family were no more exempt than strangers. Early in his Comstock career, having learned that the ore body in one of the mines was nearing exhaustion, he began to unload his stock. That night he asked his wife how much cash she had in the bank. She named the amount: about seven thousand dollars. "Don't mention this to a soul," said Fair, "but Gould & Curry is going sky high." Mrs. Fair invested her seven thousand dollars and quietly told her closest friend, who told her sister-in-law, who told someone else. On the rising market Fair profitably disposed of his holdings, whereupon news that the Gould & Curry was petering out reached the public and the market collapsed. A week later Fair innocently inquired about his wife's savings. She burst into tears and confessed that she had bought Gould & Curry and lost every penny. He restored the money to her and admonished: "My dear, I'm afraid you'll never be a speculator."

When he chose to do so, he could be affability itself. Once on Montgomery Street in San Francisco he was talking to an acquaintance when a third man stopped and exchanged greetings. Fair shook hands warmly, remarked how well the newcomer was looking, and beamingly inquired about the welfare of his family. When the flattered stranger had passed on, Fair demanded of his companion: "Who is that son-of-a-bitch?"

He owned many acres of real estate in downtown San Francisco, yet he lived frugally in two rooms in the outmoded Lick House (one of his properties) and from a cluttered office near by kept watch over his involved fortune. He had an unshakable faith in the soundness of his judgment and a corresponding conviction that most other men were fools or knaves or both. The consequence was that at no stage of his career could he bring himself to delegate authority. During his final two decades he daily spent many hours performing routine tasks that could have been done equally well by twenty-dollar-a-week clerks. When the bonanza mines were in full production, he was so enmeshed in detail that for months on end he averaged less than five hours' sleep a night. There were periods when he personally wrote and signed every check issued by the corporations controlled by the firm, some of which employed above a thousand men and all of which bought supplies in prodigious quantities. The total number of such checks must have been enormous; more than fifty years after the mines shut down, canceled checks bearing Fair's signature were being sold for ten cents each in Virginia City bars and curio shops. Only recently has the supply begun to run low, with a consequent rise in price: today on C Street Fair's autograph costs fifty cents. Signing checks was but one of a multitude of details to which he insisted on giving personal attention, to the neglect of more important matters. Once some pressing business required his presence in Carson City; he put off the trip from week to week, afraid something might go wrong if he relaxed his vigilant watch for half a day.

Periodically this load of responsibility proved too much even for his abundant vitality; his health would break down and he would have to take to his bed, sometimes for long periods. These physical breakdowns were damaging to his ego and he put them off as long as possible, meantime taking recourse to alcohol to keep himself going. His wife once stated that at such times he habitually carried a quart bottle of brandy into their bedroom and that the bottle was empty the next morning. During his bedridden periods he occupied himself by matching wits with his physician; if the latter could be hoodwinked into thinking that Fair had been following orders, visitors were likely to find the patient in high good humor. Physicians liked to pretend that the nature of the sick man's malady was known only to them and that they alone were competent to cope with it. Fair of course was too shrewd to be taken in by this solemn nonsense; he needed no help when it came to diagnosing his ailments and prescribing their cure. His method of self-treatment was ingenious. Because it was obvious that the doctors were always wrong, a sick man had only to get their advice, do the opposite, and be quickly restored to health. He did just that. If his physician ordered complete rest, he got out of bed and hurried to his office; if he was told not to touch alcohol, he sent his servant downstairs for a bottle of brandy and applied himself to emptying it; if he was put on a diet of tea and crackers, he ordered a heavy meal sent up from the Lick House kitchen. He was thoroughly convinced of the soundness of this program, recommended it highly to acquaintances, and boasted that by following it he expected to be hale and hearty at eighty.

2

HE WAS born in Dublin, Ireland, in 1831; his parents brought him to America in the early forties, and at eighteen he left the family farm in Illinois to join the migration to California. In later years he liked to recall an incident of the overland trek, the earliest recorded flowering of the native shrewdness that to his mind was ever his most valuable asset. While the party was at camp one night in northern Utah, two rough-looking strangers happened by, casually dropped a few disparaging remarks about the Mormons, and waited to hear the sentiments of the emigrants. Only Fair saw through the ruse. At once he launched into a spirited defense of the Mormon religion and of its industrious and enlightened followers. Of course the strangers were themselves Mormons. Fair and his party were warmly welcomed to Salt Lake City, where, unlike less shrewdly tactful groups, they had no trouble assembling supplies and equipment for the final dash to the gold fields.

He was a stocky, powerfully built youth, with dark skin and eyes, curly black hair, and handsome features; a typical black Irishman with all the swaggering affability of the type, but without its leavening of carefree improvidence. In the foothill gold camps he applied himself to learning the deceptively simple techniques of placer mining, "keeping his eyes and ears open and his purse-strings drawn tight." The life was exactly to his liking. The monotony and privations that so many found insupportable caused him no concern, and the back-breaking work in the creek-beds was tolerable because it was a means to an end. Above all, the gambling element that underlay all mining operations, the matching of wits with man and nature alike, appealed strongly to his devious and crafty nature. Clearly this, and not the Illinois farm he had left behind, was the proper field for his talents.

Ten years in the California gold towns sharpened his natural astuteness and proved, had he ever been in doubt on the point, that he was able to hold his own in an environment as fiercely competitive as any the nation had ever known. During that active decade the youth served his apprenticeship, laying the foundations for a career that carried him to the apex of his profession. Like tens of thousands of others he prospected the foothill streams, locating and working placer claims, and sharing the common fortunes, mostly bad. But whereas the majority, after a season or two in the diggings, abandoned hope of easy riches and returned with relief to more stable occupations, Fair was permanently enchanted by the life, its hazards and uncertainties and occasional glittering rewards. Only once did the quest lose its allure, and that but temporarily. In the middle fifties, having had a moderate run of luck, he bought a farm near Petaluma and applied himself to the less speculative pursuits of agriculture. Six months later he gladly deserted the plow and hurried back to the Sierra canyons.

By then half a decade of industrious working and reworking had about exhausted the placer claims, and interest was swinging to a more complicated technique: that of quartz mining. Here Fair's facile tongue and considerable mechanical skill found a wider sphere. Putting both gifts to use, he talked a now unknown capitalist into financing the construction of a stamp mill at Shaw's Flat and placing Fair in charge. Through no fault of its manager, this first venture proved a failure. The mill functioned efficiently and economically, and the operation would have been lucrative except for one detail: the ore it was called on to work was lamentably deficient in gold. Fair, who had put some of his own funds into the venture, wrote off his loss and moved on to other fields, resolved that next time he would inquire more closely into the quality of the ore before putting up another mill. He accordingly applied himself to a further study of gold-bearing quartz; seemingly he never had any doubt of his ability to cope with the other half of the quartz-mining operation: that of extracting the gold. This last was a mechanical problem, and machinery was not only a personal enthusiasm; it was a tradition of the family. "All the Fairs were mechanics," he once boasted, and went on to relate how, when he was sixteen, his father had urged him to study law; he had run off to Chicago instead and gone to work in a machine-shop.

Thus the Mother Lode quartz mills combined two major enthusiasms: mining, and tinkering with machinery: he was never wholly content doing anything else. During the last dozen years of his life—long after his active mining days were over—his Montgomery Street office was cluttered with specimens of ore, photographs of mining properties, and, under a table, a miniature working model

of an amalgamating mill. Through the eighties his name
was listed alternately in city directories as capitalist and
miner, and what is said to have been the only testimonial
he ever gave was, characteristically, for an ingenious piece
of machinery. "I am pleased to say your Ore Feeders . . .
have given entire satisfaction. They are durable, well
proportioned, certain in their action, and economical. . . ."
In meting out praise to fellow human beings he was sparing in the extreme, but for a mechanical contrivance that
did its job efficiently his admiration was spontaneous and
real. During the booming seventies he delighted in piloting
visitors through the underground workings of the bonanza
mines, and it was always the machines that he exhibited
with the most pride: the hoisting works and cages, the
Cornish pumps, the Root blowers, the Burleigh drills. Of
course he claimed credit for most of these mechanical
wonders: they were there only because Fair had recognized their value and had insisted on installing them, often
over the opposition of his partners. And he had had to
discover how best to use them. To an interviewer in the
nineties he stated: "I learned as I went along. That sort
of mining had never been done before. The methods I
worked out are now being followed all over the world.
Nobody has improved on them."

Like most of Fair's boasts, this claim had a basis of
solid truth. His arrogant self-glorification, his lifelong habit
of giving himself exclusive credit for whatever successful
moves the bonanza firm had made (his partners were responsible for the failures), did not obscure the fact that
he was among the ablest practical miners ever developed
in the West. He hit his stride the day he built his first
primitive quartz mill, and he did not stop until he had
made himself superintendent of the most complex mining
properties the world had ever known. This rocket-like
rise was accomplished in a little more than a decade. In
his later years he liked to point out that, unlike other
bonanza millionaires, he had been a successful mine
operator long before he saw the Comstock. Most of the
others he dismissed scornfully as "kid-glove miners," men
who managed their properties from San Francisco office

desks or from the floor of the Mining Exchange, and who could no more have followed a lead along the face of a drift than they could have read the Chinese laundry marks on their spotless linen. For these frock-coated, cane-carrying gentry who masqueraded as "miners" Fair's contempt was fathomless and obviously sincere. A miner was a man who worked a mine and who dressed the part: flannel shirt and shapeless felt hat, denim pants, and stout, mud-spattered boots. Even for the few who, like him, had served a hard apprenticeship in the California diggings he was able to maintain his sense of superiority: at least he had achieved a degree of success there. He had not, like John Mackay, spent ten unproductive years in the placer camps and, at their end, trudged up the steep trail through Gold Canyon carrying all he owned on his back.

In the last year of his life San Francisco newspapers reported that plans were afoot to bring down from the vicinity of Downieville a weather-beaten one-room shack and exhibit it as "Mackay's Cabin" at the Midwinter Fair of 1894. Fair suggested ironically that the sponsors of the project would do better to go up to Shaw's Flat and bring back "Jim Fair's Cabin." The joke was that this Calaveras County "cabin" was a pretentious two-story residence "that spreads over as much ground as a modern dwelling of twenty rooms." Fair had built it in 1856 with the profits of his first considerable strike. The story of how he had located this small but rich body of gold-bearing quartz is characteristic. A party of Indians had appeared in the village one day and exchanged a few pieces of extremely rich ore for a jug of whisky; Fair had stealthily followed them back into the hills and discovered their source of supply. In a few weeks he and a partner took $180,000 in gold from this pocket.

Later he transferred operations to the vicinity of Angels Camp, where he sank most of his capital in a series of unproductive claims and mills, but the experience gained in these enterprises was a factor in his later success on the Comstock. During his stay at Angels Camp he met and married Theresa Rooney, a pretty, dark-eyed widow who conducted a rooming-house in the neighboring town of

Carson Hills. An amiable, hospitable woman, deeply religious, Mrs. Fair was highly esteemed by their circle of friends, and when, after twenty-one years, their marriage ended sensationally in the divorce court, the sentiment of the Coast was overwhelmingly with her. But it was not until Fair attained great wealth that the marriage failed; during the first years at Angels Camp the couple lived in evident concord. There the first of their four children was born: a daughter who was named Theresa after her mother, and who a quarter century later was to marry an ornament of New York and Newport society in as brilliant a ceremony as any San Francisco had ever known.

As a substantial mine- and mill-owner, Fair did not, like most California miners, join the first headlong rush to the new silver camps. Not until 1865 was he ready to try his luck on the Comstock. His own account of the circumstances that sent him hurrying over the well-traveled Washoe trail is worth repeating. One day a prospector, back from the Nevada diggings, appeared at Fair's mill with some samples of Comstock ore. Fair examined the specimens, observed that they looked "more like common blue limestone than anything else," and, his professional interest engaged, set himself to a problem that had been baffling the Coast's metallurgical experts for six years. Assays had amply proved the richness of this soft blue ore, but means of working it on a commercially profitable scale had been evolved slowly, by the costly trial-and-error method, during which only the richest ore had been worked at all, and much silver and gold had been carried off to the dumps or allowed to drain into the Carson River. His interest captured by this problem, Fair experimented in his Angels Camp mill and—if one accepts his probably romanticized account—did not sleep until he had found the answer. Not until then was he ready to abandon his California holdings for the larger opportunities beyond the mountains. This story does not agree at every point with that told by others. Fair maintained that his Angels Camp property was valuable and that he had worked it profitably to the day he sold out. Other accounts state that, to finance his invasion of the Comstock, he had "salted" his barren California mine and disposed of it to a tenderfoot just out from the East. Which version one accepted depended on one's estimate of Fair's reliability, veracity, and business ethics. At this late date all that is known with certainty is that in 1865 he disposed of his California holdings and moved on to the Comstock.

3

HAD Fair deliberately planned it, he could not have arrived at a more opportune time. The Comstock was in one of its periodical depressions, with its leading mines barren of ore and half its mills silent: thousands had left for the booming new camps of central Nevada, and those who remained viewed the lode's future with extreme pessimism. This was a situation exactly to Fair's liking. He was by nature a nonconformist, impelled by obscure forces (which he called sound judgment and the world considered sheer contrariness) to take on every question a stand opposed to that of the majority. Had he reached Virginia City at a time when the town was enjoying one of its periods of expansiveness, it is more than likely that he would have viewed the entire picture with a jaundiced eye. But with clouds of discouragement hanging thick over Mount Davidson, Fair could see only the brightest of prospects; before he had been in town for a week he was arguing heatedly that the lode, far from heading for oblivion, was still far short of its peak, its surface barely scratched. In later years he boasted that in 1865 he was "the only man on the Comstock" who had accurately forecast its dazzling future; and as always there existed, beneath the extravagance of his pronouncements, a core of truth. He was among the few who, in the barren period of the mid-sixties, were convinced that new and richer ore bodies remained to be discovered, and he set himself to instilling this confident belief in others. In all likelihood his missionary work was attended with considerable success, for his faith in the infallibility of his judgment was so profound that skeptics were often convinced in spite of themselves.

He had two other qualities particularly useful in this emergency: a well-grounded knowledge of quartz-mining methods and an easy affability that, when he chose to exert it, could win the confidence of strangers on extremely short acquaintance. "The blarney of his race had not been omitted from his makeup," once stated the *Chronicle*. "When it suited his purpose . . . his compliments could charm a robin off a fence-post." An acquaintance wrote in like vein: "He . . . was always smiling. . . . He could scarcely speak to a woman without patting her on the back or arm and calling her 'my child.' It was a way he had. His favorite address to a man was 'my son.' He would call his deadliest enemy that. . . ."

His gift for ingratiating himself into the confidence of strangers contributed much to Fair's rapid rise on the Comstock. Less than a year after he arrived he was superintendent of the Ophir, an important mine at the northern end of the lode, where the first strike had been made in 1859. Meantime he had become acquainted with Mackay, and the close friendship that sprang up between the two is proof enough that Fair believed his fellow Irishman might prove useful in his future plans. It is unlikely, however, that even in his most sanguine imaginings he had any prevision of the successes that would attend their association. Any newcomer to the lode, anxious to orient himself as a preliminary to launching operations of his own, could not have had a better mentor than Mackay, and Fair made the most of his opportunity. Both men made rapid progress, Mackay through his development of the Kentuck, and Fair by his able work as superintendent of the Ophir. A year later, in 1866, Fair was hired by the trustees of the Hale & Norcross, charged with trying to make that unproductive mine show a profit. Fair seems to have been a sort of assistant superintendent, but of course when an important ore body was presently discovered there, he took full credit.

During the next two years the Hale & Norcross yielded

more than two million dollars, but Fair gained little from
the strike either in profit or in prestige. His connection
with the mine was abruptly terminated in the fall of 1867.
The reason is not now clear. One account states that he
was dismissed for insubordination; Fair's own version is
that, having put the mine on a paying basis, he was dis-
placed to make room for a relative of the chief owner. In
any event this setback shook Fair's resolve to remain permanently on the Comstock. New strikes had recently been
made in southern Idaho, and rumors drifting back to
Virginia City indicated that they were of surpassing richness. Fair headed for the new diggings; but the quality
of the Idaho ore fell far short of his expectations and he
soon abandoned hope of making a fortune there.

The end of 1868 found him back in Virginia City.
During his absence the town had witnessed the sharp
struggle by which Sharon had wrested control of the
Hale & Norcross from its former owners. Then had followed the coup, outlined in an earlier chapter, by which
Fair and Mackay, with the help of the San Francisco
brokers, Flood and O'Brien, had in turn ousted Sharon
and taken control of the mine—only a few weeks before
a new and greater strike put the four speculators on the
road to wealth.

4

WITH their profits from the Hale & Norcross, the Mackay-Fair-Flood-O'Brien group made a variety of investments designed to consolidate their position as a substantial new force on the Comstock. First they purchased
two mills over the divide at Gold Hill in which to work the
Hale & Norcross ore, which had formerly been reduced
at Sharon's Union Mill and Mining Company plant. More
of the Hale & Norcross profits went to purchase Sharon's
controlling interest in the Virginia & Gold Hill Water
Company. This concern supplied water, inadequately, at
high prices, to the mills and the growing towns. It is said
that Sharon was eager to unload the property because he

knew that the springs in the arid back country were drying up and that soon it would be necessary to bring water from the distant Sierra, an extremely costly enterprise of doubtful practicality. So he was well content to pass on to the amateurs this struggling company with its numerous current problems and its dubious future. In 1869 few could have foreseen that once the difficult engineering and financial feat had been accomplished, and the Sierra water was brought twenty miles across the intervening mountains and canyons, the property would return many millions of dollars in profits. It was another of Sharon's bad guesses.

Meantime both Mackay and Fair had separately embarked on ventures that added little either to their beginning renown or to their fortunes. Mackay's choice fell to the Bullion mine, which occupied a considerable area near the center of the lode, but which, despite its promising location, had never produced a ton of millable ore. Mackay bought heavily of the depressed Bullion stock, had himself elected trustee and superintendent, and spent two years and an undetermined amount of cash before he grew convinced that the mine was barren. Fair's venture was only slightly more successful. His choice fell to the Savage, a mine that adjoined Hale & Norcross to the north, and embarked on an energetic but fruitless search for a bonanza, meantime barely paying expenses by milling the low-grade ore in which the mine abounded. In 1871 both men, convinced that "even the ablest superintendents cannot find ore where none exists," tendered their resignations and prepared to embark jointly on a new enterprise.

To most observers the property of their choice seemed no more promising than those they had just abandoned. A few hundred yards beyond the Hale & Norcross lay 1,300 feet that occupied a position between two of the richest mines on the lode: the original Ophir and the Gould & Curry. The latter two mines had together produced in excess of twenty millions, but despite its uncommonly lucrative neighbors, the intervening area had returned virtually nothing to those who had impoverished themselves exploring the property from one end to the other. The search had continued intermittently for ten years, one group after another taking over the various claims and developing them, singly or in combination. In 1871 the 1,310 feet were held by five companies: the Central (150 feet), the California (300 feet), the Central No. 2 (100 feet), the Kinney (50 feet), the White & Murphy (210 feet), and the Sides (500 feet). In the middle sixties this property was described as having been "literally honey-combed with mine workings to a depth of 500 feet," without yielding a ton of profitable ore except the Central, which soon worked out its small segment of the Ophir bonanza. In 1867 a new group, amply financed, had got control of all but one hundred feet of the area, organized it as the Consolidated Virginia Mining Company, and started sinking a shaft to explore the deeper levels. Their original intention was to go down 1,500 feet, should that prove necessary. But by the time the shaft had reached only a third that distance the enthusiasm of managers and stockholders had cooled and further downward progress stopped. Instead, long crosscuts were run north and south, and when these too encountered only barren rock, the entire plan was abandoned. The stockholders, having paid out $160,000 in assessments, and seeing no future promise, wrote off their investment as a total loss. By 1870, Consolidated Virginia shares had sunk to one dollar on the San Francisco Exchange. In all, well over a million dollars was spent in these operations, with almost no return. After ten years of fruitless search the lode's experts had about concluded that the area was barren of high-grade ore.

Mackay and Fair thought otherwise, however, and when they decided to try their luck, their San Francisco partners were willing to follow their lead. It was not so foolhardy a venture as might seem at first sight, for the belief that the claims were worthless was widely held and few would touch the stock. "The entire 1,310 feet," wrote Charles H. Shinn, "was a bankrupt piece of property worth in the market less than $40,000 . . . really not worth half so much, good operators said. . . ." The firm, however, was not quite able to gain control at that bargain price. Activity in the stock of any Comstock mine, barren or not, always forced prices upward, and before the group was able to announce, in February 1872, that they had control of the two claims—the Consolidated Virginia (710 feet) and the California (600 feet)—they had made a total investment of about $100,000. Their first official act was to levy an assessment amounting to $212,000 on the stock of the Consolidated Virginia, the southernmost of the two mines, and to begin a systematic exploration.

What happened next was widely discussed in later years, for it led to the discovery of one of the richest strikes in the entire history of mining. Despite Fair's later claim that they had all along expected great things of the property—a boast to which the other partners gave tacit support—it seems clear that the primary reason for taking over the two mines was to obtain a supply of low-grade ore from the Consolidated Virginia's shallow workings in order to keep active a mill that was about to close down because of the exhaustion of the Hale & Norcross. But the fact remains that they did at once lay plans for further exploration. Because earlier owners had thoroughly explored the property above the 500-foot level, it was obvious that further search would have to be conducted lower down. Three methods of exploring the mines in depth were possible, and each in turn was considered. One was to resume work on the Consolidated Virginia shaft, which had been abandoned in 1871 at the 500-foot level, and to continue down until ore was encountered or as long as the stockholders would finance so expensive an operation. The second alternative was to explore the property on the 1100-foot level by going to the bottom of the Ophir shaft—which joined the California on the north —and running a drift southward. Both plans were rejected—fortunately, as it proved, for neither would have encountered anything but barren rock—and interest swung to the third possibility.

How the partners reached their decision to make a southerly approach was long a matter of controversy. Fair, ever willing to claim credit for any sagacious moves

of the firm, maintained that the decision was his and that
it was based on a careful study of the lode and an analysis
of its probable convolutions. In this instance, too, other
accounts differ from Fair's. One version gives the credit
to Pat McKay, superintendent of the Gould & Curry, one
of the mines controlled by the Sharon group. The Gould
& Curry lay to the south of the Consolidated Virginia, but
did not adjoin it: the Best & Belcher occupied the intervening 700 feet. McKay is said to have approached Fair
one evening and made this suggestion: "Why not go to the
bottom of the Gould & Curry and drift northward? The
shaft is 1,200 feet deep; a tunnel would be below all the
workings of the Best & Belcher, the Consolidated Virginia
and the California; it would be virgin ground and if there
are any deep ore bodies on the fissure . . . you ought to
strike them." According to the story, Fair professed to be
unimpressed. "I don't think there's anything in it," he remarked   indifferently,   and   changed   the   subject—
but "that same night" he had three shifts at work running
a drift north from the bottom of the Curry. This seems too
fast even for the impulsive Fair, yet the record shows
that such tunneling did get under way, and promptly.
Sharon, who had no reason to further the interests of Fair
and Mackay, and who might have prevented their use of
the Gould & Curry shaft, put no obstacles in their way.
On the contrary, he went out of his way to be co-
operative. He charged them only a nominal fee for hoisting the waste rock from their tunnel and hauling it to the
dump, and publicly he wished them luck. Privately, however, he jubilantly told intimates that he was helping
"those Irishmen" to blow in their Hale & Norcross profits.

For many weeks it seemed likely that Sharon's hope
would materialize. Work on the drift began in early May
of 1872, some three months after "those Irishmen" had
got control of the properties to the north. The work progressed through the spring and summer. By early September the drift was nearly a thousand feet long; it had
crossed the 700-foot Best & Belcher and penetrated well
inside the Consolidated Virginia. It was slow and expensive work, for the rock had to be run back to the end

of the drift, hoisted 1,200 feet to the surface, and carried off to the dump. Moreover, as the drift lengthened and the distance from the mine-head to the face of the tunnel increased to close to half a mile, working conditions grew steadily worse. Foul air, plus the extreme heat common to all the Comstock's lower levels, so oppressed the miners that the picked crews had to be put on progressively shorter shifts: presently to as little as fifteen minutes at the face of the tunnel, followed by half-hour rest periods. This of course slowed the rate of progress and drastically increased the expense.

Thus far every foot of the tunnel had been through barren rock. Nothing was encountered that might suggest to the most sanguine eye the possible presence of silver- or gold-bearing quartz. In view of this long run of bad luck, the expectations not only of the managers but of stockholders and the speculating public gradually waned. Confidence reached a low ebb. The value of Consolidated Virginia and California shares, which had begun an upward spurt when the Mackay-Fair group had taken over, sagged badly. Once-hopeful stockholders, seeing their assessments fruitlessly expended in Fair's will-o'-the-wisp scheme and anticipating further calls for funds to continue the work, were ready to call a halt. One writer states that by the late summer of 1872 public confidence was so low that, had another assessment been levied to extend the barren drift, the majority of the stockholders would have surrendered their shares and pocketed their losses. They would soon have regretted it.

The following is Fair's version of what happened next. Affairs had reached a critical stage when, in mid-September, he one day observed a "knife-thin" vein of ore cutting across the face of the drift. No one could say what if anything this seam might portend, but here at last was a ray of hope. Lagging spirits revived and the wavering vein was carefully traced. Anxious days followed, with Fair (who was later to claim that for weeks he had spent every hour at the end of the drift) directing operations, following the thin metallic film, losing it, picking it up again, and at last seeing it begin to widen. After that with each yard the prospect brightened. In three weeks it was a seven-foot layer of ore that assayed sixty dollars a ton; in four it had widened to twelve feet and was growing progressively richer.

Convinced by now that they had struck a considerable body of rich ore, the jubilant Irishmen rushed plans to get into production. Their first step was to begin sinking a vertical shaft that would tap the ore body at its widest point, provide ventilation to the stifling workings, and permit hoisting the ore direct to the surface. Three shifts worked round the clock and progressed so rapidly that before the end of October the shaft was broken through and the long drift back to the Gould & Curry shaft was abandoned.

Meantime exploration of their find had continued on a twenty-four-hour schedule and with ever more gratifying results. By the time the Consolidated shaft was completed, the ore body had widened to fifty feet and the four lucky gamblers knew beyond doubt that they had made a major strike. They were not yet the bonanza firm, but they were soon to be. Now began a systematic exploration of their discovery. From the bottom of the new shaft a drift was run toward the south and east for a distance of two hundred and fifty feet; nearly every foot of it was through ore of extraordinary richness.

Thus far, following the Comstock's well-established custom, the group had been at pains to minimize the importance of their find. From time to time newspapers were supplied with moderately favorable reports, nicely calculated to bolster the waning confidence of stockholders and to put them in a frame of mind to pay future assessments, but not so encouraging as to attract speculators and run prices up. Meantime the partners, who already owned more than three-quarters of the stock, quietly increased their holdings, paying a modest fifty dollars per share. Visitors of all sorts, including the experts of the Comstock papers, were excluded from the lower levels, the excuse being that the bad air and excessive heat made such visits dangerous. By then the journals of the Coast, particularly those in San Francisco, had begun to suspect that something unusual was going on in the Consolidated Virginia, and demands for information grew daily more insistent. Not until late October, however, were the partners ready to announce their discovery. Fair thereupon called in Dan De Quille, mining editor of the *Enterprise,* whose reports were widely read throughout the West and just as widely believed.

Years later De Quille wrote this account of Fair's visit:

"One day he drove up to the *Enterprise* office and came in.

" 'Those city papers have been abusing us long enough,' he remarked; 'I won't stand it! Where's Dan? I want him to go down to the mine. I'll show him what we're doing.'

"Fair spoke pretty loud, as if he only wanted to shut up the city papers, but probably he had all the stock he wanted and had just got ready to tell the truth; I don't know. Anyway . . . we drove to the mine and went down to the richest place in the bonanza.

"Fair said: 'Go in and climb around. Look all you want, measure it up, make up your own mind; I won't tell you a thing; people will say I posted you!' And so he went away. That just suited me. After I was through I went to the *Enterprise* office and wrote two articles. . . . That was the first authentic account of the big bonanza. . . ."

De Quille spent half a day below, examined closely the 200-foot segment of the lode then opened up, selected five samples of ore, and proceeded to have them assayed. They averaged $380 a ton in gold and silver, close to ten times the value of the run of Comstock ore. His report, published on October 29, under the heading "Consolidated Virginia,—A Look Through the Long Forbidden Lower Levels . . ." was all Fair could have desired. Its columns were studded with such phrases as "ores which excite the imagination of all beholders . . ." and "clusters of pure silver." When it came to estimating the value of the ore body, De Quille, although he tried hard to be conservative, could not see less than $230,000,000 in sight on this one level, which he described as "but a small section taken out of the mine of a convenient size for handling."

The *Enterprise* expert was the first of a long series of men invited to inspect the bonanza: journalists, brokers, superintendents of rival mines, mining engineers, investors eager for a personal view of the property before buying shares. It was commonly supposed that this device of throwing their mine open to the public was intended to raise the value of its stock and so to permit the owners to sell at a profit should later exploration reveal that the ore body was of limited extent. If this was the purpose, it succeeded admirably. Before the end of the year the market value had doubled; soon it went far higher.

Meantime the group had been industriously extending their holdings, gathering in one by one a variety of neighboring claims. In 1872 they bought control of both the Gould & Curry, from which their original drift had been run, and the Best & Belcher, which lay between that mine and the Consolidated Virginia. This gave them control of nearly the entire northern end of the lode, a half-mile segment that extended from the northern boundary of the Savage to the southern line of the Ophir. None of these mines returned a profit from its operation, although the new owners later disposed of their holdings at fancy prices after their Consolidated Virginia strike had sent every Comstock stock zooming skyward.

But the main business of course was the further exploration of their find. Eliot Lord in his *Comstock Mining and Miners* (1883) gives this graphic account of the gradual uncovering of the treasure trove:

"The wonder grew as its depths were searched out foot by foot. The bonanza was cut at a point 1167 feet below the surface, and as the shaft went down it was pierced again at the 1200-foot level; still the same body of ore was found, but wider and longer than above. One hundred feet deeper, and the prying pick and drill told the same story; yet another hundred feet and the mass appeared to be still swelling. When, finally, the 1500-foot level was reached and richer ore than any before met with was disclosed, the fancy of the coolest brains ran wild. . . . No discovery which matches it has been made on this earth from the day when the first miner struck a ledge with his crude pick until the present. . . ."

Other observers drew heavily on their stock of superlatives. Charles H. Shinn, in *The Story of the Mine,* described the strike as "the richest hoard of gold and silver that had ever dazzled the eyes of a treasure-seeker," and the normally conservative *Enterprise* expert, after advising caution for several weeks, joined whole-heartedly in the chorus. Of a ten-foot-square chamber excavated in one of the crosscuts, Dan De Quille wrote, under the title "The Heart of the Comstock": "Its walls on every side are a mass of the finest silver chloride ore, filled with streaks and bunches of rich glistening black sulphurets. In the roof . . . is to be seen a quantity of stephanite, shining like a whole casket of black diamonds. . . ."

It was riches unparalleled in the fourteen-year history of the Comstock. In Shinn's words, "the top had been pried off Nature's treasure-vault."

5

FOR five years the big bonanza, as this unprecedented strike came to be known, exercised a profound influence on almost every phase of life throughout the Far West. The four principal owners, two of them obscure stockbrokers in San Francisco, the others practical mine operators no better known than scores of others on the Comstock, abruptly found themselves thrust into positions of vast influence and power, with wealth beyond their expectations already in sight and every prospect of colossal fortunes lying just ahead.

How large these fortunes might eventually become was a matter that engaged the attention of the entire Coast. The four men owned outright more than three-quarters of the stock of the Consolidated Virginia and of the California, which adjoined it to the north. They therefore stood to reap three of every four dollars these mines produced. Both properties had been thrown open to inspection by any expert, qualified or not, who wished to visit them. The experts duly came, in such numbers that the work of stoping out the ore was hampered by the crowds trooping through the works.

But neither Mackay nor Fair was willing to turn them

away. They had uncovered an ore body of unparalleled richness, they were securely in control, and they had a human desire to let the world know the extent of their good fortune.

Numerous guesses were made as to the probable value of the immense ore deposits. Dan De Quille was first in the field with his statement that not less than $230,000,-000 was already in sight. This was sensational enough, but soon the estimates of other experts began to make his figures seem curiously temperate. Philip Deidesheimer, the engineer responsible for the "square-set" timbering technique, conducted a careful examination and issued this public announcement: "I assert that there is already shown in the two mines, California and Consolidated Virginia, $1,500,000,000 of ore. I make this assertion and am willing to stand by it. I should say that Consolidated Virginia and California are worth at least $5000 per share. I have been mining for twenty-four years and am very careful about my statements. . . ."

A degree of official confirmation of these astronomical estimates was presently given. Fears were expressed on the floor of Congress that so large an accession to the world's store of silver might undermine the currencies of the nations, and by authority of the Director General of the Mint a government geologist, R. E. Rogers, was sent out from Washington to report on the discovery. His findings were hardly less rose-tinted than those of the others. "On inspection of the official surveys," his report reads, "it would seem fair to conclude that with proper allowances, the ore body equals an amount which, taken at the actual assays, would give as the ultimate yield of the two mines $300,000,000; but to guard against a chance of overestimation, I take the assays at one-half, which will place the production at not less than $150,000,000. . . ."

The result of these forecasts upon a public already enamored of the Comstock's demonstrated ability to produce large returns on extremely small investments was all that might have been expected. From all over the West came a concerted rush to buy silver stocks, almost any stock at almost any price. Reviewing the picture after the boom had collapsed, the *San Francisco Chronicle* (which had earlier encouraged the buying spree by prophesying the inexhaustible riches of the bonanza mines) commented:

"Never before, in all the mining excitements of the Pacific Coast did such demoralization seize upon the community. Men and women of every class and grade of society poured in their orders for the purchase of bonanza stocks. . . . Capital was withdrawn from all the varied industries of the country, and money from depositories of safety or places of investment. Real estate was sold to procure the coin that could be invested with prospects of such immense returns, and every avenue of industry and legitimate enterprise lost supporters and operatives, who fancied they saw here a safe and speedy road to fortune."

Under such pressure the bonanza stocks, along with those of scores of other properties, rose to fantastic heights. When the four speculators had set out to get control of the Consolidated Virginia, its stock was quoted on the San Francisco Mining Exchange at around eight dollars, and Flood gathered in for himself and his partners a majority of the 11,600 shares at that figure or less. For years afterward mathematically minded citizens took a melancholy pleasure in picturing what might have happened to the man who bought a hundred shares of Consolidated Virginia in 1871 and held on to them for four years. His initial outlay would have been $800. Next year the capital stock of the mine was increased from 11,600 to 23,200, and the investor would have turned in his one hundred shares and received twice that number of the new issue. A year and a half later, in October 1873, there was another and larger increase, this time to 108,000 shares—a ratio of about five to one. Had the imaginary investor turned in his two hundred shares he would have received one thousand. Early in 1874 the controlling partners, now becoming known as the bonanza firm, reorganized the property adjoining the Consolidated Virginia on the north, and formed a new corporation, which they called the California Mining Company. Each stockholder of the Consolidated Virginia received a dividend of stock in the California consisting of seven-twelfths of a share for each share in the original company. Hence the man who three years earlier had bought a hundred shares of Consolidated Virginia would then own one thousand shares in that corporation, plus nearly six hundred shares in the California.

What meantime had been happening to the market value of the stocks? In 1874 had come the enormously rich strike on the 1,500-foot level of the Consolidated Virginia—the tapping of the big bonanza—and following closely on it one of the greatest buying booms in mining history. In January 1875 both stocks reached $800 a share on the exchanges in San Francisco, Virginia City, and Gold Hill. If the imaginary speculator had had the monumental good judgment to sell out then, his gains (plus his large dividends, less a few thousand dollars he would have paid out in assessments, and less too his original $800) would have been counted as follows:

1,000 shares of Consolidated Virginia at $800	$800,000
600 shares of California at $800	480,000
	$1,280,000

Such is the immemorial way of speculators, however, that there exists no record of any purchaser who bought at the bottom and sold at the ultimate top. None the less, during a period when every silver stock was enjoying large and sustained advances, thousands all over the Coast were fascinated (and their speculative fever heightened) by a daily quota of authenticated rags-to-riches stories: of chambermaids buying the rooming-houses in which they had worked, of suddenly affluent hack-drivers rushing from Montgomery Street brokerage offices and grandly presenting their vehicles to the first passer-by, of charwomen scrubbing office floors with three-carat diamonds glistening on their fingers.

In the early sixties two Virginia City lawyers, Thomas J. Williams and David Bixler, performed some legal business for an obscure mine called the Central No. 2. The mine was then inactive and when, unable to collect their fee (which was $1,200), the two attorneys filed suit, the owners did not contest the action. Williams and Bixler obtained judgment and took over the property at the resulting forced sale. The stock remained in their safe until 1873, when Central No. 2, along with two neighboring mines, was bought up by the Mackay-Fair group. Williams and Bixler exchanged their holdings for a substantial block of shares in the California. A few months later a realization of the extent and richness of the big bonanza caused a startling upswing in the California stock. In December of that year the *Chronicle* listed Williams and Bixler among the rich men of the Comstock, placing their fortunes at above two millions each. By then their holdings had been increased to 6,500 shares of California and 3,000 of Consolidated Virginia. Moreover, their good luck held, for they sold out near the top of the boom, pocketed some four millions in profit, and proceeded to invest it in California real estate. They were, one of their contemporaries stated, the only ones of the Washoe's bumper crop of lawyers who not only made fortunes there but carried them safely away.

In the early seventies a young man named Otto Bach decided—like thousands of other San Franciscans—to take a flier in silver stocks. He visited a Montgomery Street brokerage house and placed an order for ten shares of Consolidated Virginia, then selling at around $30. Next morning he received a routine notice from the broker recording the purchase for his account of, not ten, but one hundred shares. The young man, who was a clerk in a toy shop on Sansome Street, seized his hat and hurried off to inform the broker of his error. On the way, however, he stepped into another brokerage office and looked at the board: overnight Consolidated Virginia had jumped to $50 per share. This advance made his broker quite willing to carry him, and young Bach prudently refrained from calling attention to the mistake. Consolidated Virginia continued to advance and the amateur operator held on for several months. Then he sold out, pocketed a profit of $32,000 and returned to his native German village to enjoy his windfall.

There was of course another side to the picture. So much of the fluid wealth of the Pacific Coast had been poured into the hoppers of the brokerage offices that the financing of other enterprises became extremely difficult. A sort of creeping paralysis spread over the economy of the region, with many business failures and widespread unemployment. Thousands were impoverished, not only by the stagnation of trade but by enormous stock losses, for less than half a dozen of the Washoe mines regularly paid dividends. The great majority of speculators, after meeting a long series of assessments, disposed of their stocks for what they would bring, or were sold out by their brokers. So widespread was this experience, and so painful, that the public was eventually forced to conclude that Comstock speculation was a losing game to all except the few who controlled the producing mines and who, having day-by-day knowledge of their prospects, knew in advance of the public when to buy or sell. Realization that the cards were stacked against them came slowly to thousands of bemused and hopeful gamblers. When disillusionment came, the victims, their capital gone, their dreams of wealth shattered, looked for someone to blame for their misfortune. Since few were willing to admit that they themselves had been at fault, their resentment turned to the men who had profited most by their folly: the owners and managers of the bonanzas. The Mackay-Fair group, who in the early stages of the boom had been revered for ushering in an era of universal prosperity, gradually came to stand in quite another light. Their brief season of popularity went into a profound decline.

All four members of the firm eventually grew used to the public abuse that descended upon them; they learned to accept it, if not with pleasure, at least with outward calm, as part of the price one paid for sudden wealth and power. But they were a long time reaching this state of philosophical unconcern. At first their abrupt drop in public esteem surprised and distressed them, and they made repeated—and fruitless—attempts to counteract it. Even

Fair, whose career exhibits few instances when he courted the good opinion of his fellows, was at pains to point out that he had taken no hand in stock speculation: he was a practical miner whose business was to locate pay ore and, having found it, to send it to the surface as efficiently and economically as he knew how. He invited the public to decide how well he had succeeded. Mackay took the same general line of reasoning, but at much greater length. In one of a series of interviews he remarked of a recent drop in stocks: "It is no affair of mine. I am not speculating in stocks. My business is mining. . . . I see that my men do their work properly. . . . I make my money out of the ore." To another reporter he stated that his weekly profit from the mines, then at the top of their production, exceeded a hundred thousand dollars; why should he try to add to that tidy sum by manipulating the market? Dan De Quille quoted him in the columns of the *Enterprise* as saying: "Here and in San Francisco persons are constantly coming to me and asking 'What shall I buy?' In San Francisco they regularly besiege me. I say to all that come: 'Go and put your money in a savings bank.' "

What—if anything—the two San Francisco partners had to say has not been preserved.

6

BY HOW many millions the new kings of the Comstock enhanced their fortunes through stock deals was long a matter of debate. Despite Mackay's and Fair's reiterated claims that their sole aim was to manage their mines and mills on sound business principles, it is clear that both took full advantage of their positions to deal heavily in bonanza stocks, and to reap huge profits. Opposition newspapers, led by the once friendly *Chronicle*, frequently charged the firm with "working the Comstock from both ends." "For the purpose of stimulating the demand and market price of shares," it stated, "they published false and exaggerated reports of the extent and quality of the development. Having effected this, they sold enormous quantities. . . ." When this had been accomplished, less encouraging reports were put out designed to depress the market, whereupon they quietly bought back their shares and prepared to repeat the process. By this simple and useful technique—which San Franciscans termed "Flood's milking machine"—the group is said in three years to have realized not less than fifty million dollars.

But while it was possible to some extent to conceal the scope of the firm's stock-market operations, there was no way of keeping secret numerous other enterprises that the partners launched. The four men soon demonstrated that they were not fumbling amateurs in the complicated business of channeling the lion's share of their mines' huge yield into their personal accounts. In this they were merely following a procedure familiar enough to the industrial titans of their day. By it, the men who controlled large and lucrative corporations awarded its collateral business, on highly liberal terms, to companies they themselves had organized and owned. The bonanza group were not the first to apply this well-tested program to silver mining. It had been practiced in the Comstock for more than a decade, but none of their predecessors had brought it so close to perfection, and of course none had had so rich a field in which to operate. "The stockholders," stated the *Golden Era,* one of San Francisco's numerous and truculent weeklies, "owned an interest in the mines, but the group contracted with themselves for the timber used in the mines, for the wood that ran the engines and for the water used in reducing the ores. It owned the mills at which the ores were worked, and not only charged its own price for reduction, but left a large percentage of the gold and silver in the tailings, which it appropriated to itself. . . ."

To furnish supplies and services to the mines, the group organized four major companies. One was the Pacific Mill and Mining Company, which owned and operated the mills that reduced the bonanza ore. In capacity and efficiency of operation these exceeded any seen on the Comstock. Construction of the Consolidated Virginia Mill started in the summer of 1874; it began operating the following January. Its capacity was 250 tons of ore every twenty-four hours. A few months later, this huge plant having proved inadequate to handle the ore, work was begun on a second and larger mill a hundred yards to the north. The latter, the California Pan Mill, had eighty thousand-pound stamps, forty-six amalgamating pans, and a daily capacity of close to four hundred tons. The two mills cost the partners $800,000; they were uncommonly sound investments. For they were personally owned by Mackay, Fair, Flood, and O'Brien and the four had exclusive contracts to mill the bonanza ore.

These milling contracts were later the subject of much acrimonious debate, out of which grew a series of bitterly fought lawsuits instituted by the minority stockholders. By the terms of the agreements, the mill-owners contracted to reduce the bonanza ore for a flat fee of thirteen dollars a ton. This was the prevailing rate charged by the Comstock's custom mills; the stockholders claimed, however, that the firm's modern and efficient mills could have returned a large profit had that charge been cut in half. But the part of the contracts against which the minority stockholders protested most vehemently was that which reserved for the milling company the "slimes and tailings"; that is, the pulverized ore after it had passed once through the mills. Since in this first treatment the mills recovered but sixty-five per cent of the assayed value of the ore, the owners reaped a further large profit by reworking the tailings, for the second run commonly extracted another fifteen to twenty per cent. But the milling contracts had other clauses equally advantageous to the mill-owners. One provided that ten per cent of all the ore received from the mines would be counted as "wastage and evaporation" and the mill-owners need make no return on it; another placed in the hands of the mills the sole responsibility for keeping account of the amount of ore delivered and for assaying its value, all without any means of checking the accuracy of the mill-owners' figures.

All in all, it was an uncommonly liberal arrangement the bonanza firm members, in their capacity as trustees of the mines, had negotiated with themselves as mill-operators. When it is considered that in four years the two mines produced in excess of a million and a quarter tons of ore and paid dividends of around seventy million dollars, the extent of their milling profits becomes evident. One authority states that the mill-owners got back their $800,000 investment "every ninety days," and that this happy arrangement continued for above three years. When, in the late seventies, a minority stockholders filed suit against the Pacific Mill and Mining Company for the return to the mining corporations of these allegedly fraudulent profits, the amount was fixed at $26,015,000.

But milling the bonanza ore was not the only business to engage the bonanza firm's attention. The resourceful group presently branched out into related fields. The mines needed not only milling facilities but a variety of other supplies and services. "When a mine becomes productive," wrote Eliot Lord, "its operating expenses are reckoned by millions rather than thousands of dollars." Lord went on to state that during the year 1877 the supplies used by one of the bonanza mines, the California, cost in excess of four million dollars. One of the major items was timber, an immense quantity of which was needed to support the underground caverns after the ore was removed. To supply this, plus many thousands of cords of firewood yearly required to operate hoisting engines and other machinery, the Mackay-Fair-Flood-O'Brien group organized a second coporation, the Pacific Wood, Lumber and Flume Company, purchased vast holdings of timberlands in the Sierra, put up sawmills, built a system of flumes to convey the product down to the Carson Valley, and awarded themselves exclusive contracts to furnish lumber and firewood. When stockholders later sued to have this contract too set aside, they fixed the amount of illegal profits at four millions. A third suit was filed: against the Virginia & Gold Hill Water Company for charging allegedly excessive water rates, and again the four were named defendants.

In 1878, during a hearing of one of these suits, Flood was placed on the stand and questioned concerning the firm's ownership of these singularly lucrative enterprises.

Q: Who are the owners of the Pacific Mill and Mining Company?

FLOOD: Mackay, Fair, Flood and O'Brien are the principal stock holders.

Q: Who are the owners of the Pacific Wood, Lumber and Flume Company?

FLOOD: Mackay, Fair, Flood and O'Brien.

Q: From what source does the company procure water?

FLOOD: From the Virginia & Gold Hill Water Company.

Q: Who are the trustees of the Virginia & Gold Hill Water Company?

FLOOD: Mackay, Fair, Flood and O'Brien, Hobart, Skae and Wells.

Q: Is there any other corporation from which the company draws supplies of any character of which Mackay, Fair, Flood and O'Brien are not the trustees and principal owners?

FLOOD: I don't know of any.

By then not only shrewd and canny William Sharon, but thousands all over the West had to revise their first estimates of the capabilities of the bonanza firm's members. Originally they had looked on the partners as four lucky Irishmen who, having blundered on a fabulously rich body of ore, wholly lacked the capacity either to assume the large responsibilities it involved, or to reap the profits. When it came time to review their record, it became clear even to their critics that the four amateur promoters had not done badly.

7

As A matter of course Fair took to himself sole credit for the events that had made the partners unchallenged kings of the Comstock. Here, as usual, luck played into his hands. When he wanted to be, he was by far the most friendly and approachable of the group, and the journalists who flocked to the Comstock rarely failed to interview the affable superintendent of the Consolidated Virginia. For Fair was never so busy that he would not gladly put aside a hundred pressing duties and spend an hour regaling callers with the saga of the big bonanza, including the "inside story" of how the fabulous treasure-trove had been located. Without exception visiting scribes were delighted with this enormously wealthy man who remained bluff and hearty despite his millions. When it suited Fair to assume this forthright role, he played it with skill. Toward his partners his attitude was always generous. He was at pains to make it clear that they were hard-working and conscientious; their intentions were of the best. No fair-minded man—least of all Fair himself—would think of blaming them because, through inexperience or bad judgment or a general all-around ineptness, they were constantly getting the firm into trouble from which Fair alone was able to extricate them. True, he sometimes expressed a plaintive, half-humorous regret that so many of his hours were given over to rectifying the mistakes of the other three. There were times when these tasks were a burden; he often wished he could be free to devote all his attention to seeing that the mines and mills functioned efficiently. But these gentlemen were his friends as well as his partners, and the firm operated on a benevolent all-for-one, one-for-all principle. Fair would not have had it otherwise.

Strangers were captivated by this bluff miner's unswerving loyalty to his fumbling but well-intentioned partners; it seemed to them another instance of the traditional camaraderie of the West. After that they were quite willing to accept his version of how the big bonanza had been discovered. The consequence was that in most early accounts all the credit went to Fair, and this included not only the stories appearing in contemporary newspapers but those in such well-documented volumes as Eliot Lord's *Comstock Mining and Miners* and Charles H. Shinn's *The Story of the Mine.*

Not for many years did the work of other scholars, searching through the records of the period, shoot full of holes this picture of an all-wise and all-seeing Fair. Thus the files of Virginia City and Gold Hill newspapers revealed that during the critical weeks while the famous drift was being run from the bottom of the Hale & Norcross shaft, it was under the charge, not of Fair, but of an able

Comstock superintendent named Sam Curtis. Fair himself—who later boasted that he had lived "every hour" at the end of the drift—was absent from town on one of his periodical visits to newly discovered mining camps. Doubt was thrown too on the most dramatic chapter of all: Fair's story of how, after the drift had been blasted more than a thousand feet through barren rock, and at the moment when the hopes of the group were at their lowest ebb, his trained eye had one day observed a "knife-thin vein of ore" cutting across the face of the drift. The picture of Fair doggedly following this metallic film through yards of rock, losing the trail, picking it up again, meantime reviving the flagging spirits of his partners, and in the end bursting triumphantly into the heart of the world's mightiest bonanza—the exploit became a real-life fairy tale that charmed a generation of Westerners. One regrets that in nearly every particular it was sheer moonshine. For the evidence is overwhelming that the vein was several feet wide when it was first encountered and that it broadened steadily with each foot of progress. "A blind man driving a four-horse team could have followed it in a snowstorm," remarked Joseph T. Goodman, proprietor of the *Enterprise*.

Fair's self-glorification offended many, but few denied that he was an uncommonly able miner. All who knew him during the big bonanza's heyday paid grudging tribute to his organizational skill, his sound judgment and driving energy. Under his supervision the firm's properties were efficiently operated, with a minimum of extravagance or waste, and this in a region where the reckless squandering of stockholders' money had for years been the universal rule. Fair's correspondence of the period reveals how close a watch he kept on every dollar paid out. In July 1875 he wrote to Dan De Quille (who was visiting in the East with another Comstock veteran, Sam Clemens) that "Consolidated this month produced about $1,650,-000"—and the same week addressed a stern rebuke to a San Francisco merchant who had overcharged the firm for "sixty-five feet of eight-inch leather belting." The amount involved was less than twenty dollars, but Fair

prided himself on keeping vigilant watch over just such
trifles. "I never overlooked the smallest detail," he once
boasted, and went on to explain that the company dealt
fairly with those with whom it did business and expected
like treatment in return. This policy extended to the employees. There were periods when Fair had under his
control more than two thousand miners. He retained their
confidence and often their friendship; he drove them hard,
but they daily had evidence that he was no more inclined
to spare himself than others. He took genuine pride in his
tough and expert underground crews, whom he called the
best ever seen on the Comstock, and the men responded
by setting production records never equaled before or
since. In his ordinary contacts his affability was often assumed; in his dealings with the hard-rock miners there
is every evidence that it was genuine. Once, when the
mines' ore bodies seemed near exhaustion, Flood suggested cutting wages from their long-established level of
four dollars a day. Fair violently opposed the move, pro-
fanely scornful of what he considered the absentee partner's interference in a matter of which he knew nothing.
If Flood wanted to retrench, let him reduce dividends;
stockholders were better able to stand the loss than Fair's
pick-and-shovel men. No wage-cuts were ordered and
presently the quality of the ore improved and dividends
remained at their usual million-dollars-per-month level.

This was but one of a number of tilts between Fair
and the dominant San Francisco partner. Flood knew
nothing of the practical side of mining, and in Fair's eyes
that was enough to convict him of total incompetence.
For the men—and there were many—who presumed to
manage a mine from a city office, or even from a desk
at the shaft-head, Fair had fathomless scorn. By his creed
a mineowner belonged underground, at the far end of
whatever drift or crosscut was currently being blasted out.
There were made the decisions on which the success or
failure of the enterprise turned; it was folly to permit them
to be made by distant owners—or by subordinates on
the ground.

Fair had so little confidence in the judgment of his

foremen—and so much in his own—that he maintained vigilant watch over every phase of the operations. "Whenever anything went wrong," he once recalled, "people looked to me to put it right again. All day long and half the night men kept coming to me and asking what to do. . . ." He met twice a day with the shift bosses of the various mines: once in the morning at the mines themselves and again in the evening at his home on South B Street. His wife reported that he was with difficulty persuaded to go to bed at night; he was afraid something might go wrong during the few hours he allotted to sleep.

That he carried a heavy burden of responsibility no one denied, least of all Fair himself. In 1878 he was able to boast—truthfully—that "The receipts and expenditures of our Company total more than that of half the states in the union." His annual reports to the stockholders contained long lists of the mines' expenses, entries that ranged from millions of feet of timber costing hundreds of thousands of dollars, on down to such inconsequential items as thirty-six dollars' worth of tallow, six hundred shovels and ax-handles, thirty-one dozen lanterns, 492 buckets and dippers, 780 brooms.

Burdened though he was with detail, Fair could always find time to indulge his taste for practical jokes. During the bonanza's busiest period he often piloted groups of visitors through the underground workings. One day a Boston gentleman, with his wife and daughter, appeared at the office and asked to go below. A clerk communicated with the station at the 1,500-foot level and received permission to send the party down. A miner met them and for the next hour conducted them through the drifts and stopes, expertly explaining the various processes. The visitors were pleased to have happened on so well-posted a guide, and when they were about to go above again, the Bostonian tendered him a bright silver dollar. The miner refused the tip, explaining that the company paid him for his time and it was more pleasant to show strangers about than to do his usual work. When the visitor insisted and the miner continued to decline, the Bostonian inquired: "Tell me, my man, why do you refuse to take this dollar?" Fair sighed. "One reason is that I've got six hundred thousand of the things in the bank up the hill. It's been bothering me all morning trying to decide what to do with them."

Many of his gibes were directed against Mackay. Although the two remained close friends during the first years of their association, Mackay's stolid temperament and hesitant speech made him a natural target for his more agile-minded partner. In the spring of 1879 Fair was provided with a prime opportunity. In San Francisco an obscure citizen named William Smallman filed suit for heavy damages against Mackay, claiming that the latter had alienated the affections of Smallman's wife, Amelia. Mackay, who professed never to have seen the lady, refused to follow the customary procedure of making a cash settlement in return for having the suit dismissed. Instead he hired an attorney and fought the charge; in the end he had the satisfaction of seeing the pair sent to jail for criminal conspiracy. On the day Smallman's charges were made public, and while the Washoe towns still rocked with the news, Fair was stopped outside the Consolidated Virginia office by a young woman who explained that her family was in need, and couldn't he find a job for her brother? Fair looked thoughtfully back at the office where he had left Mackay pacing the floor in a towering rage. "My dear, John attends to all that," he announced. "Go in and tell him what you've just told me. I'm sure he'll give your brother a job if you'll do exactly as I say. He's queer and you've got to approach him properly. One of his peculiarities is that he can't refuse anything to any girl named Amelia. You go in and tell him that's your name." The young woman hastened inside; but Mackay was denying himself to visitors that morning and Fair waited in vain for the explosion.

Another of Fair's tricks was to shift to Mackay's shoulders responsibility for such company regulations as were likely to be unpopular with the employees. Fire in the underground workings was a danger that constantly had to be guarded against, for the millions of feet of timber in the stopes, plus strong air-currents, constituted an ever present menace. The rule against smoking except in designated spots was strictly enforced and the penalty for violation was instant dismissal. On his rounds one day Fair thought he detected the odor of tobacco. He approached the gang at work in the stope, leaned against an ore-car, and announced that he was tired and needed a rest. After a few affable remarks he produced a pipe and began searching through his pockets, his face gradually growing longer. He had, he explained, been looking forward to a few drags at his pipe, but he had left his pouch at the office. The miners exchanged glances; finally several produced pouches and tendered them to the boss. Fair enjoyed his smoke, gossiping socially all the while, then continued his rounds. Back at the office, he left orders that the entire gang be discharged. Next morning as he was descending the incline from C Street, he encountered the group plodding up the hill. He pretended great surprise. "What's all this?" he demanded. "I thought this was your shift." "We've been laid off," one explained. "Laid off?" repeated Fair. "That's John Mackay for you! I never get a crew of men that suit me but Mackay comes along and fires them." He sighed heavily and passed on.

That Mackay and Fair for so long remained on cordial terms was mainly due to marked differences in their temperaments. Mackay was sober, methodical, and undemonstrative, with a vein of humility in his nature that made him shun whatever would make him conspicuous. Fair on the contrary, for all his pretended indifference to public acclaim, was ever a showman at heart, never content unless he was in the center of the stage, the source of all power, the "brains" of the firm. Both were familiar figures on Virginia's steep streets as they hurried from mine to mine and from mill to mill on their daily inspection tours. For these perambulations Fair provided himself with a shining carriage drawn by a beautifully matched team of bays and driven by a coachman; Mackay's vehicle was a shabby buggy, which he drove himself. An elderly San Franciscan, J. B. Levison, recalls that during the late seventies Virginia City's small boys amused themselves on winter afternoons by long, swift sled rides down the town's tilted cross-streets. The rides ended where Sutton Avenue flattened out opposite the Consolidated Virginia's hoisting works. If Mackay's buggy was outside, the boys were in luck; the good-natured Irishman would permit them to tie their sleds on behind and ride back uptown. If only Fair's shining carriage was visible, the group started the long trek back up the hill; experience had taught them that Fair would permit no such nonsense.

Fair's house on South B Street was a square two-story building with chaste white pillars supporting an ornate balcony; Mackay lived in two rooms in the Gould & Curry office farther down the hill, attended by a single Chinese servant. One of the town's journalists, Sam Davis, recalled meeting Mackay early one morning while the latter was on his way to the Consolidated Virginia works. Davis remarked: "If I had your money, John, I wouldn't get up at five o'clock!" Mackay retorted: "If you keep going to bed at five in the morning you'll never have my money or anybody else's." Davis was sometimes invited to breakfast at Mackay's austere living-quarters. The meal was always the same: mutton chops, oatmeal mush, toast, and coffee. Davis was impressed by the Spartan simplicity of this fare; Mackay's partner up the hill was accustomed to putting before his guests far more substantial breakfasts.

Mackay was content to remain in the background while Fair indulged his taste for display, the more so because the latter never permitted his foibles to interfere with business. Fair in fact worked so hard and long that even his abundant stamina was not always equal to the strain. At times he kept himself going only by copious draughts of a brandy-bottle, and when this stimulus failed he would have to take unwanted vacations. Once, in 1875, he fell more seriously ill and was forced to spend a full two months in California. While he was away Mackay was persuaded to undertake a spectacular exploit: to mine and mill a million dollars' worth of silver in a single week. It was planned to cast this in a single cube and to put it on display at the Centennial Exposition at Philadelphia as the central feature of the Nevada exhibit. When Fair returned and learned what had happened he complained bitterly, charging that such stunts violated every principle of sound mining. Mackay had "robbed" the mine of its richest ore, leaving Fair to work ore of inferior quality.

Mackay knew well how to cope with these periodical outbursts and the two made a harmonious and efficient team during the entire period the mines were at their peak. Neither man was changed by great wealth. Mackay remained austere in his personal life (although he good-naturedly expended huge sums to provide his wife with the lavish settings her nature craved), and his millions brought him pleasure chiefly because it permitted an open-handed generosity toward old friends. Fair pursued an exactly opposite course: he counted no expenditure too great if it enhanced his importance, but to part with a dollar for any other nonproductive purpose seemed to him pernicious folly. In his later years he was no whit less close-fisted than during the years he had been fighting his way upward. He made a virtue of this, as of every other quality he chanced to possess. Traits that other men termed miserly he called by a softer name. It was not that he hated to part with his coin; he merely abhorred waste. The trustees of the Virginia & Gold Hill Water Company, engaged in bringing Sierra water to the arid towns, met one day to pass on the plans for its Virginia City office. The architect's sketch showed a modest one-story building, with cast-iron columns in front and iron shutters inside its tall windows. Fair refused to approve it. A one-story building, he stated, was an economic waste. At little more expense a second floor could be added; this could be rented out as a rooming-house and so help pay for the investment. The second story was duly added, over the pained objections of the architect. Today visitors to Virginia City look with curiosity at the tall, narrow little Water Company office, still in use on South B Street.

Fair was not concerned when his crafty business deals earned him the title of "Slippery Jim," or when his three

partners outshone him in public esteem. Popularity was
never worth the time and expense necessary to its proper
cultivation. Mackay's unobstrusive philanthropies
aroused his ridicule; any man fool enough to pass out
coin to all comers would naturally attract a horde of admirers, all loudly singing his praises. But let him stop his
hand-outs and see how many remained. Flood presently
followed Mackay's lead and began tentatively to support
San Francisco's more popular charities; Fair was at pains
to point out that the dollars so expended had been laboriously dug from the hot lower levels of the Consolidated Virginia—and would someone please tell him what
part "Old Flood" had played in the digging?

When Coast newspapers began referring to the partners
as Bonanza Kings, the title made Mackay acutely uncom-
fortable. No one ever heard Fair object to being called
a Bonanza King.

8

EXPLORATION work to determine the extent of the bonanza was carried forward almost from the day of its discovery. The diamond drill, introduced into the Comstock in the early seventies, facilitated this search, for by
this device it was possible to make test borings many
yards in advance of the tunnels and drifts. For above
three years the results were so favorable that predictions
made in 1874 that at least a decade would be required
to exhaust the bonanza seemed likely to be borne out.
From 1877 onward, however, the drills began to tell a
less gratifying story. First in one direction, then in another,
they passed beyond the outer limit of the ore bodies and
entered "country rock." By midsummer of that year it
had been established that the bonanza terminated at the
1,650-foot level and that, should further exploration fail
to pick it up again, the period of fabulously profitable
operation must soon end. Through the rest of the year
and during all of 1878 the mills continued to operate
at full capacity, for vast deposits of quartz still remained

underground. But no new strikes were made, and this, besides the fact that less valuable ore was then being worked, caused a sharp drop in the size of dividends, and the natural consequence was that the value of bonanza stocks began a long downward drift. It was not long before they were selling for fewer cents than they had once brought in dollars.

Even Fair's optimism could not long withstand constantly mounting evidence that the big bonanza was far past its heyday. He remained hopeful longer than his partners (who had begun unloading their stocks as early as 1877), but well before the decade ended he too had reconciled himself to the inevitable and begun casting about for new fields of endeavor. For a time he hesitated between a life of ease as a gentleman farmer and a career in the currently booming business of railroad construction; then suddenly his interest swung in a new and totally unexpected direction. In 1879 he announced his candidacy for a seat in the United States Senate, entering the lists against his old Comstock rival William Sharon.

He conducted his campaign exactly as he had gone about attaining other prizes on which he had set his heart: by a combination of money, guile, and shrewd common sense. He knew Nevada politics well enough to realize that a seat in the Senate was a costly luxury under any circumstances; this time, with another multimillionaire opposing him, it would be doubly so. He was told that Sharon planned to spend $100,000; Fair matched that and added $10,000, counting on the added sum to tilt the scale his way. Both men spent every dollar and much more besides; all accounts agree that Nevada's few thousands of voters never enjoyed a more liberally financed election. Fair's electioneering methods were planned with characteristic artfulness. He discarded his handsome carriage and toured the mining camps in a one-horse buckboard, wearing the boots, flannel shirt, and slouch hat of the simple hard-rock miner. He visited each camp in turn and went through the mills and underground workings, greeting the workers man to man, talking a language they understood. Evenings he made the rounds of the bars,

renewing acquaintances he had formed during the day
and cementing their loyalty with successive rounds of free
drinks. He made sly capital of the fact that he knew nothing of the ways of politicians. He had, he boasted, never
made a speech in his life, but he knew from experience
what the miners of Nevada needed in the way of legislation. He was not an orator, but if his friends were inclined to send him back to Washington he would tell
the Senate what Nevada needed, and he'd try to see that
she got it. He offered his Comstock record as proof that
he was short on talk but long on action. If what the miners
demanded in their Senator was action, he was prepared
to supply it; if it was talk they wanted, let them return
the incumbent.

Sharon, cold and dapper, constitutionally unable to un-
bend, was no match for his bluff and hearty rival. As
the campaign entered its final phase, both men sent stump
speakers into every district, while party workers, amply
supplied with cash, shepherded the electors to the polls.
Sharon headed the Republican ticket; Fair ran as a Dem-
ocrat. Sixty-one members of the legislature were to be
elected; when the votes were in, it was found that only
nine Republicans had won. Fair was elected on the first
ballot.

His Senatorial career was many degrees less than
brilliant. When his six-year term was nearing its end, a
San Francisco paper reported: "About all that can be
said for Nevada's junior Senator is that he has had the
good sense to sit silent while matters of which he knows
nothing are under debate"; and the one-time Comstock
editor Arthur McEwen (who estimated that Fair's seat
had cost him $350,000) stated that Fair's colleagues of
the Senate found him "gross, dull and greedy." Yet there
is evidence that during his first months in Washington
he took his responsibilities seriously. Like most newcomers,
he was faithful in his attendance throughout the first session; but after the novelty wore off, his chair was usually
vacant. The demonetization of silver was then a lively
issue, and of course of particular interest to Nevadans.
Fair worked with John P. Jones, the state's senior Senator,

in the fight to restore silver to a parity with gold; but this was a complex and highly technical subject and Fair prudently permitted his colleague, a former chairman of the Senate's monetary commission, to present Nevada's case on the floor. More to his taste was the Chinese Exclusion Act of 1881, in support of which he delivered his one full-scale Senatorial address. Having thus carried out a campaign pledge to maintain the supremacy of white labor in the mines, laundries, and restaurants of his state, he lapsed into an almost complete silence, which he maintained with admirable consistency the remainder of his term.

The truth was that he found the role of lawmaker distressingly tiresome and dull. To be a member of the nation's most eminent millionaires' club was flattering to his ego, but he was soon confessing that the deliberations of that body bored him to distraction. All his life he had been a man of action, accustomed to instituting bold enterprises and seeing them through to completion. A man who had recently directed the affairs of the largest mining operation in history, with thousands at his beck and call and millions in profits rolling in each month, could not, he complained, listen patiently while a group of men devoted hours of passionate debate to the question of whether or not to hire a clerk at a salary of twelve hundred a year.

Accordingly, during his brief stays in Washington he shunned the Senate floor, preferring to while away the hours in his office, where, with feet on desk and a bottle of brandy handy, he reminisced with other truant senators or entertained occasional constituents. Charles C. Goodwin, a former Comstock newspaperman and then editor of the *Salt Lake Tribune,* found him there one day when he called to urge Fair to support a proposed increase in the duty on Sicilian sulphur as a means of protecting the sulphur deposits of western Utah. The import duty on sulphur was not increased. "I had forgotten," Goodwin added, "that he had extensive refining works in San Francisco and that sulphur was an essential agent."

Through the early eighties most of his time was spent,

not in Washington, but in San Francisco, where for some
years he had been shrewdly investing his surplus profits.
He made headquarters at the Lick House on Montgomery
Street. There in the hotel's gold-and-marble lobby he
nightly entertained a circle of admirers with stories of
the Comstock's active years, tossed off opinions (mostly
derogatory) of the eminent Washington figures, and gave
his views on national and international problems, all with
the air of authority combined with mock humility he
well knew how to assume. Like many another, he had
learned that the prestige of his office grew with the distance from Washington. It was pleasant to travel about
the country, to be addressed deferentially as Senator, and
to grant interviews on grave national questions or give
wholesome advice to the young. One of his exploits captured the attention of the entire country: he bought six
nightgowns from a New York haberdasher—and paid
the fantastic sum of thirty-five dollars each for them. None
of his official acts as Senator brought him half as much
fame.

He presently achieved an even wider renown. Rumors
that the domestic life of the Fairs was far from harmonious
had been current on the Comstock for years. Although he
is said to have entered the race for the Senate on his wife's
urging (a few years in Washington, she felt, would benefit
their growing children), Fair had set out for the capital
alone, leaving his family at Virginia City. McEwen states
that Mrs. Fair, finding herself destitute, appealed to Mackay, who provided her with funds to pay household expenses—and thereby gained the enmity of his partner.
"It was years before Fair would speak to him again." Religion was said to be one of the factors contributing to the
breakup of Fair's marriage. He was Protestant, his wife a
staunch Catholic, as were also his three partners. The
faith in which the children were to be brought up was a
source of discord, but by no means the only one. This last
was made clear early in 1883 when Mrs. Fair filed suit for
divorce. Her grounds were "habitual adultery."

To level such a charge against a United States Senator
would hardly pass unnoticed even today; in the prim and

decorous eighties its effect was sensational. From coast to coast papers reported the news on front pages and analyzed it in editorial columns, while from scores of pulpits members of the Senate were exhorted to expel their erring colleague. The matter duly came up for consideration on the floor of that body, but no action was taken pending the wife's submission of corroborative evidence. Such evidence was duly forthcoming. The divorce hearing was held in early May at the district court in Virginia City. Reporters were excluded from the courtroom, but next day the papers carried accounts of the testimony, most of it damaging to the defendant. Several specific acts of infidelity to the marriage vow were charged and—seemingly—proved, stated the *San Francisco Bulletin*. "One of the women named in the complaint testified herself in Court that Fair participated with her in the carnal acts as alleged. Another filed a deposition. . . ."

For once Fair denied himself to reporters, blandly explaining that he was opposed to such public airing of private differences. He added that in due time he would establish his innocence and expose the suit for what it was: a sinister plot engineered by his political enemies. He did not contest either the divorce or the adultery charges, although he tried hard to scale down his wife's demand for half the community property and for custody of the children.

The judgment of the court, handed down on May 12, 1883, was one of the major reverses of Fair's entire career. His twenty-one-year-old marriage was dissolved. He was awarded custody of his two sons, Charley and Jim, but that was the extent of his victory. Mrs. Fair was granted the divorce, and the daughters, Theresa and Virginia, were placed in her charge; she was also awarded the newly bought family home at 1170 Pine Street in San Francisco and one third of their joint fortune: some $4,750,000 in cash and securities. This last was said to have been the largest divorce settlement ever awarded up to that time. Because he had no choice in the matter, Fair agreed "in anguish and despair" to these hard terms and set about the task of carrying them out. But he objected long and violently to the fee the Virginia City court awarded Judge R. S. Mesick, who had represented the plaintiff—a whopping $200,000. Here too he was defeated, for in the end he had to pay Mesick's bill in full. This thoroughgoing rout permanently ended Fair's regard for the silver towns; he was, he announced, "through with the Comstock."

Fair's notorious and uncommonly expensive divorce had still another result: it definitely ended the friendship between Fair and his partners. During the trial Mackay and Flood—O'Brien had died four years earlier—supported Mrs. Fair, and it was largely by their advice that she had succeeded in winning so large a settlement. The close-fisted Senator had naturally no further use for the men who had been instrumental in diminishing his fortune by close to five million dollars, yet it was not possible for him to break off relations entirely, since the interests of all three were inextricably interwoven. Thereafter Fair's enmity was deep and bitter, but it was characteristic of his devious nature that he preferred to express it by indirection. His favorite device was to damn his former partners while seeming to praise them. Once he gravely asked an interviewer to view their shortcomings leniently. After all, what was one to expect from men who had sprung from such beginnings: Flood from behind a bar, Mackay from pushing a wheelbarrow? When Flood began building an ornate residence down the peninsula from San Francisco, in the midst of the country homes of a group of conservative Southerners, Fair remarked innocently: "Flood should be popular at Menlo. There's not a bartender on the Coast who can make a better julep than Jim." Mackay liked actors, and he delighted to entertain them on their trips to the Coast. Once he gave an elaborate dinner for John McCullough and his cast. Next morning Fair observed: "John Mackay's a great admirer of geniuses. I wonder how much they borrowed from him."

In 1894 the *Examiner* reported that during the last decade of his life Uncle Jimmy had held for his former partners the same degree of kindly regard he would have bestowed on "a brace of rattlesnakes." But he patiently bided his time, never doubting that an opportunity for revenge was some day to present itself. He was not disappointed.

9

WHEN his term in the Senate ended he did not seek reelection. Six years at Washington had given him the prestige and acclaim his nature desired; nothing would be gained by another expensive campaign. Besides, he had bought much San Francisco real estate and had been embarking on a variety of other enterprises—factories, gold mines, cattle ranches, railroads—and he was never one to permit an investment to languish for lack of close personal supervision. Accordingly he abandoned Nevada, leaving that ungrateful state to whatever sorry fate it deserved, and took up residence in California. One of his San Francisco properties was the Lick House, which he had bought in the early eighties for a reported $1,225,000; he continued to live there, in modest third-floor quarters overlooking the Montgomery-Sutter corner, for the rest of his life.

During the next nine years he devoted himself assiduously to the congenial task of conserving and increasing his fortune. One of his downtown properties was a narrow, two-story building at 220 Montgomery Street, which stood on ground now occupied by the Mills Building. There he maintained his office, in two rooms so crowded and cluttered as to impress themselves permanently on all who visited them. He had two assistants, L. C. Breese and J. S. Angus; these young men sat at opposite sides of a table in the outer office. Fair's rolltop desk, perpetually bulging with a chaotic mass of papers, stood between the windows of the front room, so placed that he could keep a watchful eye on the Montgomery Street sidewalks below. From these unprepossessing quarters he ably conducted a business remarkable alike for its profits and for the variety of its ramifications. Through the middle and late eighties he systematically gathered in building after building in the business and industrial areas; by 1893 he owned *sixty acres* of the city's most desirable areas. He bought income-producing property only: stores and office buildings, rooming-houses, warehouses, and small hotels, always driving a hard bargain. What he bought he held, renting out each piece as fast as he acquired it and refusing every offer, however tempting, to part with it again. When he died his income from rents averaged close to a quarter of a million dollars a month.

Little of this sum found its way back into the properties that had produced it. Fair's leases all had clauses making his tenants responsible for the upkeep of the buildings they occupied. The consequence was that only imperative repairs were made; his buildings grew more forlorn and dilapidated year after year. A writer in the *News-Letter* stated that anyone passing along the downtown streets could easily recognize Fair's properties. "All are in a shameful state of neglect, with the paint peeling from their fronts, doors sagging on their hinges, broken sidewalks and everywhere a critical need for refurbishing." Fair had an answer to such criticisms. He would, he announced, gladly keep his buildings in repair were it not for the greed and corruption of the city officials. Let them reduce the ruinously high real-estate taxes and he would put his property in apple-pie order. He would do more: he would demolish dozens of obsolete buildings and replace them with modern structures that would reflect credit alike on him and the city. But nothing was done to relieve him of the onerous burden of taxation and he continued to buy yet other ramshackle buildings and to permit them to become more so.

Not only these lucrative holdings, but a variety of other enterprises, engaged his attention. In the early nineties he undertook an extensive development in an area of land he had picked up on San Francisco's North Beach, moving thousands of cubic yards of rock as hills were leveled and depressions filled in, in preparation for building several acres of warehouses and industrial plants. He was often off on inspection tours of his out-of-town properties, mainly ranches and mines. The gambling element of mining, which had captivated him in his youth, did not lessen, and he frequently took fliers in claims that seemed promising: not alone gold and silver, but iron, coal, quicksilver, copper, and lead. Few of these investments brought him any profit, but his losses were small. In such ventures he applied a lesson learned on the Comstock: when he wished to explore a claim, he organized a company, counting on the prestige of his name to sell stock, then levying assessments to pay the cost of development.

He never doubted his ability to compete successfully in any field of enterprise against men who had devoted years to mastering its details. More often than not the result justified his confidence. When, in the early eighties, his two ex-partners tricked him into selling his interest in the Nevada Bank, Fair organized a rival institution, the Mutual Savings Bank, and launched it on a successful career. Earlier he and a partner embarked on a still more hazardous speculation, constructing a difficult and costly railroad through the mountain canyons between Los Gatos and Santa Cruz. After several years of operation the amateur railroad magnates sold out to the expanding Southern Pacific for a round six millions; Fair's net profit on the deal exceeded a million dollars.

These exploits further inflated his ego, and year by year his self-esteem grew. He liked to boast of the size of his fortune. In the fall of 1890 he suffered a prolonged and painful attack of asthma. When he recovered he announced, through the newspapers: "I wouldn't go through another week like that for all my forty millions!" His unpopularity grew with his dollars, but this caused him little concern; in later years he got genuine pleasure out of furthering his reputation as a hard and crafty trader who neither gave quarter nor expected it. An acquaintance once remonstrated with him because he had lent money to a needy friend and, when the latter was unable to repay, had foreclosed, taking both his home and his business. Fair replied: "A man who can't afford to lose shouldn't sit in a poker game." In the eighties Flood's son contracted an indiscreet marriage, which was played up in the newspapers. Fair commented: "Well, what can you expect of a

boy who has got a fool for a father?" (This remark was
recalled a few years later when Fair's younger son got into
a similar scrape.)

As age and infirmities increased, he moved in a progressively smaller orbit. San Franciscans of the early nineties grew familiar with his short, stocky figure, his hair
and full beard now gray, shuffling between his office and
his hotel rooms, only a block apart on Montgomery Street.
These daily walks grew progressively more deliberate, for
his weight had increased with his years, and his health—
never stable—gave him growing concern. As years and
disease exacted their toll he more frequently sought solace
in alcohol. From time to time he disappeared from his
usual haunts and crossed the bay to the Marin shore.
There he put up at the Parisian House, a small and in-
expensive hotel in San Rafael; the mild climate of that
sheltered town helped him shake off recurrent sieges of
asthma. Other guests looked on curiously while the capitalist sat night after night at a corner table in the hotel bar-
room, morosely drinking himself into insensibility, whereupon his male nurse, Herbert Clarke, would summon the
proprietor and the two would carry him upstairs to bed.
The degree of luxury of this San Rafael resort may be
judged by the fact that Fair's room cost him fifty cents a
night. "After he left the hotel," the chambermaid, Caroline Serrutte, stated after one visit, "there were a great
many empty bottles in his room, some brandy, some
claret." The departing guest had left her a fifty-cent tip.
"I thought that very small for a man like Mr. Fair."

His appetite for food was on a par with his thirst. For
years his servant, Clarke, carried Fair's breakfast up to his
room from the Lick House kitchen. The meal never varied: four boiled eggs, a dozen slices of toast, coffee, beef-
steak. Once Clarke concealed his surprise when Fair's
physician, Dr. Ludington, inquired if a tonic he had pre-
scribed had improved the patient's appetite. Fair, who had
just consumed his usual breakfast, answered weakly: "A
little, Doctor."

The old man stubbornly refused to permit his infirmities
to reduce him to invalidism, yet he had moments of loneli-

ness and self-pity. One evening in the Lick House lobby he met an old Virginia City acquaintance, James McCulloch, who was passing through town on his way to Australia. "He asked if I was going alone," McCulloch recalled, "and I said no, that my wife was going with me. He said: 'You're a lucky man, McCulloch. Look at me. My wife away, my children away, and everybody calls me a son-of-a-bitch!'" McCulloch added: "Possibly he deserved it."

As the nineties advanced, Fair, then past sixty, reached the zenith of his notoriety, one of the most conspicuous of the town's bumper crop of eccentric characters. His liking for the center of the stage increased with age; journalists found him by far the most voluble of the town's rich men. He welcomed mention in the newspapers, even when —as usual—it was in connection with matters more reticent men would have given much to conceal. "He was essentially a cynic," stated the *Chronicle* after he died, "who liked to express in anything but complimentary terms his opinion of men and things." That quality was never more evident than during his extremely candid discussions of family affairs.

10

THERE was usually a great deal to discuss, for from the middle eighties until well after the turn of the century the Fairs were among the nation's most highly publicized families.

The terms of the divorce decree, granting each parent custody of two children, provided moralists with a theme for numberless homilies. Mrs. Fair devoted herself to the training of the young women, giving them the benefit of a genteel Christian home and engaging the best of tutors to instruct them in the deportment and accomplishments suitable to their time and station. Fair, immersed in the management of his involved affairs, had little time or inclination to hold an equally tight rein on the boys. He gave them liberal allowances and permitted them to follow their own devices.

The result in each case was about what might have been expected. Tessie and Birdie Fair grew up to be accomplished and conventionally minded young women who moved in the city's best social circles and in due course contracted marriages that added luster to the family name. Meanwhile, Jimmy and Charley, with too much time on their hands and too much money in their pockets, developed tastes that must have pained their well-bred sisters on Pine Street. At first their escapades were innocent enough, mere boyish pranks that were reported in humorous paragraphs in the local press. Jimmy once hired a broken-down hack and, mounting the box, attached himself to the end of a funeral procession and jogged gravely out to Laurel Hill Cemetery. Charley, two years younger, bought one of the new naphtha launches and, on his first trial cruise, ran out of fuel; he and a group of friends spent the night in a cove off Angel Island while a fleet of small craft scoured the bay searching for them. Before long the papers were recording more serious scrapes. Jimmy, nightly making the rounds of the bars and cafés, fell easy victim to the family weakness. He was so often intoxicated when he returned to his Lick House room that his father belatedly exercised paternal authority and sent him to a Los Gatos sanatorium to undergo the Keeley Cure. Back in town three months later, he proceeded to celebrate his cure by giving a party at the Palace Hotel. There, to the admiration of his cronies, he consumed twenty cocktails. He collapsed while the twenty-first was being placed before him and a doctor was summoned. Less than a year later Jimmy was dead—by suicide, stated one paper; of acute alcoholism, reported another. He was twenty-seven. His father's comment was characteristic: Jimmy had always been his own worst enemy. He did not have the strength of will to withstand the harpies and parasites that clustered about every rich man's son.

Only a few months before this tragedy, the contrast between the two sets of Fair children had been dramatically highlighted. In the fall of 1890 Tessie, the elder of the daughters, was married to Herman Oelrichs, thirty-seven-year-old bachelor and member of a prominent New York and Newport family. Next morning the *Examiner* devoted three full pages to what it termed the most brilliant social function in the city's history. It may be assumed that the bride's father plodded through those twenty-four columns of 8-point type with closer interest than most. Reporters, seeking sidelights on the wedding, hunted him up and inquired why he had not been present at his daughter's wedding. He replied with his accustomed candor: he hadn't been invited. Asked if he had sent a present, he answered yes, he had sent a check. What was its amount? A million dollars, stated Fair. The town received this news with skepticism; it was probably another of his sly jokes.

The Fair-Oelrichs marriage elevated the two silver heiresses into national prominence and an acutely interested public wondered if the younger sister would also make a brilliant match. Virginia, then sixteen, went east to live with her sister and brother-in-law. She had been named for her native Nevada town, but she was known to her friends—and presently to everyone—as Birdie. Frequent newspaper stories supplied the curious with minute details. The two sisters were unlike in appearance and temperament. Tessie was tall and reserved, with fair skin and queenly bearing; Birdie, short, plump, and vivacious, had "black eyes and a mass of curly hair worn parted in the middle." Following her Newport debut, she became a dependable source of copy for writers of social gossip all over the country, a sort of 1890 version of the glamour girl. "New York papers," stated the *Chronicle,* "published descriptions of the color of her eyes, the way of doing her hair, her figure and gowns and equipages—even pictures of the hotel where she gave a dinner and the church where she worshipped. . . ." There were estimates, too, of the number of millions she would inherit and guesses as to what lucky man would claim the privilege of helping her spend them. She was several times reported engaged, once to Prince André Poniatowski, whose visit to San Francisco in the early nineties had thrown the city's heiresses into a

state of delicious expectancy. But in the end the Polish
Prince chose Beth Sperry (whose fortune came not from
silver mines but from railroads and flour mills), and Birdie
remained fancy free. Only a few months later society
writers had her engaged to John Mackay, Jr., who, sport-
ing Bond Street clothes and a British accent, was visiting
San Francisco after long residence abroad. But this romance, too, failed to materialize and young Mackay presently recrossed the Atlantic.

Meantime other family involvements kept the Fairs in
the limelight. Mrs. Fair died in September 1891. The bulk
of her estate was left to her two daughters, but her will
established a million-dollar trust fund for Jimmy and
Charley. Each was to be given an allowance of a thousand
dollars a month until he reached the age of thirty, whereupon he would receive the principal. In the event one son
predeceased the other, the full amount would go to the
survivor. Jimmy died only five months after his mother,
and Charley thereby became eligible for the entire sum
when he reached thirty. But Charley was then only twenty-
four; he had recently bought a string of racehorses—a
notoriously expensive hobby—and he was heavily in debt.
Six years seemed a long time for his creditors to have to
wait, and at their urging (and, it was said, with his father's encouragement) he filed suit to break the trust
provision of the will. This, the first of a long series of
Fair will cases, had one immediate outcome: it caused a
complete break between Charley and his sisters.

The latter presently had a more pointed reason to deplore their surviving brother's conduct. For that young
man was then just beginning a series of exploits that were
to keep him in the public eye for a decade. Charley, third
of the four Fair children, was born at Virginia City in
1867; he was described as a quiet, studious youth with
an absorbing interest in all things mechanical. When he
was twelve he delighted his father by building, to exact
scale, a working model of a six-stamp reduction mill.
Four years later Fair announced proudly that he was
sending his gifted son to one of the country's leading technical schools to prepare himself for a career as a mining

engineer. But somewhere along the line that program was abandoned. "Too much money and alcohol, too many racehorses and women" had the expected result. Following in the wavering footsteps of his elder brother, Charley was brought up short by the other's tragic death. He too retired to Los Gatos, took the "gold cure," and on his return caused a minor sensation among habitués of the town's cafés by drinking nothing stronger than milk. To help the young man's rehabilitation, his father made some notable additions to Charley's racing stable and financed an invasion of the Eastern tracks. But Charley's horses consistently failed to win, and soon word came back that he was finding solace not only in alcohol but in the company of a young woman to whom he had recently formed an attachment. This lady, "a handsome blonde of considerable embonpoint," was variously known as Maud Nelson, Maud Thomas, Maud Ulman, and Maud Corrigan; her real name was Caroline Decker Smith. She hailed from New Jersey and was a year or two older than Charley. In San Francisco she conducted, at 404 Stockton Street, what the local papers termed, with unaccustomed delicacy, "a questionable resort."

Charley's friendship with Maud Nelson was well known in San Francisco; the town, however, was not prepared for the next development. On October 14, 1893, the *Call* reported that the couple had crossed the bay to Oakland, driven to the court house, then to the home of an Episcopal minister, then back to the station, where, while they awaited the coming of a San Francisco train, they had celebrated their marriage by drinking a bottle of beer in the garden of Barnum's Restaurant. As always when his children were in the limelight, reporters hurried to Montgomery Street and interviewed Fair. The latter received the news calmly and discussed it with philosophical detachment. Charley, he pointed out, was well past twenty-one and so presumedly had reached the age of discretion. He had long known of his son's association with the Nelson woman, but it had never occurred to him that he would be such a fool as to marry her. (Here the old man digressed to point out that he had managed these matters more prudently. "No woman ever got her hooks into me.") He disclaimed any intention of trying to break up Charley's romance: people had to learn by their own mistakes, and besides there wasn't much he could do. Charley had been for a long time under the thumb of the lady, and now that she had got him to go through a marriage ceremony, it was unlikely that she would lightly toss away her advantage. To undo the mischief would be an expensive task and Fair had other uses for his money. Of course, he added softly, if his daughter-in-law hoped to get any part of his fortune she was due for a rude awakening. He would see his lawyer at once and draw up a new will, disinheriting Charley.

What the newlyweds thought of this interview can only be guessed, for they somehow managed to shake off the town's reporters and to slip aboard an overland train. The *Examiner,* which had recently come under the control of young Mr. Hearst, thereupon engineered a coup that missed success by the narrowest of margins. Learning that bride and groom were on the Overland Limited, the paper wired the chief of police at Port Costa, demanding that Fair be taken from the train and held until a deputy sheriff arrived with a warrant charging him with grand larceny. Armed with this, the officer boarded the train and succeeded in delaying it for two hours before young Fair and the railroad officials convinced him that he was without authority to act without the warrant in hand. The train had hardly left before the *Examiner*'s reporters and artists reached the scene after a breakneck race from San Francisco; they missed scoring the biggest beat of the year by less than fifteen minutes.

Not for ten days did reporters again pick up the trail. When the elusive couple was finally located in a New York hotel, both submitted willingly enough to an interview. Charley, whom the *Telegram* described as a "well-built young man of twenty-eight, with a strong face, curly brown hair and gray eyes," announced mildly that he and his bride wanted only to be left alone. They planned to sail in a few days for Europe, where they would stay for a year. These and other questions he answered in an agreeable manner, which, however, grew less amiable when he spoke of his persecution by the San Francisco press. "Surely it is odd that a man can't choose a wife without first obtaining the consent of the editors of the newspapers," he observed plaintively. Pursuing the same vein of sarcasm, he added that he planned to start a daily newspaper and to devote it exclusively to reporting his own activities, in which the public was so tremendously interested. The *Examiner*'s attempt to detain him in California he termed an outrage; he had not, as the paper claimed, left "mountains of unpaid debts" behind. But that was nothing new; that journal had repeatedly tried to blackmail him. By way of illustrating this point, Charley told how, some months earlier, an *Examiner* reporter had visited him upon his return from a sanatorium where he had undergone a cure for alcoholism. When Charley refused to be interviewed, the reporter had stated that he was himself a victim of the bottle and wanted an opinion of the value of the treatment from one who had just taken it. Charley had accommodatingly given the desired information and the two had parted as friends. But next morning the *Examiner* had published a front-page interview that contained a garbled and sensational version of Charley's confidential remarks. It was not, he maintained, the sort of thing one expected between gentlemen. At this point the bride appeared and graciously submitted to the reporters' questions. It had been rumored, one stated, that she was the owner of a questionable resort in San Francisco; was there any truth in the story? Her answer was an unqualified no. Oddly enough, when her denial was telegraphed back to San Francisco, investigation disclosed that she had spoken the literal truth. She had disposed of her Stockton Street business three days before her marriage. The reporters next hunted up Herman Oelrichs to inquire if he planned to entertain Charley and his wife during their stay in New York. But that eminent social figure made it clear that he did not intend to see, much less entertain, the visitors. "I do not care to have my name connected with the Fairs in any way," he added, and with that the interview ended.

Bride and groom remained in Europe something less than a year, then returned to San Francisco and established themselves in a Van Ness Avenue flat. During their absence the elder Fair's health had worsened. Convinced at last that his days were numbered, he had set about putting his affairs in order. On the urging of Dr. Ludington, the erring son was permitted to visit the sickroom; a reconciliation resulted, and thereafter Charley was in faithful attendance. Newspapers kept careful watch over this family drama. They reported that Fair had again rewritten his will, reinstating Charley. They reported too that the sick man, who had steadfastly refused to see his new daughter-in-law, was showing signs of relenting. In early December he agreed, the state of his health permitting, to have Christmas dinner at the Van Ness Avenue flat. Yet another item interested the city. The pastor of Fair's church visited the Lick House and, with doubtful tact, read to the sick man the preliminary draft of a laudatory sermon he proposed to deliver at Fair's funeral. This so incensed the patient that he got out of bed, struggled into his clothes, and for three consecutive days tottered down to his Montgomery Street office. These were his last public appearances. He took to his bed again, this time permanently. On Christmas Day he was far too ill to share the Christmas dinner Charley's wife had personally prepared. He died four days later, on December 29, 1894. He was sixty-three.

Only two were at his bedside, his physician and his nurse; Charley had gone home for the night and his two sisters were in New York. Some days earlier Charley had sent his sisters a warning that their father's condition was grave, but—stated the *Examiner*—"owing to the ill feeling that exists between Charles Fair and his sisters they did not respond to him but telegraphed instead to San Francisco acquaintances." "The daughters were here only a few weeks ago," the *Examiner* continued, "but they saw little of him; their meetings were cold and formal." That journal's obituary is a good example of the style of writing encouraged by its brash young publisher: "In the darkened chamber is not a sob or a tear. No son puts back the damp locks with tender care. . . ." The account goes on to state that Fair's acquaintances gathered on the downtown sidewalks, not to express regret at his passing but to wonder when and how the struggle for his millions would begin. "Already suspicion distills a poisonous exhalation at the bier." The *Examiner* story ended with what purported to be a Persian proverb: "The gods show their contempt for riches by those on whom they bestow them."

However that might be, no one doubted that the dead man had left one of the largest fortunes ever accumulated in the West. Estimates of its size had long been a favorite journalistic guessing game (in which Fair himself was never loath to join), and all through the eighties the figure had been steadily rising, reaching a climactic forty-five millions in 1894. At the time of his divorce, a dozen years earlier, he had been worth only a beggarly fifteen millions. That this sum could in so short a time have increased threefold was no mystery to those familiar with Fair's methods. In so fast-growing a city as San Francisco any man who bought property shrewdly and refused to sell it again could hardly have avoided having riches forced upon him. Fair had so actively followed that program that when he died he was the city's largest taxpayer. All four walls of his office were crowded with photographs of buildings he owned, and the collection had steadily been augmented. A favorite boast of his later years was that he could stand on any downtown corner and point out at least a dozen buildings on which he was collecting rents.

So shrewd a businessman would naturally give careful thought to the disposition of his immense holdings. His will, the third he had written during the final year of his life, was opened the day after his funeral; it was dated September 21, 1894, a little more than three months before he died. It contained a few surprises, notably the size of its cash bequests. A sister received $250,000, two brothers were given lesser sums; $2,000 went to his nurse, Clarke, and $10,000 each to Breese and Angus, his office workers; three orphan asylums—Catholic, Protestant, and Hebrew—were given a total of $125,000. The major part of the estate was left in trust for his surviving children:

Mrs. Oelrichs, Virginia, then nineteen, and Charles, twenty-seven. But although the son's heritage was thus restored, the document made it clear that the old man's forgiveness had not extended to Charley's wife or to their possible offspring. The will provided that Charley was to receive a third of the income from the trust; on his death, however, his share of the principal would go in equal parts to his two sisters or their heirs. There were two other clauses: if any of the children filed suit to have the will set aside, his or her share would go to the other two; second, if any person laid claim to a share in the estate as a common-law wife of the deceased, or as an illegitimate child, the claimant was to be awarded fifty dollars.

Clearly, Fair had foreseen that attempts would be made to break the will. Here too he proved an accurate prophet.

11

THE will named four trustees, charged with administering the estate and carrying out the provisions of the trust fund: Fair's attorney, W. S. Goodfellow, Angus, Breese, and Thomas G. Crothers. The last named was Fair's nephew, son of his sister, Margaret Crothers. The trustees duly presented the will for probate and the document was filed with the County Clerk. There it reposed for several weeks while the Fair children—who had hoped to get direct control of their shares and who objected to having the estate administered by the trustees—made known their dissatisfaction. "We will not allow this will to go to probate without a contest," announced a spokesman for Mrs. Oelrichs and Birdie Fair. For once Charley was in agreement with his sisters. "It is the desire and intent of Charles L. Fair to contest the document," stated his attorneys. Both groups professed to believe that the trust will was illegal and that a later document would be found. The trustees on their part deprecated this talk, insisted that the document was valid, and served notice that any attempt to set it aside would be strongly opposed.

While the battle lines were being formed and the most

eminent legal talent of the Coast was being engaged by one faction or the other, occurred the first of a long series of sensations. On the morning of January 29, 1895, newspapers announced that the controversial trust will had disappeared from the safe in the County Clerk's office. The news threw the city into an uproar. All interested parties were interviewed; all had theories of how the document had disappeared, and why. The trustees believed it was a plot by the heirs to destroy the trust and so to obtain immediate possession of the estate. Attorneys for the Fair children hinted that those who stood to benefit by the trust had realized that the will was a fraud and so had spirited it away. Both sides issued statements. "We could have nothing to gain by the disappearance of the paper," stated the Fair children. "We certainly would not steal our own paper," retorted the trustees. County Clerk Curry, whose mood was described as "desperate," changed the combination on the office safe. The police prophesied an early break in the case. The grand jury met in special session and voted to investigate the conduct of the County Clerk's office.

Meantime the public had learned all that was known about how the will had disappeared. The clerk of the probate court had delivered the document to the County Clerk, who had filed it away with others in the office safe. During the next few weeks a number of persons had examined it. This was a normal procedure, wills being public documents and open to inspection by interested persons. On the afternoon of January 25 a stranger had appeared and asked for the will; on his signing the receipt book, a deputy clerk, John Whitesides, had given him an envelope containing the document. Whitesides later testified: "He returned the envelope in due time, apparently all right, and after cancelling the receipt I replaced the document in the safe." Three days later another deputy, John Heilemann, was showing a friend through the office. "I pointed out the safe where the wills were kept under lock and key and . . . asked if he would like to see the Fair will. He said he would, and so I got out the envelope and handed it to him. He took out what he supposed to be the will and it proved to be only a lot of blank paper. . . ."

The police hunted up the last person known to have asked to see the will. He proved to be a young man named W. H. Davis, an employee of a private detective employed by Knight and Heggerty, lawyers, who had been retained by Charley Fair to represent him in the impending lawsuit. Davis, badly frightened, denied any knowledge of the theft. He had been sent to compare the wording of the will with copies printed in the newspapers. He had put the document back in the envelope and returned it to Whitesides. Davis was dismissed, as were eventually a score of others rounded up by the police. All were questioned and requestioned, without eliciting a single clue. After weeks of investigation the mystery was as far as ever from solution. It remains so to this day: the trust will, stated the reporters, had "disappeared into thin air."

While this hunt was in full cry the city was startled by another sensation. In early February Mrs. Nettie Craven, a plump, middle-aged lady of the highest respectability —she was principal of the Mission Grammar School— announced that she had in her possession a second Fair will. It had, she explained, been drawn up by the capitalist in the parlor of her California Street home and given to her for safe-keeping. The new document, scrawled in pencil on two sheets of foolscap, was dated September 24, 1893, three days later than the missing trust will. The newspapers promptly christened this the "pencil will," and as such it presently became celebrated all over the Coast. It differed from the trust will in several important respects; the chief difference was that it provided, after the payment of various cash bequests (including $500,000 to Charley), that the balance of the estate pass directly to the Fair children.

This of course was precisely what the three heirs wanted: their attorneys promptly filed the pencil will with the probate court. Again heated statements pro and con were issued to the press. The executors of the trust will violently denounced the new document as a forgery, and the opposing faction just as violently defended its authenticity. Charley, who had meantime forgotten his grievance against the local press, hotly informed a reporter: "I think I ought to know my father's handwriting. . . . This talk about the will being a forgery is absurd." He went on to explain how the document had come to light. Mrs. Craven, a woman of varied interests, had been active in support of a bill then before the state legislature designed to provide pensions for superannuated schoolteachers. She had interested Senator Fair in this legislation and the old man had incorporated into the pencil will a bequest of fifty thousand dollars to be paid into the pension fund should the bill pass. "Mrs. Craven," Charley explained, "was up in Sacramento in the interest of the bill and she dropped a remark about the legacy to the pension fund. I sent for her and after a little she told me the whole story. . . . Mrs. Craven was a great friend of Senator Fair; she lived for years in the same hotel with him, and he was a frequent visitor to her home. There he wrote the will and gave it to her to keep. She came by it honestly, and we finally persuaded her to turn it over to us, which she did on Saturday last. . . ."

For several weeks the amiable schoolteacher stood high with the Fairs and their attorneys. Mrs. Craven was not mentioned in the pencil will; obviously, therefore, she had not stood to benefit by it. She had, they contended, behaved with an admirable lack of self-interest throughout; her sole concern was to see that the wishes of her dead friend were faithfully carried out. But Charley and his sisters were before long not so sure. In November 1895 the resourceful lady produced two other pencil documents, both purportedly in Fair's handwriting. These proved to be deeds to two parcels of San Francisco real estate, conveying them to Mrs. Craven. It was no small gift. The property consisted of a five-story office building at the corner of Pine and Sansome streets and a large and valuable lot on Mission Street. Their aggregate value was a million and a half dollars: they brought in between four and five thousand dollars a month from rentals. The deeds were dated September 8, 1894. Mrs. Craven stated that Fair had had them acknowledged before a notary on September 27 and had then turned them over to her. She had kept them in the bottom of her trunk (along with the pencil will) for several months; then she had taken them down to the city hall and had them recorded.

The appearance of these documents badly shook the confidence of the Fairs in the altruism of Nettie Craven. For a few days silence descended upon the pro-Craven group; even the normally voluble Charley denied himself to interviewers. The newspapers reported conferences lasting far into the night in the offices of the Fair attorneys, and at length a statement was forthcoming: The question of the authenticity of the pencil deeds, it stated, was not of present importance. But the pencil will, superseding the trust will, was clearly genuine and the heirs would continue to demand that the estate be distributed according to its provisions. Meantime the heirs were negotiating with Mrs. Craven for the surrender of her deeds. The *Call* stated: ". . . It was her [Mrs. Craven's] wish to escape notoriety in the case, and an agreement was arrived at, making Richard V. Dey, one of the executors of Mrs. Fair's will, an arbiter of her claims, with power to pay her $500,000 in settlement."

While these negotiations were in progress, however, came a new development that again threw the situation into confusion. Soon after Fair's death attorneys for his children had begun action to have the trust will declared illegal. The court's decision had been delayed for months, the matter all but forgotten in the turmoil over Mrs. Craven's successive pencil documents. In February 1896, however, Judge Slack of the Superior Court handed down a decision declaring the trust clauses of the first will invalid. Again the effect was profound. The Fairs had been opposing the trust will and supporting the pencil will because the first set up a trust and the second directed that the estate pass directly into their hands. Now that the trust feature of the first will had been pronounced invalid, they no longer had reason to oppose it; accordingly they did a complete about-face. The day after Judge Slack rendered his decision Charley informed reporters that he had withdrawn all opposition to the trust will. He added gravely that in his opinion the pencil will—which he had been vehemently supporting for months—was a forgery. Spokesmen for the two sisters issued like statements, and negotiations with Mrs. Craven for the surrender of the pencil deeds were broken off.

But that indomitable lady was not at the end of her resources. She let it be known that her collection of Fair manuscripts contained yet another item: no less than a contract of marriage between the ex-Senator and herself. This too was passed out to the newspapers and published in facsimile. It read:

San Francisco, Cal.
May 23, 1892

I take Nettie R. Craven to be my lawful wife
James G. Fair

I take for my lawful husband James G. Fair
Nettie R. Craven

More than a year and a half had elapsed since Fair's death, but the litigation he had foreseen had hardly begun. In June 1896 the executors of the trust will—now shorn of its trust provisions—began suit to have the Craven deeds declared forgeries and to restore the property to the estate. Various legal maneuvers caused a long delay and the case did not come to trial until eight months later. Meantime a number of preparatory steps had been taken. Charley had sworn out a warrant for the arrest of J. C. Cooney, the notary public who had acknowledged the Craven deeds, charging him with perjury. The Fair heirs had engaged two handwriting experts to support their charge of forgery; Mrs. Craven had countered by producing an acquaintance, Mrs. Hankins, who declared she had been present when the deeds were written and had seen Fair sign them. By then so many eminent attorneys had been engaged on both sides that the *Chronicle* pronounced them "the most brilliant galaxy of legal luminaries ever seen in the West." One of the town's weeklies paid this tribute to the group: "When the Fair will was published several years ago we remarked that a man of his vast wealth should have been more liberal in his contribution to worthy charities. We gladly withdraw the charge. For it has now become clear that a substantial part of the Fair fortune will be devoted to philanthropy of a particularly heart-warming kind. It will enable nearly a score of rich but deserving attorneys to spend the balance of their lives on the lap of luxury."

San Francisco's bumptious press had a field day at the expense of principals, witnesses and attorneys. Midway in the long trial Mrs. Craven's legal staff received a notable addition in the person of George M. Curtis, ex-judge of the New York Supreme Court, who was said to have smashed more wills than any other man in history. The *Examiner* promptly christened Judge Curtis "the Smasher" and by that name he soon became known all over the Coast. On May 27 the paper printed half a page of caricatures of the judge by its young cartoonist Jimmy Swinnerton. "He comes with a great reputation for breaking wills," stated the caption. "His smashing, however, seems to run along the lines of killing off his opponents by heaping upon them great loads of eulogy or smothering them in tubs of soft soap. His old-fashioned . . . courtesies caused a smile to flit around among the attorneys, who are accustomed to the hard scrabble, knock-down-and-drag-out style of California procedure. . . ."

The Smasher must have been an uncommonly forgiving man. After having been exposed to weeks of barbed ridicule, he was able upon his return east to pen this tribute to California: "Land of sunshine, eternal perfume and flowers, land of brave men and beautiful women, land which the Almighty has crystallized with a smile; fulfilling the destiny of your origin, you are the Elysium of the national domaine, as you have been in the days gone the treasure-house of the Republic." But he was human enough to exclude the state's newspapers from this blanket approval. "Journalism in San Francisco," he added "is personal and crude to a great degree. . . . Its conspicuous feature is in the form of caricatures, and it would be difficult to make the conservative people of the East comprehend why the artistic efforts of the daily journals should so excite and enthrall the people of California. . . ."

Although will-smasher Curtis loomed large in the public eye, he did not altogether obscure the trial itself. This moved ponderously through the spring and summer of 1897. The fortunes of the opposing sides alternately rose and fell as the parade of witnesses, attorneys, and handwriting experts presented their evidence and arguments. Counsel for the plaintiffs produced witnesses who strove to account for Fair's whereabouts during every minute of the day, three years earlier, when he was alleged to have visited Cooney and had the pencil deeds acknowledged. But this strategy collapsed when Mrs. Craven's lawyers forced from Herbert Clarke an admission that twice during the day he had left Fair alone for half an hour, ample time for him to have visited Cooney, whose office was only half a block distant down Montgomery Street. Again, detectives working in the Fairs' interest made a discovery that promised to end the case and send the unhappy notary to prison. The printing house that had produced the acknowledgment forms identified them as having first been printed in 1896. Because Cooney had testified that he had acknowledged them in 1894—and the forms were so dated—the *Call's* headline, "Outlook Dark for Cooney," seemed justified. But a week later the Cooney-Craven attorneys triumphantly put in evidence forms identical with those attached to the wills, and dated as early as 1891. Cooney remained at large and the trial continued.

The complicated proceedings were reported in the press in a vein of sustained irony; few who appeared in the courtroom escaped their barrage of ridicule. There was one shining exception: Margaret Craven, the comely twenty-year-old daughter of the defendant. Margaret's role was a minor one, for she made only one brief appearance in the witness chair. But she was faithful in her attendance, closely following from her place in the front row of spectators every word that was spoken. She must have been an uncommonly pretty girl: few of the daily newspaper reports failed to devote a sentence or two to her demure entrances and departures, her solicitude for her mother, her frequent shy smiles in the direction of the entranced jurors. That this attractive young woman (she had had an intermittent connection with the local stage) was a valuable asset to her mother's cause was recognized by both sides, and the opposing counsel vied with one another to pay her courtly compliments. Even so eminent a personage as the Smasher was not indifferent to her charms. She was, he stated, "a young woman of remarkable beauty of face and form, gifted with extraordinary mental qualities." Events were to prove, however, that she was lamentably deficient in judgment. For at the critical hour when the trial was reaching its climax, she dealt her mother's prospects a staggering blow: she eloped with one Henry Koehler, "a young man extensively engaged in the brewing interest," and the jurors saw her no more. "This was a very grave mistake of policy," commented the Smasher. "Its effect was to take from Mrs. Craven, in a great degree, the sentiment of personal sympathy she had inspired in the jury. . . . I have not the slightest doubt that this incident cost us at least three votes. . . ."

Three lost votes were enough to turn the tide against the schoolteacher. After hours of deliberation the jury confessed itself in hopeless disagreement, the court standing eight to four in favor of the authenticity of the Craven deeds. The judge thereupon took on himself responsibility for deciding the issue. "On the conspiracy issue he ruled in favor of Mrs. Craven, to wit, that no conspiracy existing between her and any other persons had been proven, either in the forgery of the deeds, or in securing their acknowledgment; but on the other two issues he found in favor of the plaintiffs. . . ." Meantime Cooney, who had sued on a motion to dismiss the action charging him with perjury, failed to convince the judge that the evidence was insufficient to justify the indictment; he was accordingly held for trial.

Still in truculent mood, Mrs. Craven filed notice of appeal to the state Supreme Court, and the Fairs prepared to fight the case all over again. But a few weeks later the schoolteacher admitted her inability to continue the expensive struggle and made known her willingness to accept an out-of-court settlement. A compromise was duly reached. In return for a small cash payment she withdrew her appeal and turned over both the marriage contract and the deeds to the Fair executors; they in turn dropped the charge of perjury against Cooney. The Fair-Craven trial —among the longest and most bitterly fought in California legal annals—thus ended in victory for the plaintiffs. It had not been a cheap victory. The *Examiner* estimated that the involved litigation had diminished the Fair estate by two million dollars.

12

A GREAT many millions remained, however, and for many months the West was entertained by a parade of claimants eager for a share of them. Hardly had Fair's body been sealed in the mausoleum he had forehandedly provided at Laurel Hill when an odd assortment of ladies claiming to have been common-law wives, affianced sweethearts, or daughters-in-law emerged from obscurity. "The Crop of Natural Heirs to the Dead Millionaire Now Making an Appearance," gleefully announced an *Examiner* headline in March 1895; thereafter there were almost weekly additions to the list.

One of the first in the field was an eighteen-year-old Los Angeles girl. Her name, appropriately enough, was Sarah Gamble, but she was known in the southern city (where she operated a flower stand in the Nedeau Hotel) by a more picturesque title: Sally the Flower Girl. Sally's story was that Fair, who had often been a guest at the Nedeau, had formed a habit of buying boutonnieres at her flower stand, had progressed to taking her on buggy rides, and had ended by asking her to become Mrs. Fair— an invitation she had promptly accepted. It does not appear whether or not the Fair executors paid her the fifty dollars his will directed to be given such claimants; at any rate no lawsuit was filed, and Sally disappeared from the public eye. She was back again three years later when the newspapers reported that she had inherited twenty thousand pounds from her paternal grandmother in England. In another brief blaze of glory she set off to claim her fortune.

She was followed in quick succession by half a dozen others. In Portland the *Oregonian* announced that a young woman had entrained there for San Francisco bearing documentary evidence that the bonanza king had seduced her under promise of marriage; there is nothing to indicate that she ever arrived to press her claim. At Oakland another lady, "now twenty-six or seven years old," came forward with a demand for a quarter interest in the estate on the ground that she was a natural daughter of the multimillionaire. In due time, she announced, her mother would furnish legal proof that James G. Fair was her father. Nothing further was heard from her, but following close on her heels appeared a young man who called himself James Fair Stevens and who claimed to have been born in Virginia City, one of the tangible results of his mother's romance with Fair during the years just prior to the latter's divorce. The *Examiner,* which made a habit of giving each claimant the benefit of every doubt, commented: "It is scarcely denied that the boy is the son of James G. Fair. Indeed, old Virginia City people ... speak of that as a certainty, as a matter of unwritten but well-known history. Many of them claim to remember the intimacy of Fair with Miss Stevens, and some know of her leaving and of Fair's settlement with her. . . . Those who have seen him declare that he bears a striking resemblance to his alleged father and to his half-brothers, Charles Fair and the late James G. Fair, Jr." Notwithstanding this family resemblance, attorneys for the Fairs were unimpressed. To have any standing in the California courts, they pointed out, the young man would have to prove that Fair had recognized him as his son, and they doubted if such proof existed. The millionaire, they explained, was "much too crafty ... to acknowledge any child born out of wedlock."

James Fair Stevens faded from the limelight and was replaced briefly by yet another young woman. Her story had a novel twist in that she claimed to be, not Fair's widow or daughter, but his daughter-in-law, the widow of his son Jimmy. She announced that she planned to press her claim on behalf of her minor son, the ex-Senator's grandchild. By this time the Fair attorneys were professing amusement at the entire proceedings. "So they have dug up a widow for young Jimmy Fair, and a child too," commented John Heggerty. "We have nothing to say. . . . She may be all right, but some things in connection with her claim appear odd." He went on to explain that by Mrs. Fair's will Jimmy was left $500,000, payable to him when he reached the age of thirty or, in the event of his earlier death, to his widow or children. "This money has been lying idle for years," Heggerty continued, "but this newly found widow never made claim to a penny of it. Really it looks as though this latest pretender wouldn't do. She is too generous. . . ." The lady must have agreed with that line of argument, for she too passed out of the picture.

Toward the end of March 1895 yet another prospective bride had a brief season of newspaper fame. This was no obscure and friendless supplicant, but a lady known from coast to coast. In a full-page story, complete with illustrations, the *Call* announced on March 24: "Miss Phoebe Couzins, the world-famed woman's rights advocate, was the affianced bride of James G. Fair at the time of his death." Miss Couzins, in San Francisco on a lecture tour, professed reluctance to discuss in public a matter so personal and private. Under the urging of the *Call*'s reporter, however, she swiftly overcame her reticence. She confided that they had met at the Riggs House in Washington when Fair was Nevada's junior Senator. The pair discovered that they held like views on social and political problems and, based on these common interests, their friendship had speedily ripened. "I took a liking to him at once . . . and I could see that he liked to be with me. . . ." Fair was never one to allow a friendship with a handsome young woman to fall into complete neglect; this one was renewed several years later in Chicago. "In the meantime I had been elected Secretary of the National Board of

Lady Managers of the Columbian Exposition, and made my home in the Grand Pacific Hotel. . . . There I received a letter from Mr. Fair in which he stated that he would see me soon, and that he wanted our acquaintance to culminate in a relationship closer and dearer than mere friendship."

Intent on furthering this ambition, the sixty-two-year-old suitor arrived at the Grand Pacific Hotel in April 1893. Their courtship was conducted under severe handicaps, for Fair had brought along not only his nurse but his secretaries, Breese and Angus, and his nephew, Thomas Crothers. Miss Couzins presently had reason to believe that Fair's children feared their father might remarry, and that members of his retinue had been bribed to nip in the bud any unfolding romance. "Mr. Breese and Mr. Angus watched the Senator like a chicken does a hawk," she recalled. "They allowed no one to see him until Mr. Crothers came, when he seemed to take charge of the matter." Herbert Clarke was also in on the plot. "Whenever anything mean was said about me in the newspapers . . . he used to mark the articles in blue pencil and place them conspicuously on the table. . . . Everything that could be done to influence him against me was done by Breese and Angus and Crothers."

It is pleasant to report that despite this vigilant group Fair and Miss Couzins managed to enjoy occasional half-hours together, "very pleasantly talking of the present, the future, and the past." Inevitably this chit-chat wandered into romantic byways, and one day—according to Miss Couzins—this dialogue ensued: Fair: "I love you and want to provide for you at all hazards so that financial troubles can never come to you. I want you to be my wife. Will you marry me?" She answered simply: "Yes." He then said: "Thank you, dearest. We must be married soon —very soon."

It was not to be. The next day, on a freezingly cold afternoon, Messrs. Angus and Crothers took the prospective bridegroom for a long ride on the lake front in an open carriage and a day later Fair took to his bed with an ear-ache and incipient pneumonia. When the sick man told Miss Couzins of this exploit she did not conceal her suspicion that the outing had been planned for the express purpose of blighting their romance. "I replied that it was criminal for anybody to take a man in his feeble health for such a drive in that kind of weather." It was the beginning of the end. On orders of Fair's physician (whom she suspected of being a party to the plot) she was refused admittance to the sickroom. She had, in fact, only one brief moment with Fair, on the day, two weeks later, when he was leaving for California. "He spoke of the many notes and cards he sent to my room after he had become convalescent and which never reached their destination. They had been intercepted by someone who had an interest in keeping us apart." Later she had sent him numerous letters to San Francisco, but no reply had ever come—Miss Couzins thought she knew why. So she had stopped writing and had tried to put the romance out of her mind. Not many months later she had read in the newspapers that her elderly admirer was dead.

On the day Miss Couzins's interview was published, a reporter hunted up Mr. Angus. Was it true, he was asked, that the men close to the capitalist were under orders to discourage his romantic tendencies? Were the Fair children afraid he might remarry, and willing to pay well to avoid such a catastrophe? To these and other questions Mr. Angus "returned only an enigmatic smile." Meantime Miss Couzins lectured before noticeably larger audiences up and down the Coast and, it may be assumed, continued to win converts to the cause of votes for women. She seems to have completely captivated the *Call* reporter, for he thus summed up his impressions of her: "She is altogether different from other women who once were passion-flames around the dead millionaire. She will ask for no compensation. She will offer no petition of any sort for a share of the millions that were once pledged to her use; she does not seek for pecuniary balm for her wounded heart. . . ."

On this rarely heard note the West took leave of the bumper crop of self-styled widows, sweethearts, and offspring who mourned at various places and with varying degrees of grief the passing of the man who had been known to a generation of Westerners as Slippery Jim.

13

THE Fair name by then had been before newspaper-readers of the Coast for nearly a quarter of a century. It did not at once pass into obscurity. In the East the two daughters moved from one social triumph to another, their successes reaching an apex with the marriage, in April 1899, of the younger daughter to William K. Vanderbilt, Jr., grandson of the redoubtable Cornelius. The news that bouncy, hoydenish Birdie Fair had carried off the nation's richest—and therefore most eligible—bachelor enchanted the West. For weeks after the engagement was announced daily stories kept millions posted on the progress of the wedding preparations, and the ceremony itself was described with an unprecedented wealth of detail. An acutely interested nation learned that the bride had been given away by her brother-in-law, Herman Oelrichs, and that the bridesmaids were daughters of men so wealthy that their combined fortunes "exceeded that of half the royal families of Europe." Following the ceremony, two hundred guests ("just the *upper half* of New York's Four Hundred") sat down to breakfast in the library of the Oelrichses' white marble mansion at Fifty-seventh Street and Fifth Avenue. There they were entertained by two orchestras and amused by a witty but overlong speech by Oelrichs. In the midst of all this magnificence the pretty bride remained the simple, unaffected girl she had been when "in simple calico she had romped about the streets of Virginia City." Vanderbilt's wedding gift was a seventy-thousand-dollar pearl necklace. When, after breakfast, the happy pair set off for Idle Hours, the Vanderbilt Long Island estate (where the groom's sister, Consuelo, and the Duke of Marlborough had recently spent their honeymoon), everyone breathed a sigh of relief. The weeks of arduous preparation for this most complicated of weddings had been happily justified. "Everything went off exactly as planned. There were no mishaps."

In San Francisco the Charley Fairs were treading a less rosy path. That young man's weakness for the bottle, which he had kept under reasonable control during the early period of his married life, again got out of hand. To cope with these recurring emergencies, his wife entered into a working agreement with Captain Lees of the San Francisco police department by which Lees periodically searched through the city's cafés and rooming-houses, located the missing husband, and returned him to the Van Ness Avenue flat. For this chore he is said to have received a monthly fee of five hundred dollars. It was money well expended. As time passed, Charley's falls from grace grew less prolonged and frequent. The entire city applauded. The *Examiner*'s prediction that, if she were left alone, the former Maud Nelson "would make a man of Charley" seemed justified: the couple lived together in evident peace and concord for nearly a decade.

Meantime, by what miracles of diplomacy, tact, and shrewdness can only be imagined, she not only had kept the erring Charley under reasonable control but had gradually won, first the toleration, then the friendship, of her sisters-in-law and their friends. During the seven years of litigation that followed the elder Fair's death she was constantly watchful over Charley's interests, lending such shrewd support as to win the respect of his corps of attorneys. As the successive legal victories put multiple millions at her disposal, she developed an interest in charity, spending two afternoons a week in the poverty-ridden areas "south of the slot," where she distributed clothing, hampers of food, and sound advice to the deserving poor.

Charley meantime was occupied with the pursuits proper for a young man of wealth and fashion. His interest in horse-racing revived and for several seasons his colors were visible on both Western and Eastern tracks. But his horses never shook off their habit of finishing in the ruck, and his interest waned. Besides, his boyish enthusiasm for mechanics had manifested itself again. He bought a fifty-foot yacht and took parties of friends on cruises up and down the coast. Tiring of this, he turned to smaller and faster boats and for a season daily churned up the waters of the bay in a series of speedy naphtha launches. But it was not until the advent of the horseless carriage that Charley found a lasting hobby. He was among the first San Franciscans to buy the contraptions and in them to bounce noisily over the city's abominable streets; he developed, too, a consuming curiosity for the mysteries concealed beneath their hoods. In those days it was customary for a man who acquired an expensive French automobile to acquire a chauffeur along with it—also French and also expensive. Charley followed the prevailing custom; but he was never content until he had made himself as familiar with the cars' mechanism as the man he had hired to take care of them.

His enthusiasm for the sport grew as the manufacturers improved their products. Each season he bought the most powerful model on the market and drove it at top speed. In the spring of 1902 he and his wife set off for Europe, where he planned to acquire one of the latest French racing cars and to spend the summer burning up the admirable French highways. In June they reached Paris, where Charley purchased the car of his dreams: a Mercédès Special, which its builder guaranteed to be capable of eighty-five miles an hour. It proved to be all he had expected. The pair made several tours out of Paris, and in mid-August set off for Trouville, where the Vanderbilts had taken a villa for the summer. The two brothers-in-law had become close friends. Young Vanderbilt shared Charley's liking for fast and powerful automobiles; he had in fact done much to further the sport by putting up the racing trophy that bears his name. A friendly rivalry existed between them—both were ardent amateur drivers—and when the Fairs left to return to Paris, Charley was bent on lowering Vanderbilt's record of two and a half hours for the run. They are said to have wagered fifty dollars on the outcome; if so, it proved to be a tragic gamble.

All went well during the early stages of the trip; Charley was at the wheel and the Mercédès ate up the miles at a speed that made victory seem certain. In mid-morning, near the village of Evreux, the chauffeur, who was riding in the back seat, observed that one of the rear tires was becoming soft. He leaned forward and shouted a warning to Charley. The highway at that point was described as "a splendid, wide road," but so great was their speed—the chauffeur later estimated it at a hundred kilometers an hour—that when Charley applied the brakes the heavy machine spun out of control. A woman gatekeeper standing at the entrance of a château across the road witnessed the accident. She saw the car careen into a tree, and two objects—which she took to be bundles of clothes—strike its trunk with great force, then fall to the ground. The chauffeur, Louis Bretry, was thrown clear and escaped injury, but both the Fairs were killed.

They did not die instantly or at the same moment. When a small group of spectators, attracted by the tremendous crash, reached the scene, they observed certain convulsive movements in the bodies of both victims. These persisting signs of life presently became the subject of countless debates in the newspapers of two continents. For the disposition of more than ten million dollars hinged on the question of which victim had died first. During his lifetime, Charley had given his wife property valued at $300,000. When her will was opened it disclosed that she had bequeathed one-third of that sum to her mother and numerous sisters; the balance was to go to Charley. Charley's will made a number of comparatively small gifts to friends and relatives and left the bulk of his large estate to his wife. Both wills had clauses providing that the bequests to husband or wife were to be canceled in the event that the prospective beneficiary predeceased the donor. In other words, should it develop that Charley had died first, all but a very small part of his estate would go to his wife and so in turn to her next of kin: the numerous tribe of Nelsons. On the other hand, if it could be proved that Charley had survived his wife, even though by only a fraction of a second, the latter's heirs would receive only the $100,000 specifically awarded them in her will.

When knowledge of this complicated situation reached

the public, few doubted that yet another of the celebrated
Fair lawsuits was in the making. In San Francisco, the
legal residence of the couple, Charley's attorney made
haste to point out that under California law when a husband and wife died of injuries simultaneously received, it
was assumed, in the absence of evidence to the contrary,
that the husband had survived longer. This was on the
theory that, being commonly stronger than the female,
the spark of life would logically remain longer in the
male. But the deaths had occurred in France, and it was
thought that if the expected lawsuit materialized, it would
be tried in the courts of that country. No one in San
Francisco could say with certainty what the law of France
might be on that point. One eminent authority hazarded a
guess that the traditional gallantry of the French might
incline the court to find in favor of the lady. This
prompted a French advocate who happened to be passing
through the city to pen a letter to the *Chronicle*'s editor
passionately denouncing the theory as a canard. Should
the case come before a French magistrate, he insisted that
it would be decided, not on sentimental grounds, but solely
in accordance with the evidence.

Signs were not long delayed that a bitter struggle for
Charley Fair's fortune was impending. Within a few hours
after news of the tragedy reached the Coast, local papers
announced that members of the Nelson clan were con-
verging on the city—from Jersey City, from Albany, from
Boulder, Colorado—all intent on protecting their interests.
Hoping to forestall another protracted lawsuit, spokesmen
for Mrs. Oelrichs and Mrs. Vanderbilt announced that
they were willing to turn over to the Nelsons the dead
woman's entire $300,000 estate. The offer was summarily
rejected. Maud Fair's relatives, warmly supported by their
attorneys, were bent on gambling for larger stakes.

Meantime the attention of the nation was divided between two villages on opposite sides of the Atlantic: Pacy-
sur-Eure on the road between Trouville and Paris, and a
New Jersey crossroads settlement called Newmarket, a few
miles from Plainfield. In the French town the Fairs' chauffeur changed his story of the accident. It had not been a

soft tire that had caused the machine to go out of control, but an error of judgment: Charley had turned the wheel too abruptly, causing the car to veer sharply to the left. More important, the gatekeeper, the only eyewitness to the tragedy, who had first declared that she had observed simultaneous signs of life in the victims, now professed to recall that the movement of the foot of the man had ceased an instant before that of the hand of the woman. These grisly details were analyzed at length in newspapers across America, while both factions charged that the other side was trying to tamper with the witnesses. A New Jersey attorney, representing the Nelsons, cabled the American ambassador in Paris asking that he personally visit the scene and question eyewitnesses, and Herman Oelrichs in New York announced that the Fairs had engaged a noted French detective and instructed him to make a thorough and impartial investigation.

While this was going on, a corps of reporters descended on Newmarket, where Maud Fair's mother, Hannah Smith Nelson, submitted to an interview. Maud, she confided, had always been a girl of ambition and spirit, generous to a fault, but headstrong and impatient of restraint. She had left the paternal roof at sixteen to seek her fortune in New York. For a long time nothing was heard of her, then a letter had reached Newmarket stating that she had gone on the stage. Another long silence had followed. After her marriage to Fair, however, the correspondence had been resumed, and thereafter each letter had contained a substantial cash gift. Then, just before the beginning of the tragic European trip, she had visited Newmarket, accompanied by her maid, and had remained several days, graciously playing Lady Bountiful to various family connections. Her half-brother, Abe Nelson, had benefited most by her largess. "She took him from the local tavern, where he was tending bar, and put him in the grocery business; she bought him a nice house, too, down the road."

Through the August evenings of 1902 the Nelsons sat in their shirt-sleeves on the porch of Abe's grocery store and gave the world their views on the accident. William, a brother, hoped only that the gatekeeper at the Château

Boisson de Mai would tell the truth and nothing but the truth. Abe's plausible theory was that, since Charley Fair was driving, he must have been in the front seat, and he therefore must have been first to strike the tree. Another brother, Henry, hazarded a guess that his sister's estate was far greater than the papers had reported: it would not surprise him to learn that it topped a million and a half. Each of the group was asked what he intended to do with his prospective fortune; all but one replied loyally that they planned to continue to live in Newmarket. The exception was Mabel Le Fier, sixteen-year-old niece of the dead woman: she announced that she planned to hire a personal maid (like Aunty Maud's) and to enroll in style at Vassar. One family connection was located in an almshouse in a near-by town. Although he was Maud Fair's brother-in-law, he did not share the prevailing optimism. He was making no grandiose plans; he doubted if any of the Nelsons would get much out of the estate. Personally he didn't expect to see a red cent.

The record does not disclose whether or not this brother-in-law's gloomy prognostications were well founded; but the Nelsons of Newmarket and elsewhere were presently dividing a very substantial amount of cash. In San Francisco long negotiations preceded the final settlement. John Heggerty represented Mrs. Vanderbilt; Herman Oelrichs came out from New York to look after his wife's interests; the Nelson clan was represented by no less than four attorneys. The horse-trading continued for a week, with day-long conferences between the two groups and periodical reports to the press. At last, on August 28, the same day the bodies of Charley and his wife left Havre for New York, both parties announced that an amicable compromise had been reached. Hannah Nelson and two of her sons signed away all interest in the estate of her late son-in-law. In return, the eight nearest relatives named in the will—mother, five brothers or half-brothers, two children of a dead sister—received Maud Fair's entire estate, plus an additional $700,000 to be paid them by Mrs. Oelrichs and Mrs. Vanderbilt; in other words, the Nelsons received a round million dollars.

Abe Nelson, the spokesman for the clan, announced himself satisfied. Three hundred thousand cash had been paid on signing the agreement; the balance would be forthcoming in thirty days. On the eve of their return to Newmarket, Abe granted a final interview. He liked San Francisco fine and hoped to visit it again. The settlement was just to all concerned and everything had turned out fine. The Fair lawyers were fine men, and that went double for Herman Oelrichs. Oelrichs was a friendly, affable fellow and a sound businessman. Abe liked him fine.

One final scene brings the saga of the Fairs to an appropriate close. The bodies of Charles and his wife, sealed in lead caskets, with outer caskets of carved oak, were placed in an improvised chapel on the steamer *Saint Louis* and brought to America. In New York the bodies were transferred to a private car and dispatched across the continent, accompanied by Charley's two sisters, his brother-in-law William K. Vanderbilt Jr., two maids, and a valet. No member of the Nelson family was with the funeral party, but several were present on the morning of September 12 when the bodies were sealed in niches in the Fair mausoleum at Laurel Hill.

One incident marred the burial ceremony. Not only relatives and friends, but a huge crowd of the curious had gathered at the vault. As the services ended, an unidentified spectator stepped forward and picked a rosebud from the nearest of the imposing array of floral pieces. Another onlooker followed this lady's lead, then another, then several together. With startling suddenness the trickle of souvenir-hunters became a stream, the stream a river, and the river a tidal wave. In the melee that followed, scores of elaborate floral tributes were ripped apart and trampled underfoot. When, ten minutes later, a squad of policemen reached the scene, the mob had dispersed, leaving the area about the vault "looking as though it had been lashed by a hurricane." The police officers returned morosely to the station, stopping en route to hustle into the patrol wagon a man they had observed struggling along the sidewalk beneath an immense wreath of lilies of the valley and maidenhair fern.

In court a few days later the culprit—an unemployed barber—explained to the judge that he had intended the wreath as a belated present to his wife, who had celebrated her thirty-ninth birthday three weeks earlier. He was fined five dollars for petty theft, lectured on the sanctity of the grave, and given a thirty-day suspended sentence.

Part Four

Flood and O'Brien

1

JAMES CLAIR FLOOD was born in New York City on October 25, 1826. His parents were poor Irish immigrants; they sent him to one of the New York public schools for a few years, then apprenticed him to a carriage-maker. In 1849 he joined the migration to California, sailing round the Horn in the packet *Elizabeth Ellen*. He was then twenty-two and a skilled artisan, already beginning a determined campaign to lift himself out of the station into which he had been born. He had spent eight years making carriages for wealthy New Yorkers; some day, he told himself, he too would drive about in just such handsome vehicles. He was proud of the fact that his taste for luxury had developed early. In after years he liked to recall that he had come west in style: he had occupied a bunk in one of the deck-cabins of the *Elizabeth Ellen* and eaten with the gentry; no cramped and airless 'tween-deck quarters for him.

But there was no demand for custom-built carriages in San Francisco, and young Flood turned his hand to carpentry, then abandoned its sixteen-dollar-a-day wage to try his luck in the placers. He spent the winter of 1850–1 on the north fork of the Yuba, where his success must

have been better than that of most, for he was presently
back in San Francisco with three thousand dollars in gold
dust. That fall he took passage for home, traveling by
steamer (not steerage) to Panama, crossing the Isthmus,
and arriving in New York toward the end of 1851. Almost
immediately he turned westward again, this time going as
far as southern Illinois, where he bought a farm and prepared to grow up with the country. But pioneering on the
Western frontier was no life for a man who liked luxuries,
and a year later he sold out and headed again for California.

Some time during his wanderings, perhaps before his
first voyage to California, but more probably after his return from Illinois, he married. His bride was the former
Mary Leary, a native of Wexford County, Ireland, who
had migrated to the United States in 1844 and settled in
Brooklyn. Tradition states that her father, a fisherman,
had financed his daughter's passage to America by selling
the family cow. In any event, Flood's wife accompanied
him on his return to the West Coast. By 1854 he was in
business in San Francisco, conducting at the corner of
Ellis and Mason streets what some accounts state was a
livery stable and others say was a shop for the repair of
wagons. The enterprise, whatever it was, prospered for a
year or two, then the slack times of the middle 1850's
forced him into bankruptcy. He went back to carpentry,
punctiliously paying in full almost four thousand dollars
in debts.

During the time he had been in business he had become
acquainted with a neighboring shopkeeper, William S.
O'Brien, who traded in marine supplies. When O'Brien's
business also fell victim to the town's first depression, the
pair decided to try again, this time in partnership. The
question of what branch of trade to engage in received
much thought; both were determined to shun a business
subject to violent fluctuations between good times and bad.
It was O'Brien who hit on the answer. He had observed
that the average San Franciscan's thirst was as constant as
it was prodigious: robust in boom times, it showed no
noticeable falling off in periods of depression. "By

O'Brien's counsel . . . the two new friends came to the conclusion that the best thing they could do was to go into the liquor business."

Accordingly, in 1857, they opened a saloon. The venture prospered moderately, but their place of business, at the corner of Pacific and Stockton streets, was far from the center of town and they soon moved to a more desirable location. This was at 509 Washington Street, a few doors west of Sansome. The spot had two advantages: it was next door to the Washington Market, the town's most popular produce emporium, and in 1862, the newly organized Mining Exchange established itself in a building only a few yards farther west. Thus this Washington Street block soon became one of the busiest in the city. The two Irishmen called their establishment the Auction Lunch, partly in compliment to the many auction houses in the vicinity and perhaps also as a tactful means of calling attention to the fact that they (like most San Francisco saloon-keepers of the day) provided their patrons with a snack of food along with their drinks.

The Auction Lunch became popular throughout the neighborhood, not only for the geniality of its owners but for the variety and quality of its free-lunch counter. Over this O'Brien presided, slicing off slabs of thirst-producing ham or corned beef for every customer who, having patronized the bar, approached his counter. Later an aged Chinese, Wong Lee, wielded the carving knife, and O'Brien devoted himself exclusively to his duties as host; Flood remained behind the bar. Both men dressed flamboyantly. Many years later the *Chronicle* stated: "It was O'Brien's fashion to array himself in broadcloth and high silk hat, and so bedecked to stand outside the saloon and do the agreeable to the passing acquaintance, a little exercise of attention that generally led to an adjournment for a drink." Not to be outdone by his partner, Flood refused to wear the traditional white apron or to serve customers in his shirt-sleeves; his working costume was described as "a conventional gray business suit of excellent material and fashionable cut." Despite the sartorial splendor of its proprietors and its bountiful free lunch, the Auction Lunch was a "bit house"—that is, the cost of drinks was two for a quarter; more elegant establishments were "two-bit houses"—twenty-five cents straight.

Flood was below medium height, with a ruddy complexion, heavy features, a short neck, and massive shoulders. In the middle 1880's an acquaintance stated that a stranger might have mistaken him for a retired gymnast. But his physical aspect was misleading; behind his phlegmatic bearing and appearance were a shrewd and calculating mind, a volatile temperament, and a driving ambition to rise in the world. Unlike his genial but unenterprising partner—who would have been quite content to remain a tavern-keeper as long as he lived—Flood seems from the beginning to have looked on the Auction Lunch merely as a means to an end. In the discovery of the Nevada silver mines in 1859 and the establishment three years later of the local Mining Exchange he found his opportunity. He made himself agreeable to the brokers, who had formed the habit of dropping in for a drink whenever trading was dull, and before long he was playing the market moderately, acting on tips dropped by his broker friends. Most of these tentative fliers turned out well, and, captivated by the rewards and excitement of the game, he applied himself to a study of its intricacies.

A considerable native keenness, plus a patient cultivation of his sources of information, presently began to bear fruit. Through the middle sixties, while the fever of mining speculation mounted all over the Coast, he prudently widened the scope of his operations. By 1868 he and O'Brien—for the two remained partners in the new venture as in the old—had amassed considerable fortunes. A further step was indicated: Flood was ready to withdraw from the saloon business. The Auction Lunch was accordingly sold and Flood and O'Brien, stockbrokers, moved round the corner to upstairs offices on Montgomery Street. Next came their meeting with the two Virginia City speculators Mackay and Fair and their gamble for control of the Hale & Norcross. That successful coup was followed a year or two later by another: the new firm took over a number of unpromising properties near the northern end of the lode and combined them into a mine called the Consolidated Virginia.

Less than four years after they had left the Auction Lunch, Flood and O'Brien were jointly enjoying an income in excess of half a million dollars a month.

2

THE uses to which they put this mighty stream of dollars long interested thousands all over the West. O'Brien, for all his picturesque garb, was a man of unshakably plebeian tastes, quite without pretensions, and with no wish to lift himself above the sphere into which he had been born. The possession of multiple millions affected his manner of life far less than that of his partners. To be sure, he moved out of the hotel room that had been his bachelor quarters for years and into a moderately elaborate residence he had bought from another Comstock millionaire, William Sharon: a square, three-story frame building at 517 Sutter Street. But he was at pains to make it clear that this was not because he planned a career in San Francisco society: it was to provide a suitable home for his widowed sister, Marie Coleman, and her three children, his nephews and nieces. His subsequent behavior bore out his announced intention not to permit wealth to become a burden. Both business cares and social responsibilities rested lightly on his shoulders, and he was far more often to be found taking his ease with friends of his saloon-keeping days than in the office of the bonanza firm or among the elegant furnishings of his Sutter Street drawing-room.

His full name was William Shoney O'Brien; like his future partner Mackay, he was born in Dublin and brought to New York as a child, an unregarded unit in the wave of Irish immigrants that washed over the country during the first third of the century. As a youth he worked in a New York grocery store until, like tens of thousands the world over, he was uprooted by the rush to California. He was twenty-three when he landed at San Francisco on

July 6, 1849. His subsequent business life became a series
of partnerships, first with William C. Hoff in a tobacco
shop and newspaper agency, next with W. J. Rosner in
ship chandlery. Then, in 1856, began his association with
Flood, a connection that progressed from saloon-keeping
to dealing in silver stocks, to the ownership of bonanza
mines, to banking and real estate. He died possessed of
about twelve million dollars.

He had neither taste nor talent for money-making; that
he amassed so considerable a fortune was due to a series
of lucky accidents. O'Brien himself was aware of this. He
had a stock answer to those who asked him to explain his
puzzling rise to affluence: he had caught hold of the tail
of an ascending kite and hung on. Geniality no less than
modesty was an outstanding O'Brien characteristic, and
through the late seventies San Franciscans came to know
him as "the jolly millionaire." The gregarious instinct, traditional with the Irish, was his in special measure: he
lived by preference in the center of a crowd. During his
first California years he was a member of one of the San
Francisco volunteer fire companies, which were primarily
social clubs and only incidentally concerned with putting
down the town's periodical holocausts. In after years he
was far more proud of having once been foreman of California Engine Company No. 4 than of his membership in
the wealthiest and most powerful mining combine ever
seen in the West. In 1862, true to his Irish heritage, he ran
for public office, but when he was badly defeated for a
seat in the state assembly, he permanently abandoned
thoughts of a career in politics.

He was the oldest and least forceful of the bonanza
group, but always the most popular. "He had more friends
in all walks of life, and fewer enemies, than falls to the
lot of most rich men," commented the *Alta California*.
It was generally understood that he had been carried to
affluence by Flood, and the latter was not averse to furthering that belief; once, soon after O'Brien's death, he
stated that all his life he had made it a rule to have nothing that Billy O'Brien didn't share. But there is evidence
that O'Brien contributed more to the partnership than he

was usually given credit for. Almost from the beginning there were quarrels among his strong-willed and acquisitive associates. Soft-spoken, mild-mannered Billy O'Brien, who had no personal axes to grind, never became involved in them, and thus he preserved to the end both the friendship and the respect of the others. Moreover, after his partners' wealth and ambition had widened the breach between them and the circles from which they had sprung, O'Brien's geniality and unassuming manner did much to soften the rancor of a suspicious and hostile public.

On the other hand, he consistently refused to carry his share of the firm's responsibilities. Although in 1875 he paid twenty-five thousand dollars for a seat in the San Francisco Stock and Exchange Board, he seldom used it, having neither taste nor aptitude for stock-trading. That aspect of the firm's operations he was content to leave in the competent hands of Flood. Instead, he devoted himself intermittently to investing the firm's surplus funds in San Francisco real estate, although it is not now clear how large his operations were in this field, or how successful. He had a quarter interest in the stock of the Nevada Bank, served on its board of directors, and maintained an office in the Nevada Block on the corner of Montgomery and Pine streets. But those who had business with him well knew that he rarely visited it. He regularly spent his afternoons in the back room of McGovern's saloon on Kearny Street, playing endless games of pedro with a group of cronies. The stakes were low, but at his elbow O'Brien kept a tall stack of silver dollars. It was understood that any habitué of the place who happened to be down on his luck was welcome to help himself. Whenever the supply of dollars ran low, O'Brien would summon the barkeep, pass him a twenty-dollar gold piece, and a new stack would appear on the table-edge.

Because he preferred to take his relaxation at McGovern's rather than in the spacious barrooms of the Palace Hotel or the Lick House, where others of the town's rich men forgathered, the public came to regard him as an ignorant fellow with a taste for low companions. This widely held view was inaccurate. O'Brien was not the un-couth, clay-pipe-smoking Irishman of the funny papers; he was in fact a man of considerable native dignity, courteous, kindly, and considerate. On the infrequent occasions when he appeared at the social functions to which his wealth gave him entrée, he "looked as though he belonged there." Gertrude Atherton, then a young ma-tron with literary ambitions, recalls seeing him once, at a fashionable ball at the Occidental Hotel, and the impres-sion that brief encounter made on her remained vividly in mind more than sixty years later. He entered the bril-liantly gas-lit ballroom with his sister Mrs. Coleman on his arm, his erect figure, graying hair, and black eyes drawing the attention of all. Mrs. Coleman was an un-commonly handsome woman, tall, blonde, and dignified, "with the bearing of an Irish princess." Mrs. Atherton thought them by far the most striking couple in the room; the O'Briens, she believed, must have come of good stock. He had another sister, Mrs. Kate McDonough; both were women of beauty and both long ornamented San Fran-cisco society. O'Brien was inordinately proud of this decorative pair and he delighted to surround them with luxuries: houses and jewels and travel, carriages and coachmen and Paris gowns. His generosity extended to his nephews and nieces, the numerous brood of Colemans and McDonoughs. But for himself he preferred the com-panions of his carefree first years in California. He stub-bornly continued to cultivate them as long as he lived.

3

THE tastes of his friend Jim Flood ran in other directions. As his wealth increased he was able to indulge his liking for luxurious living on a scale that set new standards in the West. In the spring of 1875 a New York weekly, the *Spirit of the Times,* devoted a page to the sudden rise of Flood & O'Brien, which it termed "the wealthiest firm in America and prospectively the richest in the world." Flood was then living in the modest Ellis Street house he had purchased during his saloon-keeping days; however, he had celebrated his new prosperity by buying the costliest carriage the market afforded, and the handsomest team of horses. With a liveried servant in the box and his wife and two children beside him, he took daily rides through the downtown streets and over the sandy roads to the Cliff House. Meantime he was looking about for a residence more in keeping with his station. Eventually he bought, from John Selby, ex-mayor of San Francisco, a handsome peninsula estate called Fair Oaks; the local press reported that he planned to expend a round million dollars in its enlargement and elaboration.

Fair Oaks was the first of a series of Flood mansions, each more costly than the one before, the building and furnishing of which intermittently claimed the attention of San Franciscans for nearly half a century. Fair Oaks did not satisfy him for long; after only a year or two he announced that he was abandoning that by no means unpretentious country estate in favor of a far more elaborate one. He had acquired a thirty-five-acre tract of oak-studded land at Menlo Park, encircled it with a high iron fence, and begun the construction of Linden Towers. That intricate structure long remained northern California's prize exhibit in the field of baroque architecture. It was five years building—an extraordinary mass of turrets and gables, culminating in a hundred-and-fifty-foot tower. Until it was demolished, in the early 1930's, it remained one of the show places of the San Francisco peninsula. Generations of passers-by on Middlefield Road, viewing its white-painted bulk through the oaks, knew it as "Flood's wedding cake"—a singularly apt description.

During the seventies Menlo Park was a stronghold of the conservative Southern set that had long dominated San Francisco's social life, and Flood's invasion of their bailiwick filled them with what one writer described as "a boundless lack of enthusiasm." Young Mrs. Atherton, who had recently gone to live at the Athertons' Menlo estate, Valparaiso Park, witnessed the flurry of indignation when news reached the colony that Jim Flood, late of the Auction Lunch, planned to settle in their midst. Many years later she wrote in her autobiography: "For weeks the leading topic on the verandah was whether or not the Floods should be called on when they moved in." The issue was eventually decided, not by the ladies (who well knew how to repel such "impertinent invasions"), but by their more practical-minded husbands, who foresaw that to snub a member of the powerful bonanza firm might jeopardize their business connections in the city. Accordingly, in due time the Athertons, Parrots, Howards, and Macondrays ordered their carriages and set off to pay formal calls at Linden Towers. There the ladies, having sipped tea from Dresden cups and admired the handsome service of Comstock silver, were taken on extended tours of the mansion. They duly admired the immense drawing-room finished in carved walnut with walls of embossed velvet, the music-room in rose and satinwood, the dining-room paneled in English mahogany with ceiling frescoes by a noted Italian artist whose name was unfortunately unpronounceable. Outside, the guests inspected the stable, with stalls for twenty horses, a carriage-room "as large as a hotel ballroom," and harness-room and grooms' quarters finished in primavera wood. After viewing the sixty-foot fountain and the artificial lake stocked with game fishes, the ladies withdrew; but men callers (who were understood to be interested in such matters) were taken farther afield to admire the private racetrack, the water and gas works, and the ingenious arrangement by which household sewage was conveyed a full half mile to the most costly of cesspools.

When Mrs. Flood and her daughter Jennie returned the call of the Athertons at Valparaiso Park, the young daughter-in-law of the latter family missed no detail. With the appraising eye of the budding novelist, Gertrude Atherton observed—and remembered for half a century—that Mrs. Flood wore "a flowing dark blue silk wrapper, discreetly ruffled, and 'Miss Jennie' a creation of turquoise-green flannel, trimmed with deep flounces of Valenciennes lace." Mrs. Atherton, who considered such garb unduly elaborate for informal afternoon calls in the country, imagined that the Flood ladies looked with disdain on the modest scale of life at Valparaiso Park. She watched their departure without regret. "They went away," she concluded tartly, "with the pleasant feeling of superiority that only multiple-millions can give."

But not all the peninsula residents were as hidebound as the Athertons and their neighbors; besides, the newcomers contributed liberally to all the fashionable charities, and dinners at Linden Towers were commendably long and elaborate. The social life of the Floods expanded. Through the hospitable 1880's nearly every distinguished figure who visited the Coast was carried off for a week-end at one or another of the big houses that dotted the oak-strewn plains between Belmont and Palo Alto. Few returned without at least a brief stop at Linden Towers. Thus in the reminiscences of eminent men in many fields one sometimes encounters a paragraph or two describing the magnificence of this California country estate and paying tribute to the hospitality of its host.

Sometimes the abundant refreshments set before such callers proved an embarrassment not only to the visitors but to their hosts. The entire state was amused when, in 1879, General Grant reached San Francisco after his world tour, and Senator Sharon triumphantly bore him off for a week-end at Belmont. Sharon was persuaded to bring his guests for an afternoon call on the Floods; the Senator, however, had planned an elaborate banquet at Belmont that evening, to which two hundred guests had been invited. Prudent host that he was, he had exacted a promise that the visitors would be offered only the lightest of refreshments. Mrs. Flood agreed. It would be the most insubstantial of repasts, the merest snack. Sharon and his guests arrived, were driven to Linden Towers—which Grant viewed with "unmeasured admiration"—and ushered into the dining-room. There the Senator's worst fears were realized. "A luncheon of many courses was served, and he was obliged to sit through it with an appearance of pleased enjoyment while his guests did it full justice. He watched, you might say, the edge of appetite for his surpassing dinner that night ruthlessly destroyed."

This luncheon became memorable for another reason,

for it marked the beginning of a romance that captured the attention of the entire country. In the Grant party was the general's second son, Ulysses, Jr., known to his intimates as Buck, a personable young man in his early twenties. A friendship sprang up between him and Flood's daughter Jennie, whose real name was Cora Jane. She was among the group that accompanied the Grants to Yosemite; there the romance progressed so rapidly that when the party returned to San Francisco an announcement of their engagement was daily expected. No announcement was made, however, and it was commonly believed that it was being withheld on Flood's insistence. Young Grant was penniless; Flood is said to have pointed out that for him to marry a rich girl would lay him open to the charge of being a fortune-hunter. Flood thereupon put in operation a plan he had often followed when he wished to elevate deserving friends to the ranks of the affluent: he supplied his prospective son-in-law with a stake and launched him on the stock market, telling him what stocks to deal in and exactly when to buy or sell. In six months—so runs the legend—Buck's expertly supervised operations had netted him a hundred-thousand-dollar profit, and Flood made known that he would no longer oppose an announcement of his daughter's engagement. But many weeks passed and young Grant, who had meantime returned east, showed a reluctance to return to his fiancée. Rumors began to circulate that Buck's successes had turned his head; he had come to consider himself a financial wizard, no longer in need of Flood's guiding hand. When he eventually reached California, he failed to hasten to Menlo Park. Displaying a patience extraordinary in a lover, he tarried so long in San Francisco that Jennie Flood presently lost her temper and dispatched a curt note breaking the engagement.

This version of the Flood-Grant romance was widely publicized at the time; how closely it approximates the truth cannot be known, since neither party saw fit to enlighten the avidly interested public. Buck Grant presently married, and during the next half-dozen years Jennie Flood was periodically reported engaged to a succession of highly eligible young men. But no confirmation was ever forthcoming, and gradually her interest shifted to the more sober pursuits of philanthropy. She lived until 1929 and died a confirmed spinster; she was sixty-seven.

4

THE building of Linden Towers did not long satisfy Flood's persistent liking for display. The urge to surround himself with visible evidences of his wealth and power did not grow less with the years. His early ambition to own the finest of carriages was amply realized: the Flood coupés and traps and broughams were the envy of thousands, their paneled sides and fragile wheels polished to the brilliance of mirrors; burnished silver harness fittings gleamed on his perfectly matched horses, and his coachmen were resplendent in plum-colored livery. Flood's passage through the San Francisco streets was never anonymous. "When he drives up to the entrance to the Nevada Block," stated the *Chronicle* in 1879, "a hush settles over Montgomery Street . . . it is thus that Queen Victoria arrives to open Parliament. . . ."

It was not in the Flood carriages, however, but in his succession of elaborate residences that his taste for magnificence was given full rein. Hardly had he moved into Linden Towers when he was laying plans for a town house that would overshadow its Nob Hill neighbors as completely as his country estate dominated the Menlo plains. In 1882 he bought the block bounded by California, Mason, Sacramento, and Cushman streets and began building a forty-two-room mansion: a square, three-story structure with outer walls of Connecticut sandstone, topped by an eighty-foot tower. Through the middle and late eighties every Californian who read his newspaper at all attentively was familiar with the dimensions and décor of its vast rooms: a forty-foot reception parlor finished in East Indian style; a Louis XV drawing-room forty-six feet long; a twenty-six-by-forty-six-foot dining-room paneled in carved San Domingo mahogany, and—not least—

a smoking-room done in authentic Moorish style, with domed skylight of iridescent glass.

Curiously it was not the house itself that enthralled the town, but the block-long fence that surrounded it. "Flood's thirty-thousand-dollar brass rail" remained for years a major civic landmark. "The beautifully wrought metal," wrote Amelia Neville, "flashed for the entire length of . . . the square where the brownstone mansion stood, and it was the sole task of one retainer to keep it bright. Passing any hour of the day one discovered him polishing away at some section of it." A pretty legend sprang up about this fence and did much to broaden its fame. Generations of San Franciscans believed that Flood (in a mood of humility that was hardly characteristic) had caused his Nob Hill house to be encircled by a polished brass rail as a reminder of his saloon-keeping days. Unfortunately for this pleasant fancy, the fence is in fact not brass but bronze. It passed undamaged through the 1906 fire and remains today as sound as ever, though much less highly polished. The mansion itself was gutted, but the sandstone walls suffered little damage. The interior was reconstructed and two wings were added; today it houses the most luxurious of the city's clubs, the Pacific Union.

Despite his Auction Lunch background, Flood was the least approachable of the partners, and as the firm rose in power and influence, he went to ever greater lengths to shut himself off from the clamoring hordes that swarmed about the city's multimillionaires. Mackay was notoriously an easy mark for panhandlers of every rank and hue, and men with personal axes to grind, from speculators seeking stock-market tips to promoters of wildcat mining schemes, had little difficulty gaining the ear of Fair or O'Brien. From the importunities of this gentry Flood protected himself with extreme care. His office in the Nevada Block could be reached only by passing through two outer rooms, in each of which a clerk was stationed, charged with learning the exact nature of a prospective caller's business. As an added precaution, the door to the inner office had a lock that could be opened only by the chief clerk's key. A former employee once remarked: "It is easier for an unwelcome caller to get into the vaults of the Bank of England than into Flood's *sanctum sanctorum*."

But to those who successfully ran the outer gamut, Flood was the opposite of austere. George Littleton Upshur, for several years his chief clerk, called him direct and kindly, but added that on occasion he could be implacable. The implacable moods were usually in the ascendant when he suspected that others were plotting raids on the assets of the firm. "He was daily subjected to violent personal attacks," continued Upshur. "He passed them off with an indifferent shrug. But let anyone so much as hint that the firm was withholding a disproportionate share of the bonanza profits and his cries of rage could be heard in the next county." This picture of the phlegmatic Irishman "wailing like a banshee" is hard to credit, but the fact remains that when the firm's methods were under attack it was Flood who delivered promptest counterblows. When the partners established the Nevada Bank in San Francisco and so brought to the bay city their feud with the Bank of California that had been raging on the Comstock, the rival bank's president, William C. Ralston, announced that he would "send Flood back to selling rum at the Auction." Flood retorted that if he ever returned to serving drinks it would not be at his old Washington Street bar, but over the counter of the Bank of California. A few months later, however, when the impending failure of Ralston's great banking house presented an opportunity to carry out his threat, Flood's anger had cooled. When word reached him that the rival bank was in difficulties, he disregarded the advice of friends and refused to withdraw a very large sum he had on deposit there.

Notwithstanding his lack of the affability that distinguished his three partners, Flood was not the frigid egoist he was sometimes pictured. Like Mackay—and unlike Fair and O'Brien—he recognized that the possession of a large fortune involved a certain amount of philanthropy, and his contributions to worthy charities were always liberal though seldom anonymous. In the middle seventies he inaugurated a custom of sending checks each Christmas to the city's orphan asylums and old people's homes, a practice that became a family tradition and was continued for years. But Mackay's habit of indiscriminately passing out gifts, thinly disguised as loans, to anyone with a sufficiently moving hard-luck story left his partner cold. Flood maintained that to dole out unearned cash destroyed not only the recipient's initiative but his self-respect as well—a view that Mackay himself came to share.

Flood ordered these things differently. His way of taking care of friends who were down on their luck had been demonstrated in Buck Grant's case. Usually he bought for their account a hundred shares of one of the bonanza firm's stocks that was due for a rise, later selling them and turning over the profit—which might run into the thousands—with the admonition that the money be deposited in a savings bank and used only for unavoidable expenses. This was the device he used to aid those whom he considered financially inept; men better equipped to cope with stock-market operations received more substantial aid. "To have the confidence and friendship of a great manipulator in prosperous times, is a sure road to wealth," wrote Joseph L. King, long chairman of the San Francisco Exchange. King went on to list five men whom Flood had enriched: George Wallace, Cornelius O'Conner, W. S. Lyle, George Congdon, and J. W. Brown. On this list should surely have been R. H. Follis, Flood's brother-in-law. During the years when Flood and O'Brien were operating the Auction Lunch, Follis sold butter at a booth in the Washington Market next door. Under Flood's direction he began trading in Comstock stocks, with such success that by the time Flood died, Follis was one of the town's wealthiest men, a director of the Nevada Bank, with large holdings in numerous industrial concerns.

Loyalty to his friends was an outstanding Flood trait, and it sometimes got him into hot water. One of his habits was to send up to the Comstock a great many young men, sons or nephews or sons-in-law of San Francisco acquaintances, each with a letter directing that a place be found for him in one of the firm's enterprises. For a time Fair and Mackay uncomplainingly put the newcomers on the firm's payroll. But of course few of them had any practical experience in mining, and the Virginia City partners presently grew tired of finding berths for them. At length Fair hit on a solution: the tenderfoot was given pick and miner's lantern and dispatched to the mines' deepest and hottest levels. One eight-hour shift below— where the temperature hovered around 130 degrees—was always enough: the victims willingly abandoned hopes of a career in mining and took the first train home. Fair once remarked that Flood's young men usually made the round trip in three days.

5

FLOOD'S latter years were far from tranquil. Despite the pleasure he derived from indulging his taste for display and guiding friends along the path to fortune, there must have been times when he looked back with regret to the uncomplicated days when he had addressed himself to slaking San Francisco's monumental thirst. For he early discovered that while his wealth gave him a considerable degree of influence over the fortunes of his fellow citizens, it won him neither their confidence nor their friendship. Rightly or not, he was ever the least popular of the silver kings; not even Fair was so often a target for the town's crusading newspapers. This was partly due to his austerity of manner; he could not hope to emulate the geniality of his partners, his temperamental reserve rendered impossible all such displays of warm and easy good-fellowship. But it was due too to the fact that the public recognized that in matters of finance Flood was the ablest of the quartet and they held him responsible for the manipulation of bonanza stocks that periodically disrupted the economy of the Coast, impoverishing thousands.

The discovery of the big bonanza in the fall of 1874 had of course electrified the West, and many had looked on the controlling group as the instruments by which the Pacific

Coast was to enter an era of limitless prosperity, with ease and luxury for all. Only a few months were needed to make clear the unsubstantial nature of that hope. That the discovery was creating huge fortunes for the bonanza firm soon became evident, but the expectation that any substantial share of the profits would reach the public was speedily abandoned. "It grows clear," stated a writer in the *Golden Era* in 1875, "that the policy of the mine's managers is to retain complete control of the enterprise," and he went on to cite the extremely lucrative mining and lumbering contracts the firm members had proceeded to award to the companies they owned. These developments, plus a growing conviction that Flood was using his inside knowledge of the mines' day-by-day prospects to further heavy trading on the Mining Exchange, completed the public's disillusion. The firm's popularity vanished as quickly as it had been created. Many thousands who had invested—and lost—their savings were convinced that they had been duped; their cries of fraud and chicanery grew progressively louder.

By 1876 the disgruntled stockholders had found an able spokesman in Squire P. Dewey. Dewey, once proprietor of a crockery store in New York City, had joined the rush in 1849 and, after a season as an auctioneer, had become an important San Francisco businessman. Like everyone else he had been speculating heavily in the bonanza shares and—again like everyone else—he had found nothing wrong with the mines' management so long as the large monthly dividends were paid and the market value of the stock continued to rise. In the fall of 1875, however, the great Virginia City fire destroyed both mills and hoisting works, bringing operations to a standstill until buildings and equipment could be replaced. Viewing this situation, Dewey concluded that the cost of reconstruction, plus the stoppage of production, might well exhaust the company's cash reserve and force a suspension of dividends, with a consequent decline in its stock. He accordingly visited Flood's well-guarded office and, having gained entrance, asked the amount of the company's cash balance. Flood replied that it was between $400,000 and

$500,000. Dewey, accepting that figure, calculated that the trustees must perforce pass dividends for at least two months. "I did," he stated, "what any prudent business-man would have done under similar circumstances—I sold largely of my bonanza stocks at the then depreciated market rates."

When, however, the next dividend day approached and the trustees authorized its payment as usual—the sum involved was in excess of a million dollars—Dewey returned to the bonanza office, where he was told that when he had made his first inquiry the cash on hand was not around half a million dollars, as Flood had stated, but two and a quarter millions. Dewey thereupon repurchased his shares, not at the low price he had visualized, but at a substantial advance. His loss on the transaction exceeded fifty thousand dollars, which was bad enough, but more galling was a growing suspicion that Flood had deliberately misled him. He became convinced that the bonanza firm, in order to depress the stock, had purposely spread abroad the impression that dividends were to be suspended, thereby permitting Flood to buy in at bargain prices whatever shares were forced on the market.

The truth of this charge was never established, but, plot or not, the episode won the enmity of Dewey, and during the next three years he caused the bonanza kings endless trouble. Abetted by the *Chronicle,* the *Post,* and the *Golden Era,* he kept up a steady and telling fire against the antecedents, background, personal characteristics, and business ethics of the new silver magnates. "It is one of fortune's freaks," he stated in a typical blast, "that found this mine in the control and under the administration of four men without education, business habits or experience, without standing or respectable position in the commercial, financial or social world, and possessing no qualities of mind or character adapted to the situation in which accident placed them. . . ." The *Chronicle,* having pictured the blighting effect on the community of the frenzied bonanza stock speculation, chimed in with: "The body politic is enfeebled by paralysis, while a few of its least important members are gorged with the life-blood that once gave vigor to its veins." The *Golden Era* joined the chorus with gleeful references to the "rhinoceros-like hide" of ex-saloon-keeper Flood, adding: "In future the stock business will be like Flood's old whisky shop— strictly a ten cent business."

But this was only the curtain-raiser. Other stockholders rallied to Dewey's banner and moved in force on the annual meeting of 1877. Immediately after Superintendent Fair finished reading his report, Dewey was on his feet, prepared to oppose the firm at every turn. "All we want," he announced, "is information—all the information that exists from day to day regarding the development of the mine. This alone will give all an equal chance, and preserve them from becoming the victims of designing stock manipulators." In the subsequent debate much attention was paid to a device called the diamond drill. Dewey contended that with this instrument it was possible for insiders to explore the mines far beyond the faces of the drifts, thereby gaining knowledge of the extent and quality of the ore yet to be mined—information that was kept secret from all but the controlling group.

Mackay here broke in to deny hotly that the diamond drill had ever been put to such uses. At this juncture the eyes of all were drawn to a singular figure: one James White, an elderly Englishman who had long represented the city of Brighton in Parliament, and who had invested forty thousands pounds in Consolidated Virginia stocks. White chanced to be in San Francisco on a world tour and Dewey had brought him to the meeting. It proved to be a shrewd move, for the picturesque Briton made a sensation. "His long hair, among whose gold there were many silver threads," commented the *Post,* "gave him a Druidical appearance that won the instant attention of the meeting." His remarks, however, were those of a hard-headed businessman, concerned about the yield and safety of his investment. He explained that he was appearing informally not only on his own behalf but on that of other British shareholders, who were dissatisfied with the lack of frankness exhibited by the mine's managers. This was a trait, he stated, contrary to the English habit of complete candor in all business transactions. To Mackay these remarks had the effect a red flag is supposed to have on a bull. The short-tempered Irishman sprang to his feet and, purple with rage, demanded to know what any Englishman could possibly know about the operation of an American mine. If the gentleman was so well posted on such matters, he shouted, let him come up to Virginia and give the managers the benefit of his vast knowledge.

The Mackay-White feud continued throughout the afternoon, and it was not the Englishman who came off second best. At one juncture Mackay thundered: "You are not a stockholder, Mr. White." "Yes, sir, I am," White retorted, "and a large stockholder, too, I'm sorry to say." Thereupon he drew from an inner pocket of his jacket a sheaf of certificates and, approaching Mackay, "waved them like a banner under his nose," adding: "And I have more at home; I just brought these as a sample."

"The debate at this juncture became sharp, confused and acrimonious," stated the *Chronicle*. Some of the exchanges were reported verbatim. Mackay: "It seems odd to hear an Englishman charge anybody with dishonesty." Voice in the rear: "For shame!" Mackay: "I don't believe there's an honest man in London!" White: "It is hardly fair to reproach a man on account of his country." Voice in the rear: "I think you ought to show some courtesy to this gentleman, who is a foreigner." Tempers cooled and for a time decorum prevailed. It ended abruptly when one of the adherents of the Mackay-Flood group got the floor and presented a resolution thanking the trustees for their efficient management during the year. Voice: "It should be carried." Mackay: "By a large majority." Dewey: "The idea of bringing in such a whitewashing resolution!" White: "Monstrous! Monstrous!" This brought Mackay to his feet again, shouting anathemas at meddlesome Englishmen in general and James White in particular. The resolution of thanks did not come to a vote.

Next day the town's newspapers deplored the bad manners and arrogance of the bonanza group, with special attention to Mackay's behavior. "In his eagerness to justify the conduct of the firm," stated the *Post*, "he brought to his aid bad grammar, ungentlemanly retort, and all the conceit which the consciousness of great wealth can inspire. . . ." The *News-Letter,* hardly less restrained in its language than Mackay had been, referred to the reigning King of the Comstock as "a scrub who, raised from nothing, has attained to nothing except dirty purse pride"— and proceeded to denounce his remarks to White as a "brutal assault" on that gentleman, a "vile slander" on the city of London, and a "vulgar outrage" on the British race—a comprehensive indictment indeed. The *Mail,* after a passing reference to "the indecent and outrageous demeanor of Mr. Flood," turned its full armament on "the magnificent Mackay"—who, it added, "is indignant at the public's want of appreciation of the disinterested course pursued by the firm in kindly looking after 'Con. Vir.' for a trifling remuneration of about ninety cents of every dollar it produces. . . ." In the same vein this paper concluded: "If Mr. Mackay, who condescends to exist upon an earth not peopled exclusively by millionaires . . . is really so tired of 'me and Fair's' ineffectual struggle to give satisfaction, let him resign and permit the stockholders to try someone else. . . . Let him run over to Europe and appall the effete monarchies with his wealth and weariness. There's no place like 'the continent' for satisfying display of big diamonds and small souls." The *Golden Era* concluded its account by commenting wryly: "Mr. White will return to England with an idea of American hospitality and American mining men that will reflect no credit on either."

It is likely that the ferocity of many of these journalistic onslaughts was inspired (as both Flood and Mackay contended) by the malice of owners and editors who had lost heavily through speculating in bonanza stocks. Many believed that the *Chronicle*'s enmity could be so explained. That influential journal had championed the bonanza group while they were rising to power; and its dominant owner, Charles De Young, after an inspection of the Consolidated Virginia, had invested heavily in its stock. Later he had sold out at a time when that erratic stock was at one of its periodical lows and had thereupon demanded

that Flood make good his loss. Flood refused. "It would
have cost the firm fifty thousand dollars," he explained.
"We didn't consider the *Chronicle*'s support worth that
amount of money." Perhaps there were times when Flood
regretted that decision, for the *Chronicle*'s relentless campaign continued as long as the firm remained active. That
the *Golden Era*'s opposition was not without a personal
bias its owner, Ferdinand Ewer, frankly admitted; one of
his weekly editorials on the sins of the "Nevada Block
conspirators" ended with a plaintive reference to "the
few thousands which my grandfather and my father
earned for me to lose at Mr. Flood's dead-open-and-shut
game."

But that the partners were themselves chiefly responsible for the low esteem in which they were held in San
Francisco (only two of the city's seven papers had a word
to say in their defense) is clear enough. As controlling
owners of both the Consolidated Virginia and the California they were able to elevate and depress the market at
will; and few doubted that they used this power consistently and skillfully in their heavy stock-market trading. One
writer estimated that by such operations Flood and his
partners realized a profit of three million dollars each. This
was of course in addition to their earnings from milling
fees and from their control of the sources of timber, fuel,
water, and other necessary supplies.

The revolt of 1876 was mainly an attempt to put an end
to what Dewey termed the firm's stranglehold on the
bonanza and to preserve for the benefit of stockholders
the stream of profits that flowed through their subsidiary
corporations into the pockets of Flood and his partners.
In particular, the contract with the Pacific Mill and Mining Company came under fire. Citing the annual reports
since 1874, Dewey pointed out that in thirty-two months
Consolidated Virginia stockholders had paid $5,320,000
in milling fees, of which at least one-half represented
profit. But this was only part of their gain, for the contract specified that all tailings became the property of the
mill-owners. "The great value of these tailings," Dewey
continued, "will be seen by the following: the bullion

product of the Consolidated Virginia mine has been in round numbers, $39,000,000; the percentage realized from the mills in reduction averages about seventy per cent of the assay value, which would give the enormous sum of $16,700,000 to the tailings, of which probably one half can be recovered by these mill owners. . . ."

Dewey thereupon presented a resolution instructing the trustees to enter into negotiations with the Pacific Mill and Mining Company for the purchase of its mill "at any reasonable price, and in the event of a failure to effect such a purchase, they are instructed to purchase any other desirable mill property, or to cause to be constructed without delay one or more mills adequate to the necessities of the company." The resolution never came to a vote; Judge Heydenfelt, chief of the Consolidated Virginia's legal staff, got the floor and reminded the stockholders that their recommendations were not binding on the trustees. "The stockholders delegate their power, and their only remedy is to take care whom they elect. These resolutions are simply mandatory to the attention of the board, and they won't obey the directions unless they choose to do so. They have been selected on account of their knowledge, ability and skill to manage this business. They know how to manage it, and the stockholders don't know how. At best, resolutions are but advisory."

In face of this opinion, the resolution was withdrawn. The bonanza-firm members, holding a clear majority of the stock, proceeded to re-elect themselves to the board of trustees for another year. For the time being, the revolt of the minority stockholders gained them nothing in a material sense, but their revelations focused attention on the methods of the controlling group. Opposition grew stronger month by month, and at length more effectual measures began to be taken.

Early in 1878 John H. Burke, formerly a *Chronicle* reporter, filed a series of stockholders' suits against the Consolidated Virginia trustees for the return of profits alleged to have been unlawfully appropriated by the firm. The figures were impressive: four millions from the sale of lumber; twenty-six millions in excessive milling charges;

ten millions that the firm members were said to have realized through buying with their personal funds a mine property adjacent to the bonanza and reselling it to the corporation; the total was in excess of forty millions.

The "Burke suits" attracted attention all over the Coast; for months the papers daily printed columns of testimony pro and con. The journals favorable to the partners—led by the *Alta* in San Francisco (owned by Fair) and the *Enterprise* in Virginia City (which Mackay had recently purchased)—denounced the actions as preposterous and heaped ridicule on Burke, Dewey, and their supporters, calling them indiscriminately "blackmailers," "malcontents," and "extortionists." Papers that took an opposite view were no less candid; their references to the firm members bristled with such terms as "sharks," "crooks," "scrubs," "bulldozers," and "bloated aristocrats." The *News-Letter* commented: "Such vampires deserve the emphatic and unmistakable expression of public indignation and abhorrence," while the *Chronicle* in one of its comparatively mild moods likened the four to "venomous reptiles" that, "seeking to divert public attention from the chapter of wrongs and outrages charged against them, muddy the waters in which they are floundering by ejecting inky slime against others. . . ." Not since gold-rush days had personal journalism (long a tradition on the Coast) been distinguished by so engaging a frankness.

The progress of Burke's lawsuits was closely watched elsewhere than on the Pacific Coast, and with mingled feelings. For the litigation turned on the question of the legality of the bonanza-firm members having, as managing directors of the mines, awarded extremely liberal contracts to companies that they themselves owned. It was true—as the partners did not fail to point out—that this was a strategy widely practiced at the time; it had in fact been the foundation of some of the largest fortunes amassed during the sixties and seventies. All over the nation men who had been operating such lucrative profit mills foresaw that, should the court uphold Burke's contention, they might be forced to disgorge many millions. At the same time stockholders of dozens of corporations had pleasant visions of large and totally unexpected windfalls. In the end, the fears of one group and the hopes of the other proved groundless: three of the Burke suits were decided in favor of the defendants and the fourth resulted in a compromise by which the bonanza firm returned to the Consolidated Virginia treasury some three hundred thousand dollars—and received the major share of it back again when the next dividend was paid.

But facts brought to light during the trials were damaging to the firm's prestige, and thereafter apologists for the group were hard put to it to justify their methods. Even so mild a critic as Eliot Lord, whose *Comstock Mining and Miners* is the reverse of harsh in its judgment of the Mackay-Fair group, was forced to this admission:

"It is true that bonanza mine managers have received, in various ways, the lion's share of the profits from the ore extracted; they have had the greater portion of the shares of the bonanza mines and have made large gains as mill-owners. . . . If any of their acts . . . have been illegal, measures can be taken to obtain restitution. . . . The truth of the main charge against them is admitted—that, while serving as trustees of the mining companies, they made contracts for crushing ore of these companies with themselves as mill-owners. . . . In so doing, however, they have followed notorious precedents, and in so far can plead custom, if not justification. Trustees of a mining company that considered the company's interest before their own would have erected corporation mills, or awarded contracts for milling to the lowest responsible bidders . . . but this would have been a nearer approach to ideal management than has been attempted at the Washoe mines. . . . Whether such officials exist, except in Utopia, is gravely questioned . . . and the doubt may be justified; but it is certain that no well-directed attempt to discover them has yet been made. . . ."

6

ALL through the seventies San Franciscans kept close and critical watch on the lode, for the fortunes of the metropolis had come to be inseparably linked with the ore bodies beneath the parched flank of Mount Davidson, and of course the bumptious town felt a proprietary interest in the whole enterprise. Hadn't the lode been financed by San Franciscans, men ever ready to gamble recklessly in the hope of proportionately high rewards? Wasn't San Francisco the source of supply for ninety per cent of the materials sent up, in six long trainloads a day, over Senator Sharon's fantastically crooked railroad? Goods for the Virginia City and Gold Hill merchants—all of it, staples and luxuries alike—brought the highest prices; for didn't the lordly four-dollar-a-day Comstock miner demand the best, and wasn't he able and eager to pay for it? San Francisco furnished supplies too for the mines themselves, of a quantity and at a cost that taxed the imagination. Deep mining on the lode was said to be the most highly mechanized operation in history, and here again the call was for the best and damn the expense. For fifteen years the pyramiding stacks of Comstock orders had kept scores of bay-area foundries and machine-shops running at full capacity. "Nothing is impossible nowadays," Flood had stated in 1875; "the only question is, will it show a profit?" Acting on that principle, managers coolly placed orders for mining and milling equipment running into the hundreds of thousands of dollars and, before it had been in operation a year, blithely discarded it for something newer and larger and more expensive.

Nor was that all. Spurred by the unprecedented Consolidated Virginia strike, and with speculators daily clamoring for new bonanzas, mine superintendents put triple shifts to work deepening shafts and blasting out miles of exploratory drifts. With the fever of speculation running wild, expense was literally no object. Of what consequence was an assessment of a few dollars to a man sure that his ten shares would shortly bring him riches unimagined? So the managers, urged on by their stockholders and trustees, started down another thousand feet and casually ordered the ponderous equipment needed to operate in such depth: Root blowers and ventilating systems, Cornish pumps of ever greater capacity, miles of woven steel cable on which cages were raised and lowered (at express-train speed) in vertical shafts more than half a mile deep; drills and picks and shovels by the gross, carloads of blasting powder, quicksilver by the ton, assaying equipment, trainloads of ice; timber, fuel, chemicals, miners' candles.

Most of this San Francisco furnished—and received liberal payment, in cash. Hundreds of tons of merchandise daily left her docks and warehouses, her shops and factories and produce markets, to supply the insatiable Washoe towns; and in return there poured into the coffers of her merchants a broad stream of bright minted dollars. Knee-deep in silver and never doubting that the easy profits would continue for decades, San Francisco entered into an era as grandiose as any it had known in its twenty-five-year history. Fortunes hoisted to the Comstock mine-heads were funneled over the Sierra to be expended with the same careless unconcern as they had been gathered.

Scores of San Franciscans, suddenly possessed of wealth beyond their wildest hopes, were impelled to make visible the surprising degree of their success. Beginning in the middle 1860's a building boom got under way so widespread and continued as to change the aspect of the whole central part of the city. By 1874 a writer for the *Gold Hill News* returned from a trip "down below" and reported wryly: "The Coast towns are building and rebuilding at a furious pace, compliments of the Nevada mines." The 700-room Palace Hotel had then been more than a year building, its bulk rising floor by floor above the low wooden buildings south of Market Street. The Palace was one of dozens of William Ralston's enterprises, all built with profits from the lode: the California Theatre, the Bank of California's new French Renaissance headquarters at California and Sansome streets, a cluster of factories designed to make everything from woolen blankets to railroad cars, from watches to furniture and carriages.

There was no lack of landmarks to fill visitors from Nevada's grim, unlovely towns with faintly bitter admiration. In the late seventies the huge Baldwin Hotel went up on the Market-Powell gore, providing a second luxury hotel for a city still too small to support one. Baldwin's first fortune came out of the Ophir; later he moved to San Francisco and skillfully mined the Comstock from the other end; that is, from the floor of the Mining Exchange. "Lucky" Baldwin's hotel dominated upper Market Street for twenty years, then went up in a bright bonfire one night in 1898. The site was cleared to make way for an even larger structure, and again Comstock silver was the motivating force. By then most of the first group of Washoe millionaires had died, and their heirs, seeking investments for their unwieldy fortunes, made other notable additions to the city's skyline. The ten-story Flood Building on the Baldwin Hotel site was one; another was the lofty Hobart Building on Market, a third the Sloane Building on Sutter. There were half a dozen others, but the most striking landmark put up by second-generation holders of Comstock fortunes was the Fairmont Hotel on Nob Hill. This occupies the block-square site on which Senator Fair had planned to build the West's most costly mansion; into it his two daughters, Mrs. Oelrichs and Mrs. Vanderbilt, poured five of their superfluous millions.

Comstock editors never tired of reminding San Franciscans how much they owed to the treasure laboriously dug from beneath Mount Davidson, and how meagerly and with what bad grace they acknowledged their debt. Washoe residents complained that for twenty years the Californians had skimmed the cream off the Comstock and, having made their pile, shook the dust of the silver towns from their boots and hurried westward with never a backward glance. Thus, while the new plutocrats indulged their taste for display by ornamenting San Francisco with a series of massive hotels and office buildings and residences, the bonanza towns received no part of the wealth they had produced. Virginia City and Gold Hill remained the unprepossessing settlements they had always been, clusters of boxlike, severely functional buildings that grew more weather-beaten with the passing seasons and in the end, having served their purpose, fell forlornly into decay.

The feeling that the Comstock towns have fared badly at the hands of those whom they benefited most persists to this day. A few veterans of the years when the lode hummed with activity still remain. Visitors see them sunning themselves against the sagging façades of once brightly painted hillside cottages or shuffling along the plank sidewalks of C Street in lordly disregard for the curious throngs who, for respite from Reno's bars and roulette wheels, drive the twenty steep miles from the divorce capital and spend an hour or two exclaiming over the relics of another and presumedly more heroic age. But often no more than a glass of beer and a few questions are needed to make these reticent ancients communicative. If the questioner shows a passing acquaintance with the town's history, the flow of reminiscence begins in earnest: the familiar admixture of fact and folklore, all thrown together in magnificent disregard of order or chronology.

But neither the haze of years nor the distortion of failing memory have changed the Comstocker's conviction that the lode deserved better than it ever got from the men it made rich and famous. Mention of any of the bonanza kings invariably invokes a baneful stare. Mackay? Fair? Sure, they were both big men; both got their starts here. Took fifty millions out of that shaft down the hill. Shipped it outside as fast as they made it, then left the minute the mines played out. Took along everything worth carting off and never came back, not for a day. Used to read about them running off to Europe, and about their wives hobnobbing with kings, and their daughters marrying princes or dukes, and their sons shipping racehorses across the country in Pullman cars, only the cars were fitted up with stalls instead of seats. Remember reading that Mackay gave a drinking fountain to some town in France. His wife (Mamie Bryant was her name before Mackay married her; used to run a boardinghouse up the street) once gave a half a million to take care of the London orphans. We had orphans here in those days. Could have used a drinking fountain too; still could, for that matter. Funny thing: Mackay's son was down at Reno once, maybe twenty years ago. Came out in his private car to open the mining school he built with his old man's money. Came up one day to look the town over. Lots of people with him; must have been a dozen cars came up over the grade, one after the other, like a funeral procession. Fellows from Reno took him down to the Con. Virginia works, then over to the Ophir, then up to the fire house, then on up the hill to where Mackay's old house used to stand. Peculiar little cuss with a high collar and striped pants. Went wherever they led him and stood looking about, never saying a word. Then they got in their cars and started back. Mackay kept looking at his watch; they was giving him a banquet down at Reno and he was afraid he'd be late. Can't say as I recall seeing any of the others, no Floods or Sharons or Hearsts or Haywards. Couple of years back, a party stopped at the Crystal down the street. Told the barkeep one of the ladies was a Fair, Slippery Jim's granddaughter. Seems she was stopping off at Reno changing husbands and came up to look the place over. Maybe they was just talking, though, the way people do after they've had a few. Can't blame them for not coming back to see where their money came from. Nothing here nowadays to interest a poor man, let alone a rich one. Mostly they go straight through to the Coast, like their fathers and grandfathers did. San Francisco was always the place they spent their money. Here they just made it.

The Washoe's long-standing resentment against San Francisco is easily explained; that the bay metropolis viewed the silver towns with equal hostility is harder to understand. Yet all through the period of the lode's activity Virginia City and San Francisco newspapers waged bitter warfare. The fact that San Francisco came to regard its silver profits as a dubious asset was because the Washoe business thoroughly disrupted the city's economy. Trading in Comstock shares grew so heavy that many millions of badly needed capital poured through the wickets of the brokerage offices. After a year or two of this, San Franciscans began to count the cost. Of the scores of millions invested in stocks and paid out in assessments an absurdly small percentage found its way back in the form of dividends. Immense sums were annually expended developing claims that never produced a ton of millable ore, yet the search continued for years. Buyers of such stocks held on as long as their patience or capital lasted, paying frequent assessments, and in the end sold out, nearly always at a heavy loss. More conservative gamblers, who invested only in the producing mines, seldom fared much better; such shares were forced so high that even their large and regular dividends yielded less than the same investments would have returned had they been put into less speculative enterprises closer to home. In the end San Franciscans came to realize that while the mines were enriching certain of the town's merchants and manufacturers, the result to the rest of the community was slow but inevitable impoverishment.

The blight the Comstock had cast over the Coast was frequently pictured in San Francisco newspapers through the middle and late seventies. In 1879 one stated: "These five years have brought disaster and money famine to the masses, notwithstanding the enormous yield of the precious metals." This writer went on to record that deposits in the city's savings banks had shrunk by twenty-five million dollars, and that real-estate mortgages had risen a hundred millions. He continued: "Capital, no longer generally distributed, is concentrated in colossal fortunes, which may be numbered upon the fingers. Manufactures have lessened in number, and those that still exist struggle for life. . . ."

From time to time Mackay and Flood tried to stem this torrent of abuse by pointing out that they were not personally responsible for the frenzied speculation that had gripped the Coast. Both professed to deplore gambling in bonanza stocks. Mackay had a ready answer to those who were constantly asking his advice about investments: "Put your money in a savings bank and leave it there." Flood was only slightly less conservative. If a man wanted to take a flier in Comstock stocks—and if he could afford the luxury—let him pick out a mine of known productivity and prudent management; having bought his shares, let him hold on to them, collecting his dividends and paying no attention to the erratic ups and downs on the Exchange. Fair volunteered no sage advice to the investing public, probably because he knew the folly of giving advice that would surely be disregarded, and if O'Brien ever ventured an opinion—which seems unlikely—no one saw fit to preserve it.

7

As THE ablest financier of the group and the man responsible for their heavy stock-market operations, Flood bore the brunt of the firm's unpopularity. This was not altogether deserved: all his trading was with the knowledge and consent of the other three and all shared in the profits. Yet he seems to have accepted his role of scapegoat with good grace. Loyalty to the group was the basis of his business creed, and through the years he did much to keep the firm intact, skillfully moderating differences between his two more volatile partners, Mackay and Fair, and actively repelling the raids of outsiders bent on breaking their iron-clad hold on the Comstock.

At meetings of the four he was always harping on the theme of unity. So long as they worked together, one for all and all for one, they had nothing to fear from a restless and increasingly hostile public. "I have no thought but to further the best interests of our enterprises," Flood wrote in 1876, "and this course I propose to follow as long as my connection with these companies continues." After his death a friend commented: "It was Flood who held the firm together. Without his influence the partnership would not have lasted six months. Fair was headstrong and opinionated and he could be ugly when he was crossed. Mackay was hot-tempered and quick to take offense, always threatening to walk out of the meetings. . . . They had some stormy sessions in the big corner office in the Nevada Block. Flood must have had his hands full acting as peace-maker, but in the end he always succeeded. When the four filed out they sometimes looked grim, but they were still on speaking terms."

The group's entry into the banking business enhanced their prestige, but it brought serious dissension and in the end carried two of them to the brink of bankruptcy. The idea of founding a banking house is said to have originated with Flood; Mackay and O'Brien favored the venture, but Fair was far from enthusiastic. Some years later Fair made known the reason for his reluctance: his partners totally lacked the experience and judgment needed to manage such an enterprise: he foresaw that he would have to carry the burden alone. None the less, he was won over, and in May 1875, Coast newspapers announced the incorporation of the Nevada Bank, with a paid-up capital of five million dollars. Louis McLane, chief owner of the powerful Wells, Fargo Express Company, was named president, but the four bonanza magnates were on its board of directors and owned all but a few shares of its stock. The northwest corner of Pine and Montgomery streets was bought and a handsome four-story building was put up, designed to house not only the bank but the headquarters of the firm's other enterprises.

It was understood that the partners' entry into the banking business was an outgrowth of their feud with William Sharon and that their real purpose was to challenge the long-established supremacy of the Bank of California. When, only a month or two after the incorporation of the Nevada Bank, the rival house closed its doors, many believed that the machinations of the bonanza firm had been responsible for the catastrophe. Next day the Bank of California's deposed president was dragged unconscious from the waters of the bay and died on the North Beach sands. For weeks feeling ran high, and again most of the journalistic abuse was directed at the dominant San Francisco partner. The *Golden Era* charged that Flood had deliberately plotted to wreck the bank and to impoverish its president. "Ralston was a rich man. The play was to get his money. He was confidentially supplied with points that induced him to short the bonanzas at a time when the programme was to float them away up in the hundreds. We all know the result. A large proportion of his immense fortune passed to the Nevada Block. . . ." For years the belief persisted that it was the malice of the bonanza firm, and not Ralston's unbridled extravagances, that had brought his great banking house to ruin.

While plans for the rehabilitation of the closed bank were under way, the Nevada Bank opened its doors. It had a short but eventful career. Late in 1875 a branch was established at Virginia City, on the Taylor Street corner, diagonally across C Street from the newly reopened agency of the Bank of California. During the next four years, as fiscal agent for the booming bonanza mines, it did a large business. Then came the gradual exhaustion of the Comstock's ore bodies, causing mines and mills one by one to shut down. The Virginia City branch was closed in the middle 1880's, leaving its old-time rival to carry on; not until 1917 did the Bank of California's Comstock agency give up the ghost.

Meantime, in 1881, Louis McLane had retired as the Nevada Bank's president and Flood had succeeded him. Four years later, long-standing quarrels between the three surviving owners (O'Brien had died in 1879) brought on an open break. Fair, long critical of the way the institution was being run, delivered an ultimatum: either he must be given a larger voice in its affairs or he would withdraw and organize a bank of his own. In April 1885 a compromise was worked out: both Fair and Flood sold their stock to Mackay, who thus became sole owner. There is evidence, however, that this was merely a ruse to get rid of Fair. Mackay promptly sold back a quarter interest to Flood, and the latter reassumed the presidency. The exploit widened the breach between the erstwhile partners. One day a friend sympathized with Fair for the shabby treatment he had received, referring to it as a "Machiavellian trick." Fair thought the reference was to Mackay. "Mackayavellian, hell!" he exploded. "That was a Floodavellian trick!" Fair bided his time, plotting revenge.

Toward the middle eighties Flood, whose health had begun to fail, looked about for a competent man to take some of the burdensome administrative details off his shoulders. His choice fell to George L. Brander, a young Scot of wide financial experience and excellent reputation. Flood made Brander cashier and went into semi-retirement at Linden Towers, coming up to town only once or twice a week. For many months the bank's two owners, confident that its affairs were being conducted on the usual conservative lines, gave it little attention. During the summer of 1887 Flood took his ease at Menlo, and Mackay made one of his infrequent trips across the Atlantic to visit his family.

Meantime financial circles of the town were curious to know who was behind heavy purchases of California's bumper wheat crop, then moving from the fields to the warehouses and into the holds of the clipper ships. It had begun to grow clear that someone was trying to corner the market—a bold gamble that would result either in very large winnings or correspondingly heavy losses. A few suspected that the Nevada Bank might be engineering the coup; word passed about that perhaps its owners were applying here the methods that had proved immensely profitable in their bonanza stock speculations. The fact that the bank owned wheat warehouses at Port Costa and had other large investments in the industry lent weight to such surmises. Meantime the heavy purchases continued, in the fields and warehouses, and on ships already at sea. All trading was done by a local broker, John Rosenfeld, who would supply no hint as to the identity of his client. Week by week through the spring and early summer the price was forced until it reached $2.19 a cental (one hundred pounds), well over twice its normal value. How many dollars were expended in the gamble was never made public; one estimate placed the total at twenty-two millions.

One day Flood, up from Menlo on one of his semiweekly visits, chanced to encounter William Alvord, president of the reorganized Bank of California; in the course of their conversation the latter dropped a cautious hint that the heavy borrowing of Flood's bank was causing uneasiness in the inner financial circles of the city. On that same day, Mackay returned from Europe; within an hour of landing he learned that the New York banks were "crammed with Nevada Bank paper." Both men were amazed: their bank then had a paid-up capital of ten million dollars and it was doing a diversified and profitable business. Besides, both owners had large amounts of personal funds on deposit there; neither could see any reason for outside borrowing.

Confidential telegrams were exchanged between New York and San Francisco, and Mackay boarded the first west-bound train. Flood had meantime summoned Brander to his office, confronted him with what he had learned, and demanded an explanation. The cashier was obliged to admit that from the beginning the deal had been financed with Nevada Bank funds. Under Flood's questioning, details came to light. Brander was a close friend of the broker, Rosenfeld; the latter had convinced him that it was feasible to buy up the 1887 crop at the currently low rates, to withhold it from resale until the resulting scarcity in the world's markets forced prices up, then to unload it at a huge profit.

In theory the operation had seemed sound and simple. It had failed because of a variety of unforeseen circumstances: the unusual size of the 1887 crop, and the steadily rising prices Brander and his agent had been forced to pay to maintain their control; also, the above-average yield in other wheat-producing areas, in Australia, the Argentine, in Europe itself. Brander, who seems to have gone into the deal not for personal profit but to make a handsome profit for the bank, was already heavily involved when the market began to show signs of breaking. To have withdrawn then would have meant a four-hundred-thousand-dollar loss. Afraid to admit so costly an error, he had seen no alternative but to continue to back the corner in the hope of eventual success. The amount this required was enormous. When the bank's funds were exhausted, he resorted to heavy borrowing. Even this proved insufficient to permit Rosenfeld to continue his large-scale buying, and in the end the cashier was forced to drastic expedients. For some years Mackay had kept in the bank's vault a million dollars in negotiable securities, with instructions that they be turned over to his wife in the event of his death so as to tide her over while his estate was in escrow. Brander put these up at another bank as security for a loan. Flood had similarly deposited six hundred thousand dollars in government bonds for his sister, Mrs. Follis; these went the same way.

The harassed cashier had done so thorough a job that on the morning Mackay reached San Francisco, Flood reported that the bank's liquid assets totaled $368; he could see no alternative but to close. That the two owners did not take this step was mainly because of the intercession of their old rival, the Bank of California, the managers of which feared that so spectacular a failure might drag down other Coast financial houses. To help tide them over the crisis, President Alvord offered to lend Mackay and Flood a million dollars on their personal notes. Other rich men came forward—among them Fair—and the bank remained open. But Fair, who had been waiting three years to avenge the "Floodavellian trick," exacted a high price. In mid-August it was announced that Flood was retiring as president and that Fair would succeed him. Fair's triumph over "those kindergarten bankers" was complete.

Meantime in the markets of the world the price of wheat had broken badly from its top of $2.19. By mid-August it was selling at $1.35, and the Nevada Bank set about the melancholy task of unloading its enormous holdings. Just how much the bank—that is, Flood and Mackay—lost was not revealed; perhaps it was never known. Most estimates placed the figure at between ten and twelve millions. This, plus the strain of the period when both the bank and his personal fortune had hung in the balance, is said to have hastened Flood's death, which followed less than two years later. As for Mackay, the weeks of uncertainty had no visible effect on his health, although they put a severe strain on his temper. This he relieved to some extent by firing Brander the moment he considered it prudent to do so.

Fair remained president only a year or two—Mackay and Flood still owned the majority of the stock—then retired and founded a rival house, the Merchants' Trust Company. In 1891 the Nevada Bank was purchased by I. W. Hellman, who consolidated it with his Wells, Fargo

Bank. Mackay remained a director of the combined institution until his death: Flood's son, James L., was also a director as long as he lived, and was succeeded in turn by his son, the founder's grandson. As for Brander, he was soon in hot water again. Following his curt dismissal by Mackay, he organized an insurance firm, the State Investment Company. He was again on his way to becoming a force in San Francisco finance when he was indicted on a charge of making false reports of the assets of the concern. Thereupon he sold his residence and its furnishings to Fair—at a tremendous sacrifice, it was assumed—and fled to Edinburgh. Efforts to extradite him proved futile and, so far as San Francisco was concerned, his subsequent history remained obscure.

8

At the time Brander's wheat deal nearly wrecked the Nevada Bank, William O'Brien, ever the most shadowy of the partners, had been dead almost a decade. His health had never been robust, and toward the end of 1877 he must have had an intimation that he had not long to live, for he commissioned Laver & Curett, local architects, to design a mausoleum at Calvary Cemetery. This extraordinary edifice, long unrivaled (despite stiff competition) for sheer ugliness in the field of cemetery architecture, was under construction when its prospective tenant moved from San Francisco to San Rafael in the spring of 1878, in the hope that the milder climate of the suburban town would benefit his health. There he lingered on for several weeks at the home of his nephew, James V. Coleman, and there he died on the afternoon of May 2, his partner Flood at his bedside. He was fifty-two. He was buried from St. Mary's Church at California and Dupont streets. Flood, Fair, McLane, and other distinguished citizens acted as pallbearers. Newspapers printed comparatively brief obituaries, in which the geniality that had won O'Brien the title of "the jolly millionaire" was stressed, his early death deplored, and guesses hazarded as to what disposition he had made of his fortune, estimated at from twelve to fifteen millions. Meantime the flag flew at half-mast above the Nevada Block, and the interior of the bank was draped in black crepe. His body was placed in a temporary vault pending the completion of Laver & Curett's mausoleum. Incidentally, the mausoleum was again briefly in the public eye more than half a century later. During the depression of the early 1930's a group of itinerants broke through the bronze doors and set up housekeeping inside. There they lived in comfort for several months until the police, drawn thither by the sight of smoke issuing from a stove-pipe projecting from one of the stained-glass windows, summarily ejected them.

O'Brien's will confirmed expectations that the bulk of his fortune would go to his sisters and their children. His four pretty nieces—three of them were in their teens, the fourth nine—were left tidy fortunes of $300,000 each, with the stipulation that the windfalls were for their exclusive use, not subject to control by future husbands. Three nephews (ages eleven to twenty-seven) were each given a like sum. Fifty thousand dollars were apportioned among Catholic and Protestant orphan asylums, and the balance went to O'Brien's sisters, each of whom received an estimated four millions. His early death caused the weekly *Argonaut*, then newly founded, to list more than a score of prominent San Franciscans who had recently died and to comment: "Not a man of advanced years in all the long catalogue: all were between fifty and sixty. . . . This constant, never-ceasing, never-relaxing business strain will destroy the strongest constitution. . . ." O'Brien's inclusion in this list must have puzzled many: business cares had always rested lightly on his shoulders.

Local journals saluted his passing by revealing a few characteristic anecdotes. Most of them were illustrative of how little his way of life had been changed by the multiple millions that had surprisingly been dumped into his lap. One related that during the first weeks after he had arrived, penniless and ragged, in San Francisco, he had supported himself by unloading ships in the harbor, and there a chance acquaintance, taking note of the deplorable state of his wardrobe, had presented him with a still-serviceable pair of shoes. In later years O'Brien had made persistent efforts to find the donor so that he might be suitably rewarded. In the middle fifties, when he finished his term as foreman of one of the local volunteer fire companies, fellow members presented him with a silver trumpet, suitably engraved; ever afterward it remained his most cherished possession. He had come west on the brig *Tarolinta;* in later years he was at pains to keep in touch with his fellow passengers. After he rose to affluence he annually gathered as many as he could locate and tendered them an elaborate banquet on the anniversary of their arrival. In July 1877 he transported a group of fifty on a tour of the bay in a chartered tug, climaxing it with a sumptuous repast on Angel Island. There a series of reminiscent speeches were delivered, interspersed with toasts: long after nightfall the hilarious party returned to San Francisco singing *O Susanna,* to the accompaniment of a twelve-piece band. It was the last of the *Tarolinta* reunions: O'Brien was dead before the next July rolled around.

His liberality to old-time friends was proverbial; the inventory of his estate listed some $280,000 in unpaid promissory notes, "of which about one in twenty is of any value. . . ." Family loyalty was another characteristic. As he grew prosperous it gave him pleasure to ease the lot of his sisters and their husbands and children. One by one the numerous O'Brien connections migrated from Brooklyn to San Francisco. First to arrive was his sister Kate, who had recently married one Joseph McDonough. O'Brien then was still at the Auction Lunch and in no position to play philanthropist. McDonough supported himself and his family by driving one of the city's horse-drawn street cars until his brother-in-law's stock-market operations began to yield him a handsome profit. Later McDonough went into the coal business, amassed a fortune of his own, and died in 1895, leaving a large estate that included the McDonough Theatre in Oakland. His wife, from whom he had long been separated, predeceased him by five years. The couple had three children, two sons and a daughter, each of whom shared in their rich uncle's estate. Kate McDonough herself received more than three millions. Part of this she invested in the California Theatre on Bush Street—one of William Ralston's extravagances —which she purchased for a frugal $125,000 and extensively remodeled, adding a hotel to the property. Both hotel and theater remained popular ornaments of the town until they were destroyed in the fire of 1906.

The other sister, Marie, married James L. Coleman in Brooklyn in 1850, moved to Georgetown, D.C., and in 1869 followed the McDonoughs to San Francisco. Coleman died in 1877 and his widow and their three children, Cecilia, Isabella, and James, went to live with O'Brien in his commodious house on Sutter Street. The eldest child, James V. Coleman, educated in Washington, hurried west upon his graduation in the expectation of entering the Nevada Bank. But the bank position failed to materialize (probably because of Fair, who was opposed to nepotism), and his uncle, O'Brien, set him up in the brokerage business. This arrangement must have been uncommonly liberal, for Coleman later stated: "When there was a profit we would divide; when we lost he was kind enough to stand it. . . ." James V. Coleman became a familiar figure in California and remained so for many years. He was active in mining, finance, and politics (in 1891 he ran for governor on the Democratic ticket), a forceful public speaker and ardent yachtsman, hunter, and linguist, and, finally, "the best Latin versifier in the State of California." Respected alike for his accomplishments and his large fortune, he lived to the ripe age of eighty, dying as recently as 1929.

When O'Brien's will was published, in 1878, one of his bequests caused widespread comment. Among the numerous nephews and nieces who received cash bequests appeared the name of Mary Pauline O'Brien, aged eighteen. Inquiry disclosed that Miss O'Brien was the child of Patrick O'Brien, brother of the deceased. Few knew that the latter had had a brother; it was explained that Patrick had dropped from sight years before and that the family had heard nothing of him until 1877, when word had reached San Francisco that he had died, leaving his widow and daughter destitute. William had thereupon brought the pair to San Francisco, where they were installed, along with the Coleman family, in the Sutter Street house. News of the bonanza king's passing was published all over the country, and a few weeks later the long-lost brother had arrived in San Francisco, very much alive and eager for his share of the estate. For a time it appeared that a lawsuit to break the will was about to materialize, and attorneys were engaged on both sides. An out-of-court settlement was made, however, by which the other heirs paid over some $600,000 to father and daughter, who relinquished further claim on the estate.

Meantime interest centered on Mrs. Coleman's two daughters, Cecilia and Isabella, the latter known to her intimates as Bella. Both were uncommonly pretty girls, one eighteen, the other two years younger. Mindful of the tidy fortunes each would inherit, the newspapers christened them "the two bonanzas" and speculated on who among the city's eligible young men would lead them triumphantly to the altar. But the Coleman belles disappointed the hopes of the local swains; both chose husbands far afield from San Francisco. In 1881 Bella married Harry De Courcy May, of Baltimore, and went to live there; next year Cecilia in turn married a second May brother, Frederick, a physician. Dr. May died a few years later and Cecilia married Viscount Louis d'Andigne. She died in Paris in 1922. Her sister Bella survived her by six years, dying at Baltimore in 1928.

The three McDonough children, Joseph, William, and Agnes, were aged respectively fourteen, eleven, and nine at the time of their uncle's death. The family home was on Turk Street, near Van Ness Avenue. Agnes, following the lead of her Coleman cousins, married an Easterner, John G. Agar, and San Francisco saw her no more. Meantime her two brothers had won renown by establishing a horse-breeding farm down the peninsula, not far from the estate of another eminent horse-fancier, Leland Stanford. The McDonough brothers gained international attention in the early nineties by buying a celebrated English stallion,

Ormonde, and bringing it out to their Palo Alto breeding farm; the price was $150,000, then by far the largest sum ever paid for a racehorse. The younger brother, William O'Brien McDonough, died at Palo Alto in 1914; his brother Joseph lived eighteen years longer.

9

THE bachelor O'Brien had no direct heirs and the two Fair boys had died young and childless; only Mackay and Flood left sons to carry on the family names. The younger of Flood's two children, his daughter Jennie, remained a spinster all her life, but his son's marital career intermittently interested the Coast for many years. In the latter seventies, when he had just turned twenty-one, he married Rose Fritz, formerly a singer in a light-opera company that had recently gone broke in San Francisco. The elder Flood was far from approving the marriage; he shipped the bridegroom off on a tour of the world, via Japan, and set about urging his new daughter-in-law to have the marriage annulled. He offered her a substantial inducement in the form of a $25,000 cash settlement, backing this up with the threat that should she refuse he would permanently shut off young Jimmy's allowance. These arguments must have been unanswerable, for the young woman promptly agreed to the annulment, pocketed her $25,000, and set off for Europe. But she prudently kept in touch with Jimmy by mail, and when the latter's westward progress brought him to Paris, the pair met and remarried. A few months later they were back in San Francisco.

Impressed by this exploit, the elder Flood admitted defeat and withdrew his opposition; the young couple lived in evident concord until Rose Fritz Flood's death in 1898. Meantime occurred an event that a third of a century later brought on a long and bitterly contested lawsuit. In August 1893 the childless couple took into their house at 1890 Page Street a three-month-old girl, who for the next six years lived with them both at San Francisco and at their summer home, Aqua Vale, in the Santa Cruz Mountains. In 1901, Flood having meantime married Maud Fritz, sister of his first wife, the child was sent to a convent in southern California. She remained there ten years, going under the name of Constance May Stern, and having no communication with the Floods. On her graduation, Constance Stern, then eighteen, several times wrote Flood, thanking him for having financed her education and asking his help in clearing up the mystery of her parentage. She received no direct reply, but not long after, Flood's secretary, James E. Walsh, visited her and told her what purported to be the story of her background. She was, he stated, the daughter of one Edward Stern and Eudora Forde Stern; he added that Stern had decamped soon after her birth, leaving her mother destitute, and that Mrs. Flood had generously taken the infant into her household. For a time this story satisfied the young woman, who four years later, in 1921, married a Los Angeles bank clerk, John Gavin. Lingering doubts must have persisted, however; her suspicion that she might in fact be Jim Flood's daughter gradually grew stronger and she presently set about assembling evidence to support that theory. Flood's death in 1926 brought matters to a climax; a private investigator, Eugene Aureguy, interested himself in the case, counsel was engaged, and preparations were made to press her claim to a daughter's share of Flood's estate.

Not until five years later did the case come to trial; for months it claimed the attention of thousands all over the Coast. It was the last of the long series of lawsuits involving the bonanza millions, and in many ways the most interesting. Mrs. Gavin's attorneys contended that she was an illegitimate daughter of James L. Flood and that the latter, by taking her into his home, had tacitly acknowledged the relationship. A curious array of witnesses filed through the Redwood City courtroom and gave their testimony pro and con. Counsel for the plaintiff produced a group of elderly citizens who swore they had heard Flood refer to the child as his daughter. Certain pertinent documents were put in evidence: a page from the passenger list of the steamer *Belgic,* on which Flood,

the child, Maud Fritz, her brother, and two servants had
made a trip to the Orient in 1898; here she was listed
as: "Miss C. M. Flood, 5, with father J. L. Flood."
Engraved calling cards bearing the name "Constance May
Flood" were produced, as were also a silver bowl and other
childish trinkets engraved with the initials "C. M. F."
Finally the plaintiff presented a copy of a souvenir newspaper Flood had had prepared on the party's return from
the *Belgic* cruise; this contained a photograph of the child,
the caption of which identified her as "Miss Constance M.
Flood."

Counsel for the heirs admitted that the child had lived
with the Floods during her first six years and that Flood
had paid her expenses at the convent; that she was his
child they strenuously denied. It was established that the
child's mother was Eudora Forde Stern, but there agreement ceased. Mrs. Stern's mother, Mrs. Forde (who was
ninety-four) was a key witness; her story was rambling
and confused. This ancient lady, a one-time actress, stated
that she had come from Boston to San Francisco in 1891,
where she had played in various stock companies, and that
while she was appearing at the Grove Street Theatre her
daughter, then sixteen, had met one James Cannon, the
company's property man. She added that Cannon had seduced the girl, and that, soon after she became pregnant,
her lover had sickened and died. The witness told two quite
different stories of what happened next. In her first version
she stated that soon after her daughter's child was born
she was stopped one day on the street by a stranger who
inquired if she was in trouble and, on hearing her story,
suggested that she see Mrs. Flood, a wealthy and kind-
hearted lady who might help her. This she had done and
Mrs. Flood had proved all her anonymous friend had
promised. In the presence of Flood himself she had agreed
to undertake to bring up the child; moreover, she had
promised to pay the bills of mother and daughter and to
provide them with funds to return to Boston. Later Mrs.
Forde changed this story: the person who had directed her
to Mrs. Flood was not a complete stranger who had
accosted her on the street, but a housewife on whom she

had called while she was selling tickets to a dramatic reading; Flood had not been actually present during her interview with his wife, but she had heard the latter discussing the matter in an adjoining room with a man whom she had assumed to be Flood. The girl's mother, Mrs. Eudora Stern Willette (she had acquired the extra name somewhere along the line), proved an equally unreliable witness. Before the trial opened she had made a deposition stating that Flood was the girl's father and detailing the circumstances of their meeting and intimacy; later she repudiated this document and presented herself at the office of Garret McEnerney, chief counsel for the Flood heirs, and made known her willingness to testify that she had never met Flood until after the birth of her child.

Meantime a great deal of oddly assorted information had been brought to light. It grew clear that by taking Constance into his household Flood had unknowingly incurred the obligation of supporting the child's mother and grandmother. During the next few years he was constantly called on to extricate this pair from a succession of difficulties, mostly financial. In 1893 he paid the San Francisco doctor who had brought the child into the world, settled up Mrs. Forde's past-due hotel bill, and sent mother and daughter home to Boston. A few months later they reported themselves in dire straits and eager to return west: Flood accommodatingly financed their journey back to California. It was the first of a long series of transcontinental jaunts at Flood's expense. Between times there were other emergencies: illnesses, the failure of expected theatrical engagements to materialize, their imminent eviction at the hands of stony-hearted landlords, the importunities of an army of bill-collectors. For five years Flood rescued the improvident pair from recurring financial crises; then even his good nature rebelled. In 1898, having decided formally to adopt the child, he instructed his attorney to prepare the necessary legal documents, paid the mother five thousand dollars upon her signing them, and let it be known that thereafter both mother and grandmother would have to look elsewhere for a banker. Of course the pair were soon again penniless and

once more bombarded Flood with pleas to rescue them
from abject poverty; none of their messages ever elicited
a reply.

Flood had meantime married the second of the Fritz
sisters and there is evidence that his bride opposed his
plan to adopt the child. Constance, then six, accordingly
was sent away to a convent; Flood never saw her again.

The long trial ended in defeat for Constance May
Gavin. At the close of the testimony the presiding judge
directed the jury to bring in a verdict denying the three
chief claims of the petitioner: that Flood was her father,
that he had received her into his home as his child, and
that his first wife had consented to receive the infant with
the knowledge that she was her husband's illegitimate offspring. Mrs. Gavin's attorneys appealed the case to the
California Supreme Court and both sides prepared to fight
the protracted battle over again. But the litigation was
holding up the distribution of Flood's estate, and the heirs,
foreseeing many more months of delay, were in a mood
for compromise. Accordingly, before the higher court
passed on the petition for a retrial, an out-of-court settlement was reached. By it the Flood heirs paid over a million
dollars to the plaintiff; she in turn signed away all further
claim to the estate. The last of the bonanza lawsuits
passed into history.

When Mrs. Gavin's suit for a share of the Flood fortune
was being waged at Redwood City, the man who had
amassed the millions had been dead more than forty
years. James Clair Flood died in a hotel room at Heidel-
berg, Germany, on the morning of February 21, 1889.
He was the second of the bonanza group to pass from the
scene. He lived eleven years longer than O'Brien; Fair
survived him by five years, Mackay by thirteen.

News of his death aroused curiously little interest in
San Francisco, a fact that the local papers did not fail to
point out. The *Chronicle* commented: "A few years ago
. . . the death of J. C. Flood would have created a great
sensation. . . . Yesterday, however, the telegram announcing that death had supervened after a lingering ill-

ness scarcely caused the faintest ripple of excitement. . . ."
The *News-Letter* added: "His death was not only expected
but long delayed. . . ." He was only sixty-two, but his
health had long been bad and he had gradually passed
on to his son the management of his affairs and retired
to his Menlo estate. San Francisco saw him only rarely,
shuffling out of the Nevada Block and being helped into
his carriage for the ride back to the country; his house on
the hill was closed. On Mackay's periodical visits to the
Coast he hurried down the peninsula to see his ailing
friend; after each visit he brought back progressively less
cheering reports from the sickroom at Linden Towers.
Fair made no friendly calls; by then the breach between
the erstwhile partners was permanent and unbridgeable.

In the summer of 1888, on the advice of his San
Francisco physicians, Flood set off for the Continent, accompanied by his wife and daughter. But European spe-
cialists and European spas failed to work a miracle, and
in October came word that plans to return to California
had had to be abandoned. His final weeks were passed
in a coma from which he could only intermittently be
aroused, and in newspaper offices up and down the Coast
conventional obituaries were put into type. The
Chronicle's last salute began: "His claims to fame are
simply those of a rich man, but the story of his life is
neither without its interest nor its moral. . . ."

But what the moral was, Flood's old newspaper enemy
failed to explain.

10

ALMOST a century has passed since the Washoe's vast
silver deposits first captured the nation's attention, stirring
the imagination of millions who would never see the
complex underground workings of the bonanza mines or
walk the streets of the mile-long towns that mushroomed
over the sterile slopes of Mount Davidson.

The Comstock's season of fame was as brief as it was
dramatic. Most of its activity—and all its profits—were

crowded into two decades, beginning in 1859 and tapering off sharply as the seventies ended. Its most lavish period by far was from 1873 to 1878, when well over half its total yield of a third of a billion dollars was mined. The Comstock's descent was even more rapid than its rise. For five years the immense ore body of the big bonanza was followed downward, all the while through quartz of extraordinary richness; then, more than four hundred feet from the point where it had been tapped, it suddenly terminated in barren rock—and so far as profits were concerned the Comstock had passed into history. Dividends of the California Mine ceased in 1879, those of the Consolidated Virginia a year later. From 1880 onward the silver towns lived on hopes and assessments; in Mackay's words, the lode had become "poor man's pudding."

But it has never been the nature of miners to accept defeat easily or soon; few are willing to suspend operations merely because all the ore in sight has been extracted and milled. "As many days as you spend in borrasca, that many shall you spend in bonanza"—such was the motto of those who had worked the ancient silver mines of Mexico. The Comstock embraced this philosophy, modifying it to suit different conditions: "So long as speculators can be found to pay assessments, so long shall the search for new bonanzas go on." The search—and the assessments—have continued, by fits and starts, but always hopefully, ever since. How many dollars have been expended in the six decades since the last substantial Washoe dividends were paid there is no means of knowing exactly; estimates run from a conservative ten millions to five times that sum.

Yet such is the indomitable optimism of the breed, and such the fascination of the game, that even today the sagging lode towns continue to live in hope. Under the hot desert sun the handful who remain shrug off memories of past glories and ignore the unprepossessing present; their eyes are fixed on gaudy triumphs yet to come. They tell you confidently that prodigious quantities of ore remain, far richer than was ever taken out, waiting the probing drills of a new generation of Mackays and Fairs and Joneses and Haywards. It is futile to point out that many years of search have honeycombed the lode from end to end and uniformly found—borrasca. For half a century the retort has been the same: go deeper. Always a group of wealthy and far-seeing men— in New York, or London, or Chicago, or San Francisco— are on the point of forming a syndicate. Soon this rich syndicate—Comstockers love the phrase—will take over the quiescent properties and sink shafts a mile, two miles, five miles, and run tunnels and drifts—and in the end strike bonanzas that will make Crown Point and Ophir and Gould & Curry—yes, and Con. Virginia itself—look paltry by comparison. Then the West will see a boom that is a boom; Virginia and the other lode towns will come roaring back, bigger than ever and twice as magnificent.

Should the miracle happen, Virginia and her neighbors will have a long way to come. Visitors who today follow the highway that snakes upward from Carson City, crossing and recrossing the abandoned roadbed of the Virginia & Truckee, need lively imaginations to picture the bonanza towns as they were in their heyday. Silver City's hundreds of hillside houses have shrunk to a spare cluster of shacks, sagging with age and bleached by the hot Washoe summers. Gold Hill, which once crowded its narrow canyon from floor to rim, has been all but obliterated, its very contours erased by surface workings that have scooped out great open pits. These immense glory holes occupy the sites of mills, office buildings, hotels, churches, saloons, school, newspaper plant, and brokerage offices. The road picks its way through the rubble of the vanished town and continues up the canyon, climbing steeply toward the divide, passing here the shell of a brick store, there the strangely preserved home of some forgotten mine manager, stone steps leading to its prim garden wall.

Once all the Comstock towns overlapped, their business streets joined in an unbroken line that extended three miles. Today nature—and man—have swept away all but a few short blocks. Of Virginia, once the largest city between Salt Lake and the Coast, and by far the liveliest,

only the ghost of past glories remain. On C Street a few
scores of brick buildings, in various stages of decay, mark
the center of a once widely extended business district.
Half these remaining stores are empty, some with iron
shutters still intact and drawn over the doors and show-
windows. Those still in use are mostly tenanted by merchants catering to a growing tourist trade: curio shops
offering souvenirs of the old town, bits of Victorian china
and bric-a-brac, picture postcards of vanished mills and
hoisting works, portraits of grim and bearded pioneers.
Picturesquely named bars—the Bucket of Blood, the
Sump, the Crystal, the Washoe Club—invite visitors inside
to admire their "museums of historical relics"—specimens
of Comstock ore, copies of early Washoe newspapers,
miners' tools, and similar odds and ends, and on their
walls framed views of the town in its prime are hung
above the inevitable row of slot-machines.

On B Street, higher up the mountainside, a few authentic landmarks remain: the Storey County Courthouse, the
water-company office, the brokerage house of George T.
Marye, two or three ornate residences, lone survivors of
acres of like structures put up in the booming seventies.
These, besides two churches, a school, a hospital, a mine
office, and a scant two dozen cottages are all that remain
of the original city that once boasted three thousand buildings, a hundred saloons, twenty-two restaurants, thirty-five
hotels and rooming-houses, three harness-makers', two
undertakers', six pawnbrokers', and an unspecified number of gambling-houses, Chinese opium dens, and
brothels.

Few of the landmarks that aroused the wonder of
strangers during the seventies remain today. The five-story
International Hotel, apex of Comstock luxury, dominated
the town for nearly forty years, then burned in 1914.
The scores of towering mills and hoisting works, their
smokestacks tracing the course of the lode from end to
end, have likewise disappeared, the buildings themselves
dismantled for their lumber, their hundreds of tons of
fantastically expensive machinery carted off and melted
down as scrap iron. Today only the massive foundations,

half buried in rubble and overgrown with sagebrush, mark their sites. These, and the tailings of the mines, great mesas fanning out over the lower town, are the sole visible reminders of the industry that once made Virginia the most renowned town in Western America, a wealth-producing prodigy known throughout the civilized world. For the mines themselves are sealed and hidden, their shafts covered, their lower levels flooded, their miles of stopes and tunnels a chaotic mass of fallen rock and rotted timbers. All are wrapped in silence as complete as that which long since engulfed the favored few to whom they yielded up their treasure. For men and mines arose together, together shared a transient fame, then one by one faded into the common darkness.

ACKNOWLEDGMENTS AND
BIBLIOGRAPHY

INFORMATION bearing on the lives and times of the Silver Kings was supplied by numerous individuals and institutions. In my researches I have made use of the collections and facilities of the Bancroft Library and the University of California Library, Berkeley; the San Francisco Public Library, the California Historical Society, the Society of California Pioneers, and the Wells-Fargo History Room, San Francisco; the California State Library, Sacramento; the Mackay School of Mines, the University of Nevada Library, and the Nevada Historical Society, Reno; and the Nevada State Library, Carson City.

To the many persons who supplied pertinent biographical information, assisted in running down obscure references, or provided material for illustrations, I record my appreciation. These include, among others, William Agar, Julia Cooley Altrocchi, Eugene Aureguy, Frank Brezee, Margaret Casserley, Jay A. Carpenter, Robert G. Cleland, Emily Cohen, James Daly, George Fields, Helen S. Giffen, Edwin Grabhorn, Marguerite Gray, Carroll D. Hall, Catherine Harroun, Harold Holmes, Austin S. Hutcheson, Alice Larson, Lewis F. Lengfeld, J. B. Levison, D. W. Macdonough, John J. Newbegin, Edna Martin Parratt, Robert L. Patterson, H. L. Slosson, Douglas S. Watson, Caroline Wenzel, and Jeanne Elizabeth Wier.

Much of the material of the book was drawn from the files of the following newspapers: the *Alta California,*

Chronicle, Call, Evening Bulletin, and *Daily Stock Report,* and the weekly *Golden Era, News Letter, Argonaut,* and *Arthur McEwen's Letter,* all of San Francisco; the *Record-Union,* Sacramento; the *Territorial Enterprise* and *Virginia Evening Chronicle,* Virginia City; the *Gold Hill News,* Gold Hill; and the *Tribune, Times,* and *World,* New York.

Of books on the Comstock, the first in the field, Dan De Quille's *The History of the Big Bonanza,* published in 1876, remains the most useful storehouse of information on life both above and below ground during the lode's early and middle years. Grant H. Smith's *The History of the Comstock Lode: 1850–1920* (1943), concise, thorough, and well documented, is the best factual presentation of the entire subject. Another valuable work is Eliot Lord's *Comstock Mining and Miners* (1883), which contains much carefully compiled data on historical, scientific and sociological phases of the lode. Volumes stressing the picturesque and dramatic side of life on the Comstock are more numerous. Among the best of these are George D. Lyman's *Ralston's Ring* (1937), and *The Saga of the Comstock Lode* (1944), Miriam Michelson's *The Wonderlode of Silver and Gold* (1934), M. M. Matthews's *Ten Years in Nevada* (1880), and Wells Drury's *An Editor on the Comstock Lode* (1936). Novelists who have interpreted the lode in terms of fiction include Vardis Fisher (*The City of Illusion*), Flannery Lewis (*Suns Go Down*), and James M. Cain (*Past All Dishonor*).

Following is a list of the books I found useful for the light they throw on the Silver Kings and their background:

ANGEL, MYRON (editor): *History of Nevada.* Oakland, Cal.: Thompson & West; 1881.

BANCROFT, HUBERT H.: *History of California.* San Francisco: The History Company; 1888.

——:*History of Nevada, Colorado and Wyoming.* San Francisco: The History Company; 1889.

——: *Chronicles of the Builders of the Commwealth.* San Francisco: The History Company; 1891.

BARRY, T. A., and PATTEN, B. A.: *Men and Memories of San Francisco in the "Spring of '50."* San Francisco:

A. L. Bancroft & Company; 1873.

BOWLES, SAMUEL: *Our New West.* Hartford: Hartford Publishing Company; 1869.

BROWNE, J. ROSS: *Adventures in the Apache Country, with Notes on the Silver Regions of Nevada.* New York: Harper & Brothers; 1869.

CHAMBLISS, WILLIAM H.: *Chambliss' Diary.* New York: Chambliss & Company; 1895.

CODMAN, JOHN: *The Round Trip.* New York: G. P. Putnam's Sons; 1879.

CORBETT, JAMES J.: *The Rear of the Crowd.* New York: G. P. Putnam's Sons; 1925.

DAVIS, SAM (editor): *History of Nevada.* Reno: The Elms Publishing Company; 1913.

DE GROOT, HENRY: *Sketches of the Washoe Silver Mines.* San Francisco: Hutchings & Rosenfeld; 1860.

[DEWEY, SQUIRE P.]: *The Bonanaza Mines and the Bonanza Kings.* n.p., n.d. [San Francisco, 1879.]

DOWNIE, WILLIAM: *Hunting for Gold.* San Francisco: The California Publishing Company; 1893.

DRURY, WELLS: *An Editor on the Comstock Lode.* New York: Farrar & Rinehart; 1936.

ELDREDGE, ZOETH SKINNER (editor): *History of California.* New York: The Century History Company; 1915.

GLASSCOCK, C. B.: *The Big Bonanza.* Indianapolis: The Bobbs-Merrill Company; 1931.

GOODWIN, C. C.: *As I Remember Them.* Salt Lake City: Salt Lake Commercial Club; 1913.

——: *The Wedge of Gold.* Salt Lake City: Tribune Printing Company; 1893.

GORMAN, HENRY M.: *My Memories of the Comstock.* Los Angeles: Suttonhouse; 1939.

HALÉVY, LUDOVIC: *The Abbé Constantin.* New York: A. L. Burt Company; 1895.

HART, ANN CLARK: *Lone Mountain.* San Francisco: The Pioneer Press; 1937.

HITTELL, JOHN S.: *A History of the City of San Fran-*

cisco. San Francisco: A. L. Bancroft & Company; 1878.

HITTELL, THEODORE H.: *History of California*. San Francisco: Pacific Press Publishing House; 1897.

KEMBLE, JOHN HASKELL: *The Panama Route: 1848 –1869*. Berkeley, Cal.: University of California Press; 1943.

KING, JOSEPH L.: *History of the San Francisco Stock and Exchange Board*. San Francisco: Joseph L. King; 1910.

LEVISON, J. B.: *Memories for My Family*. San Francisco: John Henry Nash; 1933.

LILLARD, RICHARD G.: *Desert Challenge: An Interpretation of Nevada*. New York: Alfred A. Knopf; 1942.

LORD, ELIOT: *Comstock Mining and Miners*. Washington, D.C.: Government Printing Office; 1883.

LYMAN, GEORGE D.: *Ralston's Ring*. New York: Charles Scribner's Sons; 1937.

———: *The Saga of the Comstock Lode*. New York: Charles Scribner's Sons; 1944.

MARYE, GEORGE THOMAS, JR.: *From '49 to '83 in California and Nevada*. San Francisco: A. M. Robertson; 1923.

MATTHEWS, MRS. M. M.: *Ten Years in Nevada*. Buffalo: Baker, Jones & Company; 1880.

MICHELSON, MIRIAM: *The Wonderlode of Silver and Gold*. Boston: The Stratford Company; 1934.

MURPHY, I. I.: *Life of Colonel Daniel E. Hungerford*. Hartford: Press of The Chase, Lockwood & Brainard Company; 1891.

Nevada: A Guide to the Silver State. American Guide Series. Portland, Ore.: Binfords & Mort; 1940.

NEVILLE, AMELIA RANSOME: *The Fantastic City*. Boston: Houghton Mifflin Company; 1932.

PAINE, SWIFT: *Eilley Orrum: Queen of the Comstock*. Indianapolis: The Bobbs-Merrill Company; 1929.

PHELPS, ALONZO: *Contemporary Biography of California's Representative Men*. San Francisco: A. L. Bancroft & Company; 1882.

QUIETT, GLENN CHESNEY: *They Built the West*. New York: D. Appleton-Century Company; 1934.

QUIGLEY, HUGH: *The Irish Race in California*. San Francisco: A. Roman & Company; 1878.

RENSCH, H. E. and E. G., and HOOVER, MILDRED BROOKE: *Historic Spots in California: Valley and Sierra Counties*. Stanford University, Cal.: Stanford University Press; 1933.

SHINN, CHARLES HOWARD: *The Story of the Mine*. New York: D. Appleton & Company; 1896.

SHUCK, OSCAR T.: *History of the Bench and Bar of California*. Los Angeles: The Commercial Printing House; 1901.

SKINNER, EMORY FISKE: *Reminiscences*. Chicago: Vestal Printing Company; 1908.

SMITH, GRANT H.: *The History of the Comstock Lode: 1850–1920*. Reno: Nevada State Bureau of Mines; 1943.

STEWART, WILLIAM M.: *Reminiscences*. New York: The Neale Publishing Company; 1908.

TILTON, CECIL G.: *William Chapman Ralston: Courageous Builder*. Boston: The Christopher Publishing House; 1935.

TWAIN, MARK: *Roughing It*. Hartford: The American Publishing Company; 1872.

UPSHUR, GEORGE LITTLETON: *As I Recall Them*. New York: Wilson-Erickson; 1936.

VIVIAN, A. PENDARVES: *Wanderings in the Western Land*. London: Samson Low, Marston, Searle, & Rivington; 1879.

WOODS, SAMUEL D.: *Lights and Shadows on the Pacific Coast*. New York: Funk & Wagnalls Company; 1910.

WRIGHT, WILLIAM (DAN DE QUILLE): *The History of the Big Bonanza*. Hartford: The American Publishing Company; 1876.

INDEX